BLACK RELIGION

The Negro and
Christianity in
the United States

Joseph R. Washington, Jr.

UNIVERSITY
PRESS OF
AMERICA

Lanham • New York • London

Copyright © 1984 by

University Press of America,® Inc.

4720 Boston Way
Lanham, MD 20706

3 Henrietta Street
London WC2E 8LU England

British Cataloging in Publication Information Available

© 1964 by

Joseph R. Washington, Jr.

Originally published by Beacon Press in 1966.

Library of Congress Cataloging-in-Publication Data

Washington, Joseph R.
Black religion.

Reprint. Originally published: Boston : Beacon Press, 1964.
Bibliography: p.
Includes index.
1. Afro–Americans—Religion.   I. Title.
BR563.N4W3   1984   277.3'008996073   84–5659

ISBN 0–8191–3907–6 (pbk. : alk. paper

From Faith: Joseph and Susie

For Hope: Bryan

With Love: Sophia

PREFACE

The aim of this work is to evaluate critically the religion of the Negro in America. What were the forces which produced it? How do its present forms further the original intention? Why does it differ from and yet adhere to patterns developed in white Protestantism? Is there a relationship between the content of Negro religion and its white counterparts? Has the religion of the Negro a creative potential? Does it have a sense of mission?

Many of my contemporaries, spiritually arrested in various Negro religious organizations, have raised these questions concerning our past underdevelopment and its effect upon us and our children. This book is a response to these penetrating questions, at once symbolic of our hope and our frustration.

Among an increasing number of Negroes, decided obliviousness to the life and mission of the Church is evident. Why? Because, I believe, the religion of the Negro lacks the following: a sense of the historic Church, authentic roots in the Christian tradition, a meaningful theological frame of reference, a search for renewal, an ecumenical spirit, and a commitment to an inclusive Church.

The ethical emphasis which dominates the religious life of Negro congregations has been generally attributed to the inevitable tension of being both a Negro and a Christian in the American milieu, where the Negro is only a partial member of either the secular or the Christian community without full participation in either. Consequently, the Negro develops sub-cultures and sub-religions. His non-acceptance into

vii

the Christian mainstream produces a preference for an ethical religion, which endeavors to provide some relief from the tensions of being a Negro in America, but also tends to exclude other equally indispensable dimensions of the Christian faith.

The ethical preoccupation in the religion of the Negro has been accepted by many as merely a one-sided emphasis; with the decrease of social problems and the increase in educated Negro leaders, it is assumed that the slightly askew religion of the Negro will be corrected. Rather than being diagnosed and treated as a symptom of a critical malignancy, the religious expressions of the Negro have been dismissed as understandable nervous disorders.

This nearly universal view runs counter to my experience and its repetition has never rung true for me. If the Negro is a victim of discrimination and segregation, of a pervasive malaise affecting the entire society, it appears incredible that the religious life of the Negro should be mysteriously delivered from this bondage. It is considerably more helpful to acknowledge that the socio-economic forces excluding the Negro from full participation in the society also exclude him from full participation in the Christian faith. To insist upon this portrayal of the predicament is to indict neither the Negro nor the Church but to disclose the unalterable disrepair of Negro qua Negro religion.

I have been immeasurably aided in this work by numerous authors, and although we may not always be in agreement, I wish particularly to acknowledge my indebtedness to the following: St. Clair Drake and Horace R. Cayton, *Black Metropolis*; Miles Mark Fisher, *Negro Slave Songs in the United States*; John Hope Franklin, *From Slavery to Freedom*; E. Franklin Frazier, *The Negro in the United States*; Ruby F. Johnston, *The Development of Negro Religion* and *The Religion of Negro Protestants*; Benjamin E.

Mays and Joseph W. Nicholson, *The Negro's Church;* W. D. Weatherford, *American Churches and the Negro;* and Carter G. Woodson, *The History of the Negro Church.* I am also indebted to conversations with Negroes and whites who have understood the difference between tolerating segregated congregations and excluding the Negro from the historic Christian faith and tradition.

Joseph R. Washington, Jr.
Chaplain, Dickinson College
Carlisle, Pennsylvania

PREFACE TO THE PAPERBACK EDITION

Black Religion is not a dispassionate, erudite treatment of the Negro and his American Christian tradition. It is not unique as a criticism of white institutional influences within religion in general and Negro responses to Christianity in particular. But *Black Religion* is, I believe, the first work which challenges simultaneously and equally white and Negro congregations and denominations to close the gap between creed and deed. What hopefully makes this book unique is its revelation of the weaknesses in Negro qua Negro religious life. The Negro and his religion are here taken seriously because to fail to do so only protects the Negro by hiding his failures, by treating him as immature. Respect comes when it is assumed people are mature enough to answer charges and responsible enough to meet a negative challenge with positive change.

Hitherto, American whites harbored overwhelmingly romantic notions about both the exotic and the unusually deep religious character of Christians who are Negroes. Negroes have known better but felt it to be high treason to lay bare the realities. The nonviolent movement and its development in the southern churches of the drive for civil rights has practically made Negro congregations "untouchables," or organizations not to be criticized. A lieutenant in the SCLC could not get past the first chapter of *Black Religion* and was so incensed that on a radio interview he declared that I had given ammunition to the critics of the movement. Many whites have felt that *Black Religion's* criticisms of Negro religious life are precisely the criticisms they would make of their own churches. They have asked what is "new"? The answer is: nothing in practice; a great deal in purpose and meaning. Negro congregations have become less than their original intention demanded—by accident rather than design, by poverty rather than by an overabundance of well-being, by a paucity of rootedness and widespread uprootedness.

If the overstatements in this book stimulate both people and institutions to change, this is sufficient reason not to re-work the text. These pages are, I believe, filled with essentially correct destructive indictments. If Negro religious institutions are to continue to exist they need a purpose for existing meaningfully. It is now my hope to soon write as a complement to *Black Religion* a constructive statement suggesting a theology, a destiny, and a hope for Negroes in religious structures.

Joseph R. Washington, Jr.

A REVIEW
BY MARTIN E. MARTY

"The emergence of the militant Negro, insisting upon his rights as a human being and equality as a citizen, is the great, new fact of this half of the American twentieth century." With this sentence Joseph R. Washington, Jr., begins his original analysis of the spiritual factor in the Negro revolution.

Chronicles of the revolution are appearing with weary-ing frequency. Defenses of the American Negro are commonplace. Indictments of white Christian America are a dime a dozen. Washington's book is another chronicle, another defense, another indictment. But it is more than any of these and that "more" casts a different light on all of them. At last someone has examined what has happened theologically to Negro and white Christianity, to American life, and even to Western culture because of racial segregation.

Who cares about theology? Chaplain Washington of Dickinson College, who defines theology as "the interpretation of and response to the will of God for the faithful," cares. He is convinced that a church without theology is a contradiction in terms; that "black religion" is the Negro substitute for authentic faith and church life; that white Christianity is sick unto death because it cut Negroes off from the history of faith and the tradition of theology and because it does not experience the fullness of that history and tradition since it has been so busy remaining paternalistic or oppressive. Washington, more than any other Negro interpreter to date, has been informed by the Christian theological renewal of the 20th century. He draws deeply on the language of that renewal. Since to most people theology represents a rather crabby, specialized science practiced by pettily precise men in seminaries, it is remote from their experience. They will not immediately empathize with Chaplain Washington and may soon lose patience with him. If they do, if they fail to try to pursue his interpretation to its logical conclusions, they may miss the opportunity to see an enrichment of our whole cultural tradition.

Since so little has been written on the Negro revolution from the specialized theological viewpoint, it is necessary for readers to recognize Washington's specialized use of terms. "Religion," for one, is almost a dirty word in contrast to "faith." Religion is an impoverished and partial expression of a kind of faith. It is a purely human construction, designed by man to justify his own actions. In the case of *Black Religion*, it serves to create institutions which are "amusement centers for the disengaged," "arenas for power politics," and "organs for recognition." These institutions have not now and have never had any real reason for separate existence apart from race, either before or after Negro emancipation a century ago. They have succeeded in helping the Negro come to terms with his subordinate place in society. They have succeeded in cutting the typical Negro church member off from the rich resources of faith and tradition, have left him disinherited in Protestantism, impoverished in Christianity, homeless in Western culture.

Black Religion will have to be an unpopular book. The mere segregationist will reject it out of hand. The segregationist Christian will be enraged in the presence of Washington's convincing demonstration that segregated Christianity is a contradiction in terms and that separated white Christianity has not been and is not yet a full expression of the faith. Moderately liberal whites and white Christians will be bewildered over his argument that integration is an unsatisfactory and static resolution. It implies that white culture and white Christianity are healthy and intact and the Negro need merely be "fit in." Negro leaders will be embarrassed or angered. Washington has little sympathy, of course, for the Black Muslims as leaders, the Father Divines as exploiters, the Adam Clayton Powells as typical entrepreneurs in the field of "black religion."

Most painful of all are his searching criticisms of the finest Negro Christian leaders like Benjamin E. Mays of Morehouse College, the deeply spiritual Howard Thurman of Boston University, and Martin Luther King, Jr. He clearly admires all three, but uses each of them to suggest ways in which Negro Americans have been cut off from cultural and religious resources.

Take the example of Dr. King. In the public imagery, King represents the quality, depth and energy of Negro church life. He is accepted as the man who most of all contributes pure-form Christianity and the ideal of love to the racial revolution. But to a theologian like Washington, King is a syncretist. Washington defines the term popularly (a "hodge-podge," a "mixed salad bowl") when he says that King has tried to fuse Jesus' revelation of divine love with Gandhi's practice of non-violence; to confuse Christian love with the demand for justice—in short, to misunderstand the center of the Christian faith.

Chaplain Washington does not blame these Negro leaders for their failings; rather, he uses them to illustrate his grand theme:

When the Christian enterprise selfishly reserves the tradition and its dynamics, channeling the spirit of Christ and His Church to white people only, that is the greatest crime against man and defiance of God ever perpetrated in the name of love, justice, and mercy. This is the peculiar and primary sin of white Christians in

America and it cannot be laid at the door of socio-economic pressures. White churchmen alone are responsible for the creation of an exclusively white Christian community of faith. Negro Christians have a Christianity divorced from the mainstream of the Christian faith.

If *Black Religion* represented merely a prissy theological interpretation of Negro life, it could safely be dismissed by the leaders of the Negro revolt, who are increasingly secular in orientation, and by the majority of Americans, who care little about the details of Christian definition. But the book actually succeeds in involving all of us, all who live in and profit from and hope for Western culture. It reveals the malignancy at the core of that culture, a malignancy which shows itself on the surface in the tumor of segregated Christianity but which actually courses through our whole system. My metaphor of malignancy may suggest that it is too late for the tumor and the system. Sometimes Chaplain Washington speaks as if it is. But since he draws on a tradition that blends realism with hope, he looks ahead to therapy.

Complete, dynamic, profound assimilation of Negro religionists into the body of the Christian faithful and complete assimilation of all black cultural compartments into the cultural whole are the only possible hopes for therapy.

Those hopes are dimmed, and Washington's book is limited, by the fact that neither the Christian experience nor the cultural tradition are so vivid or vital as he sometimes makes them out to be. His descriptions of Black Religion, with its self-seeking institutionalism, its trivial goals, its ersatz spiritual appeals, its thoughtless and history-less devotion to short-range, local programs sound like nothing so much as the accepted pictures of much of mainstream middle-class Christianity. What good does it do the Negro to be assimilated with *that?* Will the people who worry about the tickets to the Christmas bazaar care about the tradition, the history, the quality and character of authentic faith? Washington anticipates this argument. He knows white Christianity is that sick. But, he contends, it at least has a memory, a history, a font for renewal. Black religion has none of these. It is alone, with only race to unite it.

If there is pathos in Washington's description of a white Christianity that does not know or use its spiritual and cultural resources, there is hope beyond his overly gloomy picture of the Negroes' religion. Everything he says about their systematic cultural deprivation is true, so far as theology and formal history are concerned. But Christianity is a faith which centers in events, sufferings, experiences, actions. The Negro believers represent a people on the move; they represent a memory of suffering. "Nothing ever seems to happen" in the bland, pale settlements of the white establishment. Negroes and Negro religionists have happenings to spare. Assimilation, therefore, could mean that the once-segregated factions each might bring distinctive and valid gifts.

If new political fanaticisms develop today, if forces of unreason prevail, if those impatient with history and unaware of guilt overcome, assimilation and sharing will be retarded. Indeed, they will not occur at all. *Black Religion* has given us fair warning of the price we will pay by citing the fearful price we have paid.

CONTENTS

Chapter 1

RELIGION AND
THE PROTEST MOVEMENT

The emergence of the militant Negro, insisting upon his rights as a human being and equality as a citizen, is the great, new fact of this half of the American twentieth century. This dynamic, creative revolution of a deprived people erupted in Montgomery, Alabama on Thursday, December 1, 1955; the momentous events which followed this historic date need not be retold here. Nonviolent, direct action has proven itself an effective moral force in the lives of Negro and white residents by urging the Supreme Court, the President of the United States, the local power structures, and communities, and individual consciences to action. The rising Negro is a victory for the human spirit. America in particular and the world in general are gaining new life with the Negro.

The nonviolent movement has brought about abrupt and sweeping changes in the patterns of discrimination and segregation. Shaken by this reality, many have sought the causes. Frequently it is attributed to the transforming power of religion, and it is often said that the Negro is winning the white man with love. This confusion of Christian terminology with passive resistance has certainly not hampered the movement; whether or not it has been an indispensable factor in it, is more difficult to determine. Almost all Negro and white Americans believe that Negroes are authentically and historically rooted in the Christian tradition, and the nonviolent movement provides an opportunity to ascertain the truth of this nearly universal assumption.

1

Montgomery and Martin Luther King, Jr.

Montgomery, Alabama is in the heart of the Bible Belt, in Dixie. Negroes attend church in this section in great numbers, with the same religious zeal as their separated white brethren. Of course the rigidity of segregation requires the Negro congregations to organize and support most of the community activities and social festivities, while members of white congregations are free to use a variety of municipal facilities. The social role of Negro churches is of great importance, especially among the Baptists, the denomination of the masses, whose members are not inclined to develop a distinctive social life in sororities, fraternities, social clubs, or community organizations. No less important is the position of the Baptist minister as the news medium of the community. He is expected to gather the local news and circulate it through his sermons on Sunday. In fact, almost all ministers in southern Negro communities are looked to as the disseminators of information, and the pipeline of the community leads directly to them.

When Mrs. Rosa Parks of Montgomery, Alabama decided that it was in her best interest to rest her weary body in a seat designated for white patrons and to ignore the segregated bus signs, she was arrested. It was not unusual that E. D. Nixon, the railroad porter who posted the bond for Mrs. Parks, also telephoned the ministers, informing them of the consensus to boycott the buses. It was natural, too, that the initial and subsequent mass meetings were held in church buildings, and were presided over by ministers. The ground swell to boycott the buses did not originate with the ministers, but they supported it. Of the 50,000 Negroes in Montgomery, 17,500 depended upon public transportation twice a day. This fact aided the unanimity of the decision; the leadership of this successful boycott was thrust upon the shoulders of the ministers, particularly those of the Reverend Dr. Martin Luther King, Jr.

King is a remarkable product of the South; barely tainted by his academic exposure in the North. He is a charming, quiet, well-groomed southern gentleman. A native of the South who graduated from Morehouse College in Atlanta, he earned further degrees from the Crozer Theological Seminary and Boston University. Extremely well qualified and prepared for his role as the leader in the area of civil rights, he is not an intellectual in the usual sense of this term. The environment of the South, his duties as a minister, and the work of mass noncooperation have not provided him with the oportunity to live with men and women of all races at every level. He is a solid product of the South in the sense that its history of segregation has kept him from the give and take of an open society, an advantage that, for instance, Harlem has despite its multitude of handicaps.

In fact, King is an outstanding example of the Baptist preacher. He has that Baptist hum which makes what is said only as important as how it is said. The key to being a successful Baptist preacher is being able to speak at once as a philosopher and as a man of religion, without distinguishing between the two. This is accomplished by using a tone of voice which so absorbs one's audience in the emotion that anything which is said is cushioned. The usual approach is to begin a sermon with a philosophical statement such as, "One of the great glories of democracy is the right to protest for right." This is followed by numerous examples of the present situation: "We have no alternative but to protest. For many years, we have shown amazing patience. We have sometimes given our white brothers the feeling that we liked the way we were being treated." Then comes the Biblical injunction "to turn the other cheek." Other scriptural passages are added to suggest the way in which one would thereupon enter jail, "as a bridegroom enters the bride's chamber." As the climax nears there is an admonition to love drawn not only from the Bible but perhaps from some past tower of strength such as Booker T. Washington, who said, "Let no man pull you so low as to make you hate him." As the sermon or lecture is concluded, such words as these may be heard:

If you will protest courageously, and yet with dignity and Christian love, when the history books are written in future generations, the historians will have to pause and say, "There lived a great people—a black people—who injected new meaning and dignity into the veins of civilization." This is our challenge and our overwhelming responsibility.

Then comes the climax: "In this spirit the victory is assured. Glory hallelujah! Glory hallelujah!"

The boycott in Montgomery was the result of an unplanned incident, the arrest of Mrs. Parks. King and various other ministers were given the reins in guiding the ensuing Negro protest; the mass meetings were steeped in religious imagery and shot through with Biblical themes. It was natural for them to fall back upon their convictions in time of trouble, and King is proud of the fact that the movement was first spoken of in terms of "Christian love." Although the moral justification for civil disobedience and nonviolence had shaped the movement from its beginning,

. . . it was the Sermon on the Mount, rather than a doctrine of passive resistance, that initially inspired the Negroes of Montgomery to dignified social action. It was Jesus of Nazareth that stirred the Negroes to protest with the creative weapon of love.[1]

In his first speech to the demonstrators on December 5, 1955, King attempted to combine what he called "two apparent irreconcilables." He sought to "arouse the group to action by insisting that their self-respect was at stake." This was balanced by "a strong affirmation of the Christian doctrine of love" as a means to "keep this fervor within controllable and Christian bounds."

Our actions must be guided by the deepest principles of Christian faith. Love must be our regulating ideal. Once again we must hear the words of Jesus echoing across the centuries: "Love your enemies, bless them that curse you, and pray for them that despitefully use you."

Despite the words used, the absence of any real theological understanding here is blatant. But King's problem was a boycott. Was "boycott" the right word for a Christian minister? What should be done? How should it be done? These were King's problems and, as we shall see, in his espousal of passive resistance, King was thinking basically as a philosopher and not as a theologian. Far from being a criticism of King's Christian stature or the quality of the movement, this discussion is simply an investigation of the roots of nonviolent resistance.

In his impressive book *Stride Toward Freedom*, King points out that the term "boycott" was immediately accepted by everyone including himself. The appeal of "massive noncooperation" did not prevent the use of coercion in the transportation boycott, the avowed purpose of which was to gain a more just seating and hiring policy. King first turned to Thoreau's essay "On the Duty of Civil Disobedience," where he found a precedent for noncooperation with the evil system of segregation as strongly evidenced in the Montgomery bus company. Apparently, he had already begun to consider noncooperation within the whole segregated pattern in Montgomery. Yet, neither the Montgomery Improvement Association nor the Southern Christian Leadership Conference were able to gain equality in any area other than public transportation.

Although the Montgomery movement began as a boycott of buses and moved to a massive noncooperative platform, the latter was more philosophical.

In an effort to clarify the just aim of the movement, every attempt was made to differentiate its method and objective from that of the boycotts aided by the White Citizens Council: "Our method will be that of persuasion, not coercion." But a boycott cannot be camouflaged and the claim of persuasion as distinguished from coercion is meaningless. While the aim of the militant movement may certainly be favorably contrasted with that of the Ku Klux Klan, it cannot be denied that the immediate way of reaching the goal of non-discriminatory seating and hiring was based on the use of power.

This distinction between persuasion and coercion was a response to the peculiar situation. First, it represented a clear-cut severance from the purposes of retaliation vis-à-vis the forces of oppression. Second, there was a need to develop a sound philosophy and strategy to guide and direct the movement. Third, it was desirable to maintain the high interest and enthusiasm of the masses without resorting to violence. Fourth, there was the hope of gaining universal support via a positive interpretation by the widely represented mass media. To meet this situation, basic principles of nonviolence were set forth and guided the movement: (1) to offer active yet nonviolent resistance to evil; (2) to awaken moral shame in the opponent as a means of redeeming and reconciling him; (3) to attack an evil system rather than the persons involved in its perpetuation; (4) to accept but not inflict or avoid violence and retaliation; (5) to act out of love, whereby the broken community can be restored on a more genuine basis; and (6) to have faith that justice is at the heart of the universe.

Nonviolence has been thoroughly accepted as a technique, even by those in the majority who do not adhere to it as a philosophy of life. King repeatedly affirms that violence is both immoral and impractical, and at least this feeling has won the day.

Love as the Regulating Ideal

The reason why the preachers of nonviolence originally attempted to use love as a tool of massive noncooperation is understandable. They considered this the best means of controlling the masses in the movement for justice. The nonviolent movement was and is a positive one, yet its Christian ingredient remains a restraining, negative one— that is why Christian love is termed the "regulating ideal." "Christian love" represents the kingdom of God theme; it is heaven contrasted with the hell of hate, and it is other-worldly in its implications. In a sense, the Christian theme is an expression of the desire to be all things to all men. Apparently, faith in the nonviolent movement was so shaky as to demand religious sanction, but precious little thought was given to rooting it in the Christian faith. To do so would have probably confused the movement on its philosophical side, as surely as the failure to do so has confused it on its religious side. Apparently, too, there was a woeful lack of confidence that the masses would take to the nonviolent movement without the dangling of "sugar plums"—"no cross, no crown."

In addition, King assumed that nonviolence would produce guilt on the part of the influential white minority. Guilt, in response to the unjust suffering of the Negro, would presumably cause a great wave of sentiment. This sentiment would create a climate in which the just demands of the Negro would be met, and would thus provide the condition for the healing or redemption of the broken community through reconciliation or love. Thus King viewed love as "passive" and nonviolence as "resistance" and attempted to wed what he had earlier called two "apparent irreconcilables."

But the reason they are irreconcilable is not apparent to King. Love and the strategy of nonviolence are two different forces. One is not more weak or passive than the other. They are both to be distinguished from sentiment and affection. They may both be best described as "passionate resistance," not "passive resistance." Love is the greater of the two, for love is not afraid of either physical or spiritual violence and, indeed, may use them creatively for its good end. But nonviolence fears violence; indeed, it is not nonviolence in violence, while love is love even in violence.

Love and nonviolence may work together but they cannot be fused. The root of love is in God, interpreted through theology. The root of nonviolence is in philosophy and it need not rely upon God. Love and theology need philosophy to operate in the context of the human community, to determine the content and quality of justice. But love and theology always transcend, or bear a corrective on, philosophy; just as God must always transcend man and correct him.

Why did King attempt to fuse love with nonviolence? He has always insisted upon "love as the regulating ideal" of the movement. He feared that a militant movement would generate hate and bloodshed administered at the hands of Negroes (he already expected them to be the victims of bloodshed). To prevent this, he mixed with non-violence a dash of love. Love, as a universal principle, was induced to control hate and bloodshed, as well as to prevent conflict. Instead of constituting a positive factor, love was injected as a negative factor.

Now, the reason King did not follow the path of love is that love cannot be motivated, forced, contrived, or demanded. Regardless of the situation, however clear and obvious the need, it must always be a free response. Love is neither calculating nor calculable. Given the Montgomery situation King made the decision that the Negro could not wait for love. He needed an immediate means of forcing the Negro to act in behalf of justice. He found the method in Mahatma Gandhi's massive noncooperation and militant nonviolence. If this method had been followed to its logical conclusion, it would have borne all the freight from the beginning, as it now does in the present. The philosophy of nonviolence was and is a sufficient guide. But King added a religious element, naming it the "Christian doctrine of love." He was able to do this only by seeing the love expressed in Jesus through the eyes of Gandhi. Gandhi had previously turned the ethic of love into a principle and King merely accepted this syncretism.

King borrowed more than nonviolence from Gandhi. He accepted his syncretic spirit, and it is as though Socrates, Thoreau, Hegel, and Jesus were all dumped together into one philosophical bowl like tossed salad. It is this syncretistic inclination combined with King's undoubted impact that continues to make Negroes mistake religion for faith.

Religion is always a partial expression of some faith. Religion, or more precisely some of its practitioners, may seek to harmonize or syncretize some of its elements with other religions. Faith does seek to acknowledge the common ground it shares with other faiths, but it does not seek to reduce itself to them or vice versa. Christianity acknowl-

edges its roots in Judaism and their common areas of agreement—it does not seek to equate the two. The error in syncretism is that it is blind to the honest differences inherent
in various faiths. In seeking the lowest common denominator
among religions there is the risk of rubbing out the authentic
dimension in each. This is the grave error of all Negro
religion, and it is due to lack of theology, as we shall discover. For the present it is sufficient to point out that the
syncretistical element in King is due to the dominance of
philosophy over systematic theology.

Negro Baptist preachers like King are expected to generate more heat than light. In this tradition, sermons and
speeches tend to be inspirational and are virtually unprepared. One draws upon all his resources to make a point.
Often this resource tends to be more philosophical than theological. King makes a point of the enthusiasm which followed his initial speech as head of the Montgomery movement. It was not well-planned, but it evoked such a response
that he said: "I came to see for the first time what the older
preachers meant when they said, 'Open your mouth and
God will speak for you.'" Of course, King prepares his sermons and addresses, but his comment suggests one reason
for the fuzziness of his blend of philosophy with theology.
Moreover, as a Baptist, King is not disciplined by a theology
or a community of faith and thus is free to interpret the
Bible as he feels led. The influence that such a spirit has on
the Negro as a whole is enormous.

A clear-cut instance of his syncretism is in the endeavor
to fuse Christian love and nonviolence. King declares that
Christian love, the Sermon on the Mount, and Jesus of Nazareth sparked the Negroes in Montgomery to "protest with
the creative weapon of love." He continues by pointing out
that prior to reading Gandhi he had viewed the ethics of
Jesus as effective only in a one-to-one relationship: "But
after reading Gandhi, I saw how utterly mistaken I was."

He concludes his homage to Gandhi and "pilgrimage to nonviolence" with these revealing lines: "Gandhi was probably the first person in history to lift the love ethic of Jesus above mere interaction between individuals to a powerful and effective social force on a large scale. Love for Gandhi was a potent instrument for social and collective transformation." Elsewhere too he speaks of love as a principle or a weapon.

King has come to understand love through the syncretistical religion of Gandhi. His philosophy has led him to see Jesus of Nazareth as a man who taught love in his Sermon on the Mount. King did not come to love or to Jesus through the eyes of the Christian faith.

The Christian understanding and support of revolution, at least in the Protestant tradition which King represents, has never been plumbed. Thus King, in the midst of the crisis, was in no position to add to the theological dimension —he was in need of a guide to action. As we have seen, he turned in his need to the inspired example of Gandhi and the method of nonviolence. He thus combined what he believed were two necessary and potent weapons for the Negro—"the Christian doctrine of love operating through the Gandhian method of nonviolence." He drew upon a well-tested philosophy and method, supported by an underdeveloped theological doctrine.

Love as the "regulating ideal" was irrelevant from the beginning. Love and Christ may have been indispensable to the ministers and leaders of the Montgomery movement, but if the Montgomery story has any validity, it is this: the spirit was Martin Luther King, Jr. It is doubtful that the people were motivated by love. But that they were motivated by the will to dignity and justice—without humiliation by a transportation system they largely supported—is indubitable. King is quite convincing when he describes the spirit and the motivation in his own words, to his own people: "We are tired . . . tired! . . . tired of being kicked

about by the brutal feet of oppression. Now we have no
alternative but to protest." Anyone who has heard the ring-
ing "Amens" which always follow such an oration knows
that therein is spirit and motivation enough.

Love as redemptive, understanding, disinterested good
will in action—to create a just and equitable community in
which all men are brothers—is, in principle, the center of
nonviolence. The ideal of loving the enemy and the equation of the strategy of love with the technique of nonviolence
may have been promoted in Montgomery in the very early
stages of the militant movement. But in Birmingham now,
love is at best peripheral and at worst excluded. Dr. King
speaks less of love and more of "legitimate and unavoidable
impatience":

Frankly, I have never yet engaged in a direct-action movement
that was "well timed," according to the timetable of those who
have not suffered unduly from the disease of segregation. For
years now I have heard the word "wait!" It rings in the ear of
every Negro with a piercing familiarity. This "wait" has almost
always meant "never." It has been a tranquilizing Thalidomide,
relieving the emotional stress for a moment only to give birth to
an ill-formed infant of frustration. We must come to see with the
distinguished jurist of yesterday that "justice too long delayed
is justice denied." We have waited more than 340 years for our
constitutional and God-given rights. The nations of Asia and
Africa are moving with jet-like speed toward the goal of political
independence, and we still creep at horse and buggy pace toward
the gaining of a cup of coffee at a lunch counter.

Obviously, the honeymoon with love has given way to a
pragmatic emphasis upon justice. The religion of love is no
longer at the center of the nonviolent movement. Instead
of reconciliation and the Man on the Cross, there is the image
of the cup of endurance running over.

The Montgomery Improvement Association, headed

by King, was unable to live up to its name. It grew out of the optimism of the effective bus boycott, but the hope that the MIA would be extended for the purposes of desegregation in other areas of the community was not realized. King had developed a dynamic philosophy and method which he was unable to put into further practice there. The opportunity to implement the decisions of the Supreme Court on a regional rather than a local basis presented itself in January of 1957. When King left Montgomery to head the Atlanta-based Southern Christian Leadership Conference (SCLC), it was already incumbent upon him to determine the nature of his direction. The choice was between presenting an image of a militant civil rights leader with a deep and private religious faith, or one of a spiritual leader with a concern for civil rights.

Rise of the Militant Negro

The religious movement which began in isolation in Montgomery has spread into a nationwide revolution, increasingly independent of religious emphases. Insofar as the Negro in America is militant, the religious dimension of his cry of "freedom now" is in the background rather than the foreground.

Prayers, Biblical themes, ministerial personalities, and hymn singing have all added a religious aura to the nonviolent movement. The experimental nature of the beginning in Montgomery was conducive to the mixing of religion with nonviolence. The leaders of the movement were also the ministers of the people, who were open to a pinch of holy sanction.

To some extent, religious prayer and singing continue

as a technique. But the infusion of religion into the basic method of the militant movement began and ended in the 1950's. The legal end of bus segregation in Montgomery came December 21, 1956. The remainder of the 1950's was comparatively inconspicuous. Disenchantment and nation-wide spread of the movement began in the 1960's.

The sit-ins started on February 1, 1960, in Greensboro, North Carolina. Four freshman students from the North Carolina Agricultural and Technical College initiated a chain reaction of stand-ins, kneel-ins, wade-ins, and lie-ins. They spontaneously seated themselves at the all-white counter of the Woolworth dime store in Greensboro. Within a matter of hours they were joined by other students. By the spring of 1960, sit-ins were commonplace throughout the South and in many urban communities in the North.

From this event on, the nonviolent movement developed into what is acknowledged as the American Revolution of 1963. In the face of increasing white pressure the students requested help, which was immediately forthcoming from the Congress of Racial Equality (CORE).

CORE had experience in the technique of nonviolent, direct mass action in the desegregating of facilities in northern metropolitan communities. Len Holt and several other field representatives were dispatched to Greensboro, where they conducted intensive institutes in the method of non-violent mass protests. King went to Greensboro to lend his support. Herbert Wright, then youth secretary for the National Association for the Advancement of Colored People (NAACP), was also in Greensboro.

The key to the sit-ins was the resolution of the students to advance the cause of justice and equality through the method of nonviolence. King was an incalculable inspiration to them as a man of nonviolence—but not as a man of God. The sit-in movement quickly spread both North and South and inspired the participation of white, as well as Negro, students. The seriousness with which the students subscribed to the direct mass action approach is seen in the organization of the Student Non Violent Coordinating Committee (SNICK).

Students were largely responsible for the desegregation of lunch counters in the chain drug stores and dime stores in about ten cities. Enthusiasm, a clear-cut issue and a belief in practical results motivated these young college men and women. If there had previously been any question as to whether the method of nonviolent mass protest was sufficient without its confusion with Christian love, it ended with the student protests. Indeed, the student protests took the initiative away from King and the Southern Christian Leadership Conference for a number of months. They also influenced the non-religious pattern of the movement in the 1960's.

This generation of students is cast in a mold different from that of their inspirers in Montgomery. They exhibit the refreshing candidness of youth, and there is exhilaration in their new-found boldness, cohesiveness and lack of inhibitions. This youthful Negro tends to be disarmingly direct, impatient, and militant in his demand for equality. He has infected his white peers with the urgency of action, while maintaining his distinction through such tendencies as his preference for gospel songs over folk music. Negro students of today differ from previous generations in their liking of Scotch, hitchhikes and CORE, as compared with the less exciting world of soda pop, picnics and compulsory chapel.

The old-time religious fervor is still valuable. It is transposed, however, from hymns to soul music, expressed in the passion of rallies and postgraduate seminars against a background of gospel tunes, rhythm, and blues. The moralities which once dictated that female students be occupied with the wearing of a bonnet to Sunday Vespers, and refraining from smoking, have given way to a deep concern about at least one ethical issue. The past virtues of formality, rigidity, dedication to sublime ideals, and imitation of ephemeral middle-class phoniness have withered. In their stead is a serious commitment to informality, flexibility, the immediacy of living from moment to moment, and the pride of being a Negro.

King is the inimitable symbol of the nonviolent movement—he is the undisputed spokesman for the masses. But he does not speak the language of the students, cut as he is from the old pattern of Baptist preachers. There is greatness in King, but there is also a stiffness. He knows the world of Baptist congregations and the medium of the cloistered halls of academia—he does not know the fullness of life. This is to be expected since he followed his twenty-seven years of education with the pastorate of the Dexter Avenue Baptist Church in Montgomery. In this post he enjoyed a meteoric rise to international acclaim. Yet the religious phrases he has been forced to depend upon fail to impress students.

Contemporary students are preoccupied with their cultural roots and the search for identity. If they have a spokesman, it is James Baldwin. He is unmistakably and unashamedly a Negro; this much he has in common with King. An intellectual, Baldwin is honest, perceptive, and freewheeling. He enjoys life, all of life, and he is a man of conviction and courage with a power over words dictated by thought as well as by emotion. He has been thrust into the role of lecturer, speaking to the student mind in a way withheld from King. On the other hand, he would be readily dismissed from the minds of the Negro masses. Baldwin is determined to face the real issue of the Negro question at its roots without blurring the American dilemma. Fortunately for him and for Americans in general, he is not limited by ministerial or political habits. He is able to be himself and not what others would expect or like for him to be.

Philosophically, James Baldwin is decidedly bent in the direction of existentialism, now greatly in vogue among college students. He speaks in the current idiom, avoiding the classical terminology of philosophy or religion. His appeal is to the head and to the heart. While he does not advocate hate, neither does he hide the rage and anger of the Negro. King has been described as the patron saint of the student protesters. This is undoubtedly true. But when he speaks to them in the idiom of religion there is no immediate communication. The great majority of Negro college students, like most college students, are anti-religious in the formal sense. The language of religion and the example of the churches do not meet them where they are. There is a community of feeling among student resisters and their success tends to prompt this question: "Who needs religion?" Though they sing spirituals—"We Shall Overcome"— and pray before the oppressor, this is a way of fortifying their nonviolence, not an affirmation of their faith in Christian love. The interracial, interreligious and intercultural bond of student protests transcends any common religious commitment.

There is a new religion among Negro students, but not a renewal of faith. The religion is that of belief in direct mass action as the shortest distance to equality. They do not operate from the platform of Christian love. For students, Christian love is ambiguous; it does not commend itself with justice to the student mind. Love is not needed as a control factor for them; they are bright enough to see that nonviolence is the only practical method. The example of King and the training they have received allows them to see that nonviolence is a powerful technique and, as a technique, is independent of Christian love. Moreover, love concerns itself with the post-revolutionary period; it is the way of life in the millennium. Students realistically see the present task as breaking through the barriers, for they do not believe the brotherhood of man will come immediately. This realism has infected King. Nevertheless, since these students sing spirituals and kneel-in at houses of worship, the claim is still held that the movement is a religious one.

When one looks at the nature of the organizations involved in the protest movement, it is difficult to see it as other than a secular one. The NAACP, CORE, SNICK, and the SCLC can hardly be said to have grown out of a religious revival. If they have a belief in common, it is belief in justice and the moral potential of man. Their leaders may use religious terms, but this is part of the American speaking pattern. The healthy factor in the student witness is that when they sing "Lord, I want to be a Christian" within jail cells it is a morale booster and they neither intend nor pretend it to be more.

It is also clear that when they kneel-in at houses of worship the furthermost thing from their minds is worship. They are attempting to bring shame to and illuminate the sham of the congregation that claims to believe in love while excluding the Negro. This is a powerful witness because these students kneel-in in interracial fellowship. They know what real love is. They have eaten, lived, marched, and gone to jail together.

The clearest indication that Negro students do not equate this new religion with the old religion of empty gestures came to light in May of 1963. The students who marched silently in the streets of Greensboro were teeming with resistance. The authorities permitted them to march unmolested. Primed for nonviolent action but provided with no opportunity for expression, they were frustrated by the nonviolent method of the police force. (Incidentally, it cannot be readily assumed that these policemen were motivated by Christian love—nonetheless, they were effective.) Frustration could have led to overt action on the part of the students.

Happily, their leaders did not allow the disappointment to spill over into destructive violence—in the city or on the campus. The students were led back to the meeting house. There they were allowed to relieve their anxieties through the rocking and rolling singing of gospel tunes to which they put their own words born of the situation. The powerful cohesion produced by the singing of hymns and spirituals as a morale builder, aiding protestors to withstand the pellets of the street or the confinement of jail, was not necessary in Greensboro. Not spiritual uplift, but emotional release, was the technique of this situation.

A further instance of the non-religious motivation occurred in this same month in Birmingham. There, for the first time, children poured out of schools instead of adults out of meeting houses. This left the semi-liberal white person limp. But these children had heard their brothers and sisters, fathers and mothers, and aunts and uncles speaking about their resistance during the previous days. They had seen them facing dogs, fire hoses, the local police, and the state militia. They were eager to join this emancipation from docility. For the first time in their lives they could be proud of their elders. Few would claim that these children put up their lives by reason of faith or overblown arguments.

The example followed by the resisting children and students was not Jesus Christ. The spirit of Montgomery, as manifested by King, was the real guide. Indeed, the grandeur and misery of being a Negro is sufficient motivation. To be a young Negro facing a lifetime of indignities is too bitter a pill to swallow passively in a day of universal achievement in human dignity. A large majority of the students graduating from Negro colleges in the South will remain there. The minority of students forming the protest movement believe that their improved economic status as, for example, teachers, rather than domestic workers, the lot of many parents, means they can buy more things than their fathers and mothers were able to purchase—but without any increase in their rights as citizens. It is this awareness which supplies the courage to sit-in. The price for dignity is not too high—abuse from the white community and expulsion from the pressured Negro institutions.

Students are extremely sensitive to their deprivation, even as they attend Negro institutions of higher learning. They are burning with the realization that segregated college life separates them from the main currents of democratic thought, owing to the economic and social regimentation which prevails even as they gain something like a liberal education. In their direct action they seek the immediate goals of dignity with opportunity. They willingly follow ministers because they trust their example in civil liberties, not their views on ultimate goals and theological questions.

As the movement spreads North, it is undeniably enkindled by discrimination. Adults, students, and children think in terms of the method of nonviolence, not the strategy of love. Ministers, alone, speak in terms of the strategy of love —but, as the movement spreads and the resistance stiffens, even they recognize that justice is the present goal. There is acknowledgment on the part of all nonviolent participants that the power of love may be a transforming reality. Less and less it is claimed as the force of change in *de facto* and *de jure* segregation-discrimination.

In their attack upon the socio-economic system, Negroes are angry. This is a wholesome emotion, a far cry from docility. They are on the offensive rather than the defensive. Negroes neither hate nor love their enemies, the former being impractical and the latter impossible. Negroes simply know their enemies, and in this knowledge lies their strength. Sensitive to the need of pulling together, comedians (Dick Gregory), executives (Jackie Robinson), fighters (Floyd Patterson), and singers (Al Hibbler) gladly join ministers, housewives, social workers, teachers, and children. They are not motivated by Christian love, but by the cause of justice and are united under King's slogan—repeated even in the poolrooms of Birmingham: "Violence is not only immoral but impractical." The dynamic of the revolution is neither love nor hate but the truth expressed in this dictum: "Might and right rule the world; fight 'til right is ready."

Relevance of Massive Noncooperation

From its inception, the nonviolent method has been concerned with justice at the same time that it has been confused with love. Admittedly, this move toward justice has not been hampered by the red herring of love evoked in conversations, speeches, and sermons. What is unfortunate, however, is that the tension between justice and love, or action and thought, has added one more nail to the coffin of faith among Negroes—*and* given a new lease on life to a withering Negro religion.

The cohesive forces of militant nonviolence have not created a new religion among the Negro so much as a new shape for the old black or folk religion. This new shape of folk religion, militant identity for the purposes of justice, is amazingly successful. Negroes have always been attracted by the religion of success, although previously the success seemed to be relegated to the world beyond this one. Now that black religion may be equated with success in this world it is in danger of becoming enough. Religion is always more immediately rewarding and glamorous than is faith, but religion is not faith. Religion requires a little discipline and some restraint, but no fundamental change, to ascertain the goal. For example, persons who join in the nonviolent movement are required only to suffer without retaliation, but in every other regard they are free to be and to do as they will. Religion is concerned with neither justice nor love, but with technique.

On the other hand, justice and love are distinct but indispensable dimensions of faith. Faith demands a fundamental change in the individual. Its direction is shaped and tested by a community of believers instructed by tradition and history. Faith must always be a response to God. Religion may be a response to whatever the individual desires. Faith stands in judgment on all religion, and is the critic of every religion. It is the concern with *the* Ultimate above every limited or limiting concern. Thus, faith is not concerned solely with one aspect of a man's life but with the whole of life. It is out of faith that one makes every decision and wills to be loyal to God in every moment. But in religion a man may place his value on some goal or god which he confuses with God.

When King speaks of the redemptive, reconciling, and healing nature of Christian love, he is speaking about faith. But in reducing this Christian love to a technique and equating it with dignity and massive noncooperation he turns faith into a religion.

In the heat of battle one does not have time to make every shot count, and rapid fire may be more immediately effective—it may at least throw the enemy off guard and lead him to believe that behind the smoke there is real power. This is what King has done on the firing line of civil rights. As a result, he has not only advanced Negroes in the areas of real and urgent concerns; he has also led them to assume that the religion of the nonviolent mass movement is the Christian faith, or certainly *a* faith. A ready instance of this misunderstanding is found in the writing of Louis Lomax. He prides himself upon being a critic and a knowledgeable man. Yet, like so many of his more humble brethren, he interchanges religion with faith. In *The Negro Revolt* Lomax speaks of direct mass action as the new religion of the Negro and then follows with this spurious description:

This faith, given incipient articulation by Martin Luther King, was the culmination of a hundred years of folk suffering. Like all faiths, it is peculiar to the people who fashioned it; it was a hodgepodge, as every faith is, of every ethical principle absorbed by my people from other cultures. And so the best of Confucius, Moses, Jesus, Gandhi and Thoreau was extracted, then mixed with the peculiar experience of the Negro in America. The result was a faith that justified the bus boycott and inspired Negro college students to make a moral crusade out of their right to sit down in a restaurant owned by a white man and eat a hamburger.[3]

While Lomax does not understand the meaning of faith (though he was reared by his uncle, a fellow Baptist minister with the Reverend Martin Luther King, Sr., in Georgia), he articulates the poverty of faith in a majority of Negroes. This pithy statement is directed toward Martin Luther King, Jr. It is obvious from the reading of *Stride Toward Freedom* that King has to bear the responsibility for a "hodgepodge" interpretation of faith. His impact upon the American Negro has led too many to continue to equate religiosity with faith.

For Martin Luther King, Jr., and for many others, the Sermon on the Mount is the key to the teachings of Jesus and serves as shorthand for Christian principles. In this way love as a principle is interpreted as the "Christian doctrine of love" without sensitivity to the fact that the use of the Christian understanding of love apart from the Christian faith is a violent distortion.

Faith begins with the cross and resurrection of Jesus Christ, not with the man from Nazareth or with the Sermon on the Mount. The Christian is one who has faith in Jesus Christ as Lord. He affirms this faith not by beginning with the ministry of Jesus, but, like the disciples, from the vantage point of the cross and the resurrection. From this perspective the teachings of Jesus are revealing in a way they are not when one begins at the point of Jesus' ministry. Beginning with faith in the Lordship of Jesus Christ, the Christian understands that he cannot interpret the teachings of Jesus as he wishes and must interpret them in the light of the cross and resurrection. The teachings of Jesus are not manipulative principles which can be taken out of the context of faith and used for whatever purposes are at hand.

The syncretist is aware that the teachings of Jesus are readily available to anyone who wishes to live by them, or wishes to use them as a basis for principles. The syncretist who also happens to be interested in civil rights is free to interpret the teachings of Jesus as principles and to use them to spark action in the realm of civil liberties. But he is not free to assume that by so pulling the ethic of love out of context, for example, he is thus "emphasizing the Christian doctrine of love." This can only be expressed through the medium of the community of faith.

To say that the nonviolent movement is based upon Christian principles is no more significant than to say that pacifism stems from the same source. It is quite possible to be involved in either or both of these movements without adhering to the Christian faith, however loyal one may be to Christian principles. Christian principles are no more peculiar to the faithful Christian than the principles of democracy are unique to the people of America. The principles of Christianity, like those of democracy, belong to those who appropriate them. They are forms without specific content—to be shaped by the respective heritages of those who embrace them.

The Christian is not motivated by principles, even those expressed in the Sermon on the Mount. He is committed to responding to God, as Jesus Christ before him, in the best interest of his fellowman. Such a response is without an exact formula, but nevertheless it is imperative. It is based upon a love relationship between God, man, and fellowman, a love relationship which calls forth a unique response in every situation, for every situation is unique. The Christian understands that the imitation of Jesus is valid only at the point where he submits his will to the will of God.

Consequently, the Christian faith is irrelevant to the nonviolent movement. This has been true from its inception. It has been proved beyond all doubt in the explosion of the revolution in the 1960's.

The principle of love, disguised as the Christian doctrine of love, was added to the militant movement of direct action as an insurance policy. It was not invalid to introduce love as a principle. Certainly Gandhi had done so before King. The only invalidity is the equation of the principle of love, which is truly universal, with love as it is understood in the Christian faith.

Militant noncooperation is an overwhelming success in its dignity, objective, effectiveness, and intrinsic worth. The failure of the movement is its by-product as a religion, a religion which in the eyes of an influential number of Negroes is equated with the Christian faith. The form of the movement and the content of its language, expressed by persons held in esteem, have unconsciously, but no less effectively, preserved a status quo Negro religion.

It is difficult to measure the impact of King and other Negro ministers upon their followers. They are raising to new heights the historical role of the Negro minister as the leader in civil rights. The price of leadership is that it entails following the people. The danger is that the effectiveness in one area produces the effect of "expertise" in every other area the leader considers worthy of his involvement.

Nonviolence as a technique is acceptable. It is declared *the way* to justice and equality and marches under the protection of the virtually unassailable banner which reads "It is *the* Christian way." To cast the nonviolent movement in the role of being the only Christian approach implies that any other way is not Christian. This leads to the inference that the Christian faith is devoid of justice and/or punishment; that it allows only the acceptance of voluntary suffering. At the root of this interpretation of Christianity is the cross, where God in Christ voluntarily accepted crucifixion as a means of His love and His will to redeem the world. But the cross was not contrived. God did not force men to act in any particular way. The truth of the cross is not only that God's way is the way of reconciliation—but that God's way is the way of freedom of choice. Men still have the right to choose for or against God, for or against suffering, for or against love. The way of nonviolence provides no choice because it preempts freedom of will. In this light even its method is not *the* Christian way, though it may be *a* Christian way (and more clearly a way of some Christians).

Anything which is Christian may be more than, but it cannot be less than, what is human. It is not inhuman to strike out for what is right—herein lies the strength of the nonviolent attack for equality. But the nonviolent movement claims to be Christian in its pressuring of others to the point where they react in violence and then the argument is that *the* Christian response to precipitated violence is to accept it—as if in punishment for guilt-ridden action. That is, the nonviolent argument claims to be both in the battle and above the battle. This is an attempt to be God, and the Christian faith declares that this is the persistent sin of man. It is both Christian and human to choose to do what is clearly right, but nonviolence does not allow for this choice in either its methods or its results. Nonviolence as a philosophy wishes to be God in defining the boundaries, a desire which is not Christian though it is perhaps human.

The Christian way is freedom of choice; it is this way

which is held in common with what is fully human or moral. Nonviolence seeks this Christian and human way for the Negro. But nonviolence is predicated on the assumption that the Negro has no freedom of choice, and it seeks to gain this choice by claiming that its method is both Christian and human—or moral. The right of the Negro to this choice is certainly Christian and human. What is not clear is that the nonviolent *technique* (as it is realistically and rightly called) is Christian and human.

Nonviolent resisters are urged to protest with "dignity and Christian love." Dignity is the human counterpart to what is Christian. Nonviolence clearly lost any claim to what is Christian in its coercive tactics. The emphasis upon dignity is indicative of its religious pretensions—for the non-violent movement attempts to be more than human; it calls followers to be superhuman—which is not a Christian admonition. When a pregnant woman is kicked in the streets of Birmingham, dignity demands that neither she nor anyone else protect either her or the unborn innocent child. At this point nonviolence loses any claim to being human and takes on superhuman qualities. For one clear criterion of being human and having dignity is self-defense. It is the human thing to do to protect oneself if one is attacked. But nonviolence robs the resister of this dignity or humanity and turns him into a superman. This is accomplished by advancing a situation to the point of violence and then claiming innocence, whereupon the resister becomes a sacrificial lamb. Yet a sacrificial lamb, in the classic sense, is innocent in a way that the resister is not.

The goal of justice and equality for the Negro is both Christian and human. The means to this end, massive and militant noncooperation in nonviolence, is both unChristian and inhuman. What is more important, nonviolence is an effective weapon which does not require the universal and unanimous approval which it deceptively seeks under the banners of being both Christian and human.

Christianity continues to be viewed as an indefatigable factor in Negro life. The argument is that the Negro is inherently Christian and that the best indicator of this is the protest movement. The contrary is true. Christianity as a factor in nonviolence is involved in its end, but merely alluded to in its means. The massive noncooperation movement may be the clearest evidence available that Christianity has always been of less than primary importance for the Negro. Just as Christianity is perverted in this movement for the purposes of control and morale, so it may have been with black religion all along.

A defense for the religion of the Negro race has been made on the basis that it constituted the first Negro institution of proven value throughout its history—the present being its finest hour. The nonviolent movement has added to the evidence that Negro houses of worship are essential as meeting places and that black religion is a source of Negro leadership. But the movement has also declared that every other aspect of Christianity is of limited value and interest. Christianity has served as a cohesive force in the Negro community—but the content was such that this force might well have been derived from another source. And although the congregations of the Negro filled this vacuum, the nonviolent movement intends to dispose of the vacuum. (The question is whether the revolution will also dispose of Negro religiosity). It is generally agreed that the Negro congregations in the South are still needed as organs of comunication, as they are in the urban North. But this is at best temporary and at worst a prostitution.

The story of the protest movement is that the trappings of religion are increasingly playing a minor role in the life of the Negro—insofar as religion involves commitment to the

Christian faith. In the wake of this commitment, the revolution is injecting new vitality into an old form of black religion.

Unhappily, as the Negro advances on the front of civil rights there is a comparative retreat in the sphere of Church equality. As a result of the success of the revolution, mixed as it is with pseudo-faith, it is more difficult to immerse the Negro into another area from which he has been excluded—the Christian faith and community. The same point may be made another way—Negro qua Negro denominational institutions and congregations are distinct from their white counterparts in ecclesiastical separation as well as in their failure to contribute anything to the Christian community they claim to represent. Instead of the Christian faith, the principle of love keeps black religion alive. This unfortunate fact is a deterrent to the full participation of the Negro (as a whole people) in the mainstream of the Church universal and the American culture.

But the revolution will accomplish its objective and fade from the scene. It will be inevitably, if deliberately, followed by the withering of Negro religiosity. This withering process may yet be realized as being in the best interest of all, particularly the Negro. It will become clear that the real folk religon of the Negro is his commitment to freedom and equality *with* equality; this he can contribute to the Church and the community. The first step in this direction is for him to disentangle his authentic black religion from the psuedo-religion to which Negro institutions and congregations pledge allegiance. For only in the strength of the authentic folk religion of the Negro can there be added the imperative direction with responsibility in the mainstream of the Christian Church and the American society.

Rather than the beginning of the end, I see the withering of Negro religion—quasi-Christian communities of race —as the end of the beginning for the Negro.

Chapter 2

FOLK RELIGION
AND NEGRO CONGREGATIONS

The Fifth Religion

In many places today, as in Montgomery in 1956, the reality of Negro folk religion can be seen in its uniqueness, supported in part by Negro Protestants and Negro Christians but in full by Negroes of the most diversified persuasions. The common suffering of segregation and discrimination is the crucible out of which the folk religion was created in the past; it creates the unity and power of Negroes in the present and in an effort to tap this resource Negro ministers have been particularly guilty of equating the folk religon with "the Negro church." The folk religion is not an institutional one. It is a spirit which binds Negroes in a way they are not bound to other Americans because of their different histories. Here and there this folk religion may be identifiable with a given congregation, yet, wherever and whenever the suffering is acute, it transcends all religious and socio-economic barriers which separate Negroes from Negroes. There are Negroes who are Protestants, there are Negroes who are Christians, there are Negroes in churches —but there is no Negro Protestantism, Negro Christianity, or Negro church. There are Negro religious institutions which developed out of the folk religion. And it is this historical folk religion which unites all Negroes in a brotherhood which takes precedence over their individual patterns for the worship of God, or the lack thereof. The root of this folk religion, as we shall see in Chapter 3, is racial unity for freedom and equality. Every ecclesiastical expression of Negro congregations and institutions is but a variation or frustration of this theme.

It is unusual to think in terms of Negro folk religion, but it constitutes the fifth major religion functioning in the American culture. Generally acknowledged are Judaism, Protestantism, and Roman Catholicism.[1] The impact of these religions on the Negro has varied in quantity and quality. A religion less widely acknowledged, but nevertheless influential in American culture, is secularism. Secularism is rooted in humanitarianism, philosophical ideals, democracy, science, and human progress. Its impact upon the Negro, less widely heralded, has been impressive. In the sense that secularism is a religion, so also is the folk religion. The folk religion holds in common with secularism a non-ecclesiastical affirmation, but the singularity of the folk or black religion is its hereditariness. As individuals, Negroes are adherents of the other dominant religions in this country. The majority are secularists; of those who have formal commitments the greater number are Protestants, usually in independent Baptist and Methodist communions—institutionally and racially segregated from white congregations of the same name.

Black religion is unique to the Negro folk, born as it was of slavery, and it ties them each to the other in times of stress by a racial bond which cuts across all other variables. Given enough facts about his ecclesiastical affiliation and his status we are often able to generalize accurately about the beliefs and attitudes of any particular non-Negro person with whom we are concerned. The fact that a Negro, however, is Protestant, Roman Catholic, or in rare instances Jewish is of minor and less predictable value in determining his beliefs and attitudes.

Regardless of the congregational expression in which he may be involved side by side with his white neighbor, the Negro knows the dimension of separation from the white which leads him to seek fulfillment in fellowships primarily concerned with the folk religion: freedom and equality.

The white American prefers to repress, and the Negro American often does, the truth of a people involuntarily uprooted from their environment, herded together like animals and treated so on their way to an entirely different environment where the animal treatment was reinforced and its stigma perpetuated. This is the common history of the Negro from the early seventeenth century on. Once he landed on these shores he was quickly separated from his family and sold to the highest bidder. Thrown together with other slaves with whom he had in common only the bonds of slavery and race, he was forced to start a life without a history, a religion, or a family, and with a most precarious future. For the first two and a half centuries the majority of Negroes were denied freedom of body and for three and a half centuries they have all been denied freedom of choice (Negroes who have been able to advance on the basis of merit in one locale are still subject to being treated as undesirables when they move out of their restricted situation of privilege).

As a consequence, Negroes have chosen to make their way on pride of race as they strive to be respected on the basis of quality, since they are invariably viewed first as black men rather than as men. This is especially true in congregational life.

Black religion began amidst polygamy in the cotton fields. It was an adaptation of the white master's religion. Slaves were not initially permitted to raise families of their own, nor to protect their women from the desires of the plantation owners and their associates. But they were permitted, from the earliest days, to work out their own peculiar religion. The slave songs which antedated the Negro family, and which the Negro used to articulate his overwhelming concern with freedom, were the key feature of this folk or black religion. Deprived of the natural right of a family, exposed to moralities shorn of ethics through the religion the whites introduced into the lives of the slaves to ease the pain of a non-ethical system, Negroes fused race and the meaning they gave to slave songs into a religion which provided their sole sense of identity.

Born in slavery, weaned in segregation and reared in discrimination, the religion of the Negro folk was chosen to bear roles of both protest and relief. Thus, the uniqueness of black religion is the racial bond which seeks to risk its life for the elusive but ultimate goal of freedom and equality by means of protest and action. It does so through the only avenues to which its members have always been permitted a measure of access, religious convocations in the fields or in houses of worship.

The genius of the Negro folk religion is not readily understandable apart from the awareness of the black and white streams of which it is constituted. The white stream began with the missionaries who beat a path to the door of the Negro slave. Their main purpose was to extoll the virtues of the next world. From the earliest days, the Negro was much more concerned with the freedom of this world than with the religion of the next. He listened attentively to the religious and moral teachings of the whites, but his mind was elsewhere. He was resourceful enough to perceive that the best way to freedom in this world was through the religion of the whites, sanctioned by his masters and overseers as a means of harnessing his energy for production.

The black stream began under the camouflage of camp meetings during the day and singing at night, in which the religion of the whites and the concern of the slaves were blended to create the Negro spirituals which provided a cover for Negro preachers to lead insurrections and escapes. The fermentation of the folk religion began in the shadows of the plantation.

Inspired by the hope which accompanied the end of slavery, the Negro created out of his black religion a relief agency to aid the Freedman, centered in the congregation and the preacher. The hope of equal opportunity continued in the aftermath of Reconstruction, as well as the intention of the Negro that his religion of militancy and his minister serve him in the "advancement of the race."

This black stream of the Negro folk religion was given leadership by the free Negro ministers of the North who had instituted Negro congregations independent of their white sponsors. This independent movement was a response to segregation in, and, later, exclusion from, white congregational communions, first in the North and then in the South. Frustrated by their inability to express in open ways the militant drive for freedom which in slavery was channeled through escapes to the North, the post-Civil War Negro folk put their trust in and merged with the independents, who, like the folk, were instructed by whites, but, unlike the folk, brought to this union the institutional procedures of whites. The independents intended and carried out no innovations in ecclesiology, doctrine, ritual, polity, or theology which distinguished them from white denominations; instead, they assumed the names of white denominations, prefacing them with "African." Direction came from Negroes who had long yearned for freedom and equality; their folk religion supplied the independents with a needed, unique, inner dynamic. The union of the folk religion and independents created in the Negro congregation a center for the relief of the Freedman. This was assumed to be a temporary need and the folk anticipated the day when the preacher and the fellowship would bring about freedom and equality.

But the hope for the minister and fellowship was not realized. Following Reconstruction the old practice of segregation was resumed with a vengeance in the South and discrimination continued in the North. These twin evils curbed the militancy of the folk religion. In that era of decline in the quest for freedom, the Negro minister remained the spokesman for the people with this difference—faced by insurmountable obstacles, he succumbed to the cajolery and bribery of the white power structure and became its foil. Instead of freedom, he preached moralities and emphasized rewards in the life beyond, in much the same manner as the white missionaries. The Negro minister increased his control and redirected the enthusiasm of the folk religion for the purpose of gaining personal power.

From this point on, the black contribution lay dormant while the white contribution was active and dominant. The burning zeal for liberty and justice, the *raison d'être* of the folk religion, was dimmed in the darkness of the whole society's disarrangement. The dominant theme was stymied and could not be articulated in the society at large. Frustrated, the vitality of the repressed black religion was expressed through the hope of a world beyond—the only other outlet available to the Negro.

The disappointment with the Negro minister and the independent fellowships became apparent early in this century with the loss of widespread support of Negro congregations and the rise of organizations such as the National Association for the Advancement of Colored People and the National Urban League. These racial organizatons, led by social workers, took over the leadership of the central concern of the Negro people and channeled their desires more satisfactorily in creative and positive achievements. Increasingly, since the 1920's, the Negro minister has been an object of disgust. The deprecation of the Negro minister and his

thwarting of black religion reached its height during the
Depression, as noted by St. Clair Drake and Horace R. Cayton in *Black Metropolis*:[2]

You take some of these preachers, they're living like kings—
got great big Packard automobiles and ten or twelve suits and a
bunch of sisters putting food in their pantry. Do you call that
religion? Naw! It ain't nothing but a bunch of damn monkey
foolishness.

Blood-suckers! they'll take the food out of your mouth and make
you think they are doing you a favor.

The preachers want to line their pockets with gold. They are
supposed to be the leaders of the people, but they are fake
leaders.

Ministers are not as conscientious as they used to be. They are
money-mad nowadays. All they want is the almighty dollar and
that is all they talk about.

I used to be active in the church; I thought we could work out
our salvation that way. But I found out better. These Negro
preachers are not bothered about the Race—about all they think
of is themselves.

There were always a few ministers and congregations which
continued to work along the lines expected of the folk religion:[3]

I am a member of the Solid Rock A.M.E. Church. Churches are
a necessity, for I believe that it is through them that our people
got the idea that we must co-operate with each other.

My whole family belongs to St. Simon's Baptist Church. I am
of the opinion that the church fills a great need. It is hard to
picture the amount of evil that would take hold of the world if
the church were done away with. I also believe that many of our
folks have learned from the church that big things can be accomplished only by the joining of forces of a large group of people.

It is precisely this function of religion, which Negroes everywhere have always adhered to, that white Protestants do not understand and Negro ministers forget when they claim that Negro congregations are evidence of "the Negro church," instead of the affirmation of black religion. They may have never realized or forgotten what the folk have always known, that the meeting house is the gathering point, where alone the brotherhood is free to be about its primary business: working together to pursue and achieve equal rights and opportunity for each and all.

Since the 1920's, black religion, the religion of the folk, has been dysfunctional. From this period on the once subordinate and latent stream of white Protestant evangelicalism has been dominant and manifest, relegating the uniqueness of black religion to verbal expression from the pulpit in such a way that action was stifled. But all the while the folk religion has been seething. It came to a head with the nonviolent movement. Once again, some of the Negro ministers resumed their expected roles as leaders of the race. With the protest movement black religion has come full circle and its vitality has never been more pronounced. For historic reasons, American Negro folk religion employs the meeting house to advance the race through brotherhood and to make its presence felt in politics, education, economics, and the fight for justice and equality. Black religion has never been primarily concerned with contributing to worship, liturgy, theology, or the ecumenical movement in Protestantism, nor has it assumed responsibility in the specific concerns of the Christian faith such as missionary work. Ecclesiastical expressions are rooted not in black religion but in the white heritage.

The dysfunction of the folk religion was caused by its suppression within institutional and evangelical Negro religious organizations. Militancy was frustrated or considered repellent. On the strength of the repressed militant and folk religion, the independent movement among Negroes who adhered to white religion expanded into the major Negro institution. Today, there are over thirty Negro religious organizations, bearing names similar to the white institutions from which they are independent. But from the beginning the major ones were committed to double duty. To provide an outlet for equality in religious leadership and worship and to be the primary institution for the advancement of the Negro in the society, in the interim between freedom hoped for and freedom realized, was the *raison d'être* of the independent movement.

Unfortunately, for several generations now, Negro ministers and their organizations have misconstrued the historic intent of the folk religion. It is clear that black religion has always been deeply committed to the central concern of Christianity, which was not learned from white Protestants —love-justice-equality. Instead of focusing on this concern and bringing it to fruition, Negro ministers have concentrated on the maintenance of independent organizations for the sake of independence. They have forgotten that black religion is a tradition interested not in pseudo-Protestantism but in freedom with equality.

Surprisingly enough, while Negro religious institutions of the independent variety have been dysfunctional in the realm of the black stream running through the folk religion they have been equally dysfunctional in the realm of the white stream. Negroes have failed to make real contributions to Protestantism, the Christian faith, or the Christian Church, or to suggest any ecclesiastical change in the white organizations after which they are modeled. The reason for this failure is not inherent inability; it is primarily because of the fact that Negro institutions were not established to propound theology or liturgical matters. Negro independent religious life has been shaped within structures whose power is perverted, as clearly as black religion perverted the historic Christian

faith. Independent Negro congregations and institutions are
ineffective among Negroes because they have failed in faithfulness to black religion and to the communion they represent.

Of the independents, the Baptists are numerically in
the majority and now boast of about 7,268,800 members—
divided into two National Baptist Conventions (an indeter-
minate number exists in a third one organized in 1962). The
African Methodist Episcopal Church lists 1,166,300 and the
African Methodist Episcopal Zion Church 770,000. Each of
these institutions grew out of conflicts within white bodies.
They were the carriers of the black religion with which they
have infected latter-day independents, as well as dependent
Negro congregations within white denominations. Congregations of Negroes in white Presbyterian, Episcopal, Lutheran, Roman Catholic, Methodist, and Baptist denominations have all been permeated with the dynamic of the
Negro folk religion—most particularly in the sermons of the
minister and the social fellowship. While these dependent
institutions have been financially underwritten, to various
degrees, in their educational and building programs by
whites, the independents have been supported to a far less
degree by the white communities. For instance, African
Methodist Episcopalians claim they are a completely Negro
organization with no white backing. Baptists in the South
are sometimes aligned with and more often supported by
the Southern Baptists (white) and Negro Baptists in the
North are aided by the American Baptist Convention
(white), but even among Baptists it is clear that congregations are largely independent.

Considering this independence, the dysfunction of black
religion is the more startling. A tremendous amount of energy is spent to keep these organizations alive for the sole
purpose of providing a place of worship and fellowship for
Negroes. Pride in the past history of these independent

groups as militant communities aiding the advancement of
the Negro is now only a ritual, recalled to support their continuation for religious exercises. The real purpose of Negro
independents, promotion of freedom and equality, is no
longer a primary concern. Indeed, in many ways, these independents have become separatists or reactionaries who
dampen the contemporary drive for freedom, fearing it will
disturb the institutional program. Against this lethargy the
massive nonviolent protest movement has striven, and it has
drawn into its ranks those Negroes who affirm black religion
and deplore the maintenance of institutionalism. Strange as
it is, the protest movement represents the last "big push" for
the justification of separate Negro religious organizations.
Insofar as the movement is successful in pulling Negroes
together, independents will have ammunition for the restoration of pride in racial institutions. It is accurate to state
that racial pride and personal interests are now the distorted
characteristics of independents and are the only reasons for
which these organizations exist.

If we consider the role of the independents throughout
the first half of this century, the dysfunction of the folk religion is a matter of record. The Negro's emotional involvement in black religion has been manipulated by these organizations for their own benefit. In return, they have provided
an opportunity to worship, primarily through emotional release and fellowship.

But the vestiges of this once imaginative and unique
black religion are here and there identifiable. To see the
present dysfunction of black religion in proper perspective,
it is helpful to recall this fact: it is as the Negro social organization for the advancement of the race—not the "Negro
church"—that the folk intended the meeting house, although
their belief in the divine sanction of their endeavors is obvious. In addition to their will to worship—though the majority of Negroes from the days of slavery have never been

involved—there is good reason why Negroes have identified their destiny with the meeting house:

The church was the first community or public organization that the Negro actually owned and completely controlled. And it is possibly true to this day that the Negro church is the most thoroughly owned and controlled public institution of the race. Nothing can compare with this ownership and control except ownership of the home and possibly control of the Negro lodge. It is to be doubted whether Negro control is as complete in any other area of Negro life, except these two, as it is in the church.[4]

By any theological standard, "the church" is the people of God and cannot be "owned" as if it were a "community organization" unless it is intended to be the Negro's "community or public organization." In varying degrees, the meeting house is an honored symbol for some Negroes, an improvident one for others, and the source of imprecation for still others. However, the meeting house of the folk still enables one to see in isolated instances a once indispensable site for an experimental black religion.

In spite of the failure of the folk religion, Negro congregations appear to flourish, which is not explained by the white man's belief that the Negro is all emotionalism in religion. Given a Negro and a white person, or two congregations of the same socio-economic background and cultural sensitivity, the emotional output in religion, as elsewhere, would not vary significantly. And while the degree of frenzy of religion varies in proportion to the class station of white and Negro Americans, the Negro may be slower but no less sure in abandoning this frenzy because he is impeded in his endeavor to participate fully in the culture. (The word "station' is deliberately used here to indicate the difficulty of using the term "status" when speaking of Negroes in America, because they have no status except as they make their own within Negro subcultures—and it is this imitation

which reinforces the will to separate religious societies.)
Moreover, the Negro is not inherently fixated upon the supernatural; there are, comparatively, at least as many Negroes as whites who do not feel this compunction. Whatever
prosperity Negro congregations realize, in the near obliteration of black religion, is due to the lack of choice and the
curtailment of community diversions. Both the oldest and
wealthiest organization in the Negro community, the religious fellowship has moved into this vacuum, offering a wide
variety of activities which give a fundamental rhythm to existence. The obvious need filled by religious organizations is
at once the glory and doom of the folk religion. Its glory lies
in its proper function within the framework of the folk religion; its doom is in its being the consuming interest of the
organization. These activities are stepped up in the large
urban areas, whose milieu offers increasing competition to
Negro congregations. In small towns, they meet less competition from the taverns, poolrooms, police stations, movies,
clubs, and dance halls.[5] In rural areas the meeting house
remains the dominant outlet for the excluded people.

What follows is illustrative of Negro congregations today, which are dysfunctional with regard both to this fifth
or black religion to which all Negroes pledge allegiance and
to white religion (institutional and evangelical Protestantism), with which Negroes lack ultimate concern.

Amusement Centers for the Disengaged

Members of the local congregations affiliated with independent Negro organizations can be depended upon to be
more serious about the "religious fellowship" than any other
area of their individual and corporate life.

The main event of the week is Sunday morning worship. Those in attendance are there because they like good singing, good speaking, and good fellowship in a restful atmosphere filled with beauty. The popularity of a given church is heavily dependent upon the pastor, who is expected to transcend immediate conditions through sermons filled with imagery, humor, contemporary illustration, good jokes, and original "portraits" of the "wages of sin" presented through exhilarating oratory. The popular preacher is able to identify with the experiences of "Aunt Jane" yet speak the language of her grandson. In addition to being an authority on all things experiential, the pastor who is a showman with a program "has a following."

The people want to be entertained. The church, depending upon its size and location, is an activities center complete with "Rally Day," "Men's Day," "Children's Day," and special Sunday afternoon and evening programs. Musicales, dramas, pageants, movies, concerts, suppers, and "gospel singers" are offered as free entertainment throughout the week and are enjoyed by the churched and the unchurched without discrimination. The value and quality of the entertainment varies from locale to locale.

In the small towns of the North, Negroes dwell for the most part as a minor cluster in a designated section. They are able to vote, engage in the recreational facilities, attend the public schools, sit wherever they choose on the buses which carry them to their menial employment, enjoy the refreshment of the local theaters and restaurants and generally refresh themselves through the modes of entertainment provided by the community. These Negroes, from New England to California, take a good deal of pleasure in the advantages they have over their friends whom they have left in the South or migrated from in the cities. Oddly enough, these very community activities to which they have access are but nominally taken advantage of, and Negroes can only

occasionally be seen by day or by night outside their habitat
—and then in inconspicuous numbers. The isolated and
sparse Negroes of Northern towns are lulled into a false security; they are, in fact, no more accommodated to the open
society of the North than their fellows are to the closed society of the South. It is something to be in the North and
to be vigorously content. On the other hand, the small population, menial jobs, and discriminatory housing reinforce
a deep sense of inferiority which drives them to seek relief
in "togetherness," instead of making a concerted effort for significant improvement. In towns like Beloit and Racine, Wisconsin; Chester and Carlisle, Pennsylvania; Woburn and
Brockton, Massachusetts; Waterloo and Dubuque, Iowa;
Great Falls and Butte, Montana; Springfield, Washington,
and Stockton, California; Negroes are moving backwards.
One fundamental symptom of this is that the folk religion
has become dissipated into entertainment and the church
has been relegated to the status of an amusement center.

Negroes in these towns are noticeable only when they
congregate at the churches. They constitute the "good people" yet, increasingly, the ineffective people of the community. The one place where they feel at home is the church,
which becomes more than a place to "make a joyful noise
unto the Lord." It is a place to have a good time and not
necessarily "in the Lord."

Often the pastor is a laborer-preacher of limited education who holds down a regular job and spends his leisure
hours in the ministry. Infrequently a graduate of a Bible
Training School, such as the Moody Bible Institute, or a
correspondence school, the pastor in a small town makes up
in inspiration and perspiration what he lacks in preparation.
Usually this is insufficient to perceive the real needs of the
people and lead them to cooperate with each other and the
community power structure toward their fulfillment. The
pastor is often the only "professional," but, given his back-

ground, he is not respected by the local authorities nor expected by his people to be more than the "spiritual leader." The incapacities which curtail his leadership in the community are reflected in his sermons and programs. As a result he thinks of himself as and is expected to be an impresario.

In these small towns, with a small number of Negroes, there are seldom denominations other than Baptists and Methodists, but there are always several varieties of each. The minister and the people are cut from the same mold, which accounts not only for the flow of participants from one congregation to another, depending upon the variety of excitement known to be developing in a particular center, but also for the interchange of ministers for a special program. Frequently, a gospel chorus will be imported from a nearby city. Less frequently, the congregation will sponsor a visitation to a church of the same denomination in a neighboring community or in a larger city where the choir will sing and the minister will preach. On these occasions, following the morning service, there will be a caravan of cars or a chartered bus which transports the members and their friends to this "inspirational service."

The maladies of these Negro congregations in the small towns of the North are many, notably: a sparse population of lower-class people, isolation in one or more districts of the town, insulation from the winds of change which would enable them to pull together to form one solid congregation to attract a well-trained minister or join the stronger churches of the community, and a festering sense of inferiority mistaken for "pride of race" or "pride of denomination." Tradition and stiff-neckedness have long held sway after the cause for their independence is inoperative and unproductive. These congregations persist despite underdevelopment and duplication of effort, supported by a handful of the Negro community, as amusement centers for the entertainment of disengaged Negroes. There is no question about their intent to worship. But when Deacon Thomas responds to the "rousements" of Pastor Allen and Deaconness Margie Jones breaks out in a "shout," falling limp in Deacon Thomas' arms, while resisting the attempts of her faithful husband to console her—that is more than worship, it is the talk of the community and those who missed the event will be on hand the following week. Without this nonreligious function the quality of the moral instruction and worship would hardly be attractive even for those who have been reared from childhood to attend church.

Those who do attend these congregations in the North do so voluntarily, choosing this form of diversion among other possibilities, and their numbers are often replenished by migrants from the South who are still in the habit of going to the meeting house as the only opportunity for fellowship and relaxation.

In the rural areas of the South, Negroes are scattered and poverty-stricken. They do not need to dismiss the thought of entering into the existing community life, because for all practical purposes the very idea is a rare occurrence. Authentic currents of creative conflict in the religion of the folk were uprooted with Reconstruction. It is wellnigh impossible for preachers to penetrate on any regular basis into the remote areas where rural Southern Negroes live. These Negroes take great delight in the bi-weekly services, which continue throughout the day. Such occasions call for more than the praise of God. They are the one opportunity for banter, fun, and frolic as well as the refreshment of a meal prepared by someone other than the "good madam." These deprived migratory workers and farmers are pleased to accept whatever pastoral care is obtainable. Sometimes the preacher is a chaplain in a college or a student in a seminary within commuting distance of less than a hundred miles, but for the most part they welcome one of their own who "feels called of God" to preach.

In the small cities and towns of the South the meeting house is no longer the only Negro institution where the people can be assured of a lively atmosphere, and this much it has in common with the congregation in the North as distinct from that in the rural South. There are a great many Negroes in these areas, and there are many more who attend congregational services than in the North, to some extent because the general community facilities are not open to them and the meeting house is the only Negro institution with a wholesome environment for recreation. The pastors of these Baptist and Methodist congregations often hold bachelor of divinity degrees from such "respectable" institutions among Negroes as Dickerson Theological Seminary in Columbia, South Carolina; Bishop College in Dallas, Texas; E. W. Lampton School of Religion in Jackson, Mississippi; and Johnson C. Smith University Theological Seminary in Charlotte, North Carolina. For more than a generation these pastors of no mean potential have been raising the standards of the ministry, while the educational standard and economic well-being of their constituents have also improved. But the Southern system of segregated education, along with the job ceiling, has only installed a more sophisticated system of fringe benefits offered by society. Consequently, the minister and his people make up a large minority, in some cases the majority, of the community excluded from the channels of communication and participation, of which the right to vote is only one. Thus, the Negro minister spends an excessive amount of energy in staging a carnival of events for a people coerced to make the most of what may charitably be called incessant incestuousness. There is some evidence that the nonviolent movement is stimulating a rebirth of the folk religion in these ill-contrived communities.

Of course, the epitome of insularity is to be found in the all-Negro towns of Grambling, Louisiana and Tuskegee Institute, Alabama. The ministry of amusement is properly subordinated in these unusual towns for these reasons: (1) Grambling and Tuskegee Institute are towns dominated by their colleges, where a good deal of the cultural life originates and is open to the community at large; (2) the towns are largely populated and governed by Negroes whose per capita educational level is among the highest in the nation; (3) Negroes own and support amusement and recreational facilities; and (4) these Negroes are oriented toward the collegiate and middle-class life, demanding and obtaining equally capable ministers engaged for spiritual direction and prophetic witness in the Protestant traditions. While Grambling was planned and grew without altercation, the origin of Tuskegee Institute was a real test of the creative power of the American Negro folk religion. Prior to the 1950's, Tuskegee Institute was a segregated college colony within the town of Tuskegee, Alabama. Through the cooperation of the Institute and the local ministers the Negroes united their resources into a self-sufficient community. Because they represented the economic heart of Tuskegee, the Negroes were backed by strength in their militant request for equality and justice. Their request denied, they besieged the town of Tuskegee with a boycott which culminated in the corporation of Tuskegee Institute, Alabama.

Although there has been a considerable Negro population of affluence in certain metropolises of the South, such as Atlanta, the socio-religo-economic stratification of Negroes has been too extensive to spawn self-sufficient Negro cities within them. Negroes have developed separate colleges, theaters, churches, stores, automotive concerns, and various forms of other retail, personal, and professional businesses. Such establishments are symbolic of racial progress, and are intended as incentives for the Negro and not as capitulation to the Jim Crow system. Moreover, they are businesses as opposed to the common property of recreational developments. While a minority of Negroes can afford an enviable "style of living" and support private clubs, fraternities, and sororities for the good of themselves and the "advancement of the race," the vast majority of Negroes are not as fortunate. The Negroes in Houston, New Orleans, Birmingham, Augusta, and many other large cities of the South must find their amusement within their restricted environs. In the Bible Belt of the South Negroes seek out the meeting house with regularity and in larger numbers than elsewhere in the country. It follows that the independent congregations should provide a ministry of entertainment and amusement to take care of this basic need for diversion, though they are limited as to what can be structured in the meeting house.

The Berean Seventh-day Adventist Church in Atlanta exhibited a billboard-size multi-colored advertisement in July of 1963 which described the variety show during its Revival Meeting:

THE ATLANTA EVANGELISTIC CENTER
INVITES YOU TO ATTEND
YOUR BIBLE SPEAKS

Hear nightly H. L. Cleveland "He makes the Bible plain"	Pictures on Screen in Color
Hear Barbour at 7:15	Family Counseling Service
Sing with Lukes at 7:45	Atlanta String Quartet
Guest Soloist Joyce Bryant "Her Songs will stir your soul"	Air-Conditioned For your comfort
Outstanding Lectures	Tonight's subject: "The Wisest Negro who ever lived"
Free Bibles and other Gifts	
Free Nursery during services	

The variety of offerings in these large metropolitan churches are matched only by their counterparts in the North, where the amusement emphasis of the Negro congregations reach a frenzied height in competition with red-light districts, the policy racket and a seemingly inexhaustible variety of entertainment.

Circumscribed by psychologically or legally imposed conditions and stranded in the mire of poverty or stagnant sociabilty, Negroes have stretched the sacred nearly beyond recognition into extremes of secularity. In Chicago, New York, and Los Angeles there is a conscious effort, on the part of promoters garbed as ministers, to exploit the sacred for secular purposes. Given the compartmentalization of the Negro and his ambitious entrepreneurs, severed from the integrity of the folk religion and unexposed to the Protestant or Christian tradition, the combination of manipulation and ingenuity is deadly in its seriousness. For curious spectators and undernourished participants the nightly spectaculars in urban centers of shaking, rattling, rolling, and rollicking is kaleidoscopic entertainment.

The folk religion of the American Negro is essentially the spirit of freedom-loving men. It has been negated through decades of instilling the curse of inferiority into the Negro masses. One effect of this methodical inhumaneness was the withholding of community resources for refreshment from the great mass of Negroes. Because of this disarrangement, the minister, the titular leader of the Negro community, was unable to perform his primary function. The people looked to him and together they turned to what was far less significant, and was the most objectionable element in their religious heritage—eschatological exuberance. The meeting house became the first center for refreshment in perfect freedom. The joy which poured forth from these meetings was released in African rhythm. In the face of deprivation in this world, Negroes soared off into heights of ecstasy, cuting loose their ties by singing Negro spirituals—the songs of freedom and free men. As they migrated from the rural to the urban South, on the heels of Reconstruction, this joyous ecstasy and African rhythm were carried out of the meeting houses and into the streets of daily drudgery. There in the cesspools of poverty and ignorance the spirit of the new Negro religion gave relief to the captive and birth to the blues. Jazz was born of this spirit, too. "When the Saints Go Marching In" is not only a good secular tune based on a solid Negro spiritual. It is more. "When the Saints Go Marching In" is evidence that the religion of the Negro has been less preoccupied with the sacred than is generally supposed. Were this a sacred song, instead of a song of freedom, the Negro community would have protested.* Rather, this spirited jazz arrangement is symbolic of the dedication to joy in the infectious religion of a disinherited people.

However, the conservative members of the masses preferred their blues and jazz expressed through more "orthodox" religious forms. With the migration of Negroes from the rural and urban South to the North, which began with the job inducements offered in World War I, the meeting house continued as their mainstay in a strange and frustrating environment. Negro ministers were often unequal to the task of aiding their people. The masses accepted the anguish of the ghetto, a significant number of them being sustained by its congregations. The joy expressed in these sessions was sealed within, giving birth to the most degenerate form of Negro religion—gospel music.

Gospel music is the creation of a disengaged people. Shorn from the roots of the folk religion, gospel music has turned the freedom theme in Negro spirituals into licentiousness. The African rhythm distracts from the almost unintelligible "sacred" texts. It is commonplace now; it is sheer entertainment by commercial opportunists. When

---

* For an analysis of the actual role of Negro spirituals, see Chapter 3.

Mahalia Jackson sings "How Great Thou Art" all America
may listen enthralled, but, though she is more humble, she
is no less symbolic of crass commercialism than are the
bouncing Clara Ward Singers in the rendition of "Joy, Joy,
Joy." Ministers who urge their people to seek their amusement in gospel music and the hoards of singers who profit
from it lead the masses down the road of religious frenzy
and escapism.

Arena for Power Politics

The dynamics of prejudice in conjunction with ostra-
cism produce an American environment in which the authentic intent of the Negro folk religion is largely inoperative. This climate of dispossession all but destined that the
political life of the desolate Negro masses be forced into the
meeting house.

Independent Negro religious organizations, born of exclusion to meet the needs of the people and give structure
to their religion, soon showed signs of their powerlessness.
Symptomatic of the inadequacy of their efforts to advance
the cause of Negroes in the community was the internal
strife of these groups. The Baptists, the congregations of
the masses, represent both the earliest and clearest example.

The Negro Baptist attempts at national organization
began as early as 1880 and followed the pattern of white
Baptist bodies to the last detail. The unity of Negro Baptists
reached its climax in Atlanta in 1895 with the creation of
the National Baptist Convention of the United States of
America. This national organ, then the most extensive and
powerful organization, emerged from the social expectancy
of the Negro folk religion. For reasons to be fully explained

in Chapter 3 it failed, however; the optimism became pessimism, the unity disunity, and the righteous cause one of corruption. In 1915 the organization split into two conven-tions. As we shall see in Chapter 3, there was a more pervasive cause for this permanent separation than the legal entanglements over the adoption of a charter and the exclusive ownership of a publishing house.

This legal explosion of Negro Baptists into two groups with identical ecclesiastical nomenclature and social motivation can be accounted for in large measure by external socio-economic pressures. With no higher loyalty than to the race and its progress, and with little or no success in advancing against the seemingly invulnerable common enemy, Negro Baptists turned their wrath and hostility inward upon themselves. The only channel at the disposal of the Negro for implosion was religion. Baptists, constituting the vast majority of Negroes, were accustomed to local autonomy, and their congregations provided the perfect medium for the free airing of personal disappointments, discontent and disillusionment. Dashed hopes, feuds, factions, and fights created Negro politicians. In this atmosphere of tension the Baptist preacher arose as the master politician who continued as the leader of the people by diverting them from their external failures in society through practical politics in a religious setting. Since 1915, the heavy concentration of Negroes in the South has been largely denied the privilege of political expression. The local congregation has filled this need and has created through city, county, state, and national Baptist associations a political outlet for the Negro. The explosion which created two national conventions continued down through county, state, city, and local bodies. On the local level, this division of Baptists persists, partly because the external forces have not substantially changed and partly because splits are the habitual way of Negro Baptists. (Baptists would say that division is the simplest way to make more Baptists; historically, there is more truth than error in this view.) *

It is clear that this absorption in politics extends beyond normal political activity, vital for the healthy development of all organizations, to produce an exasperating treadmill operation. Instead of "advancing the race," the politics of the folk religion creates an overabundance of small congregations for a surplus number of untrained preachers who are always seeking a position and almost invariably become dictators—until the deacons meet to vote the minister out of the pulpit while he is preaching in it. (Baptists can and do launch a new congregation at the slightest provocation without deference to any ecclesiastical or coordinating hierarchy.) Individuals are provided with a medium for the release of tension and anxieties in this religion of politics, but at the same time their effective participation in community politics is circumvented.[6]

A partial history of one congregation is sufficient to illustrate what is well known as the paralysis of National Baptists.** Prairieville, a midwestern town, has a population of about 100,000, including at a generous estimate 2,000 Negroes, ten per cent of whom constitute the membership of four struggling congregations. There are one each of the Holiness-Sanctified and African Methodist Episcopal bodies and two of Baptists, one aligned with the American Baptist Convention (white) and the other with the National Baptist Convention of the U.S.A.

The Mount Moriah Baptist Church is the focal community for Negroes in Prairieville and is largely the congrega-

---

* See Benjamin E. Mays and Joseph W. Nicholson, *The Negro's Church*, Chapter 11, "Is the Negro Overchurched?" and Chapter 16, "Overchurching in Rural Areas," for a statistical analysis. Without allegiance to principles higher than personal gain and local autonomy, the changing society does not modify to any significant degree the present situation in which political profit issues in too many churches, as it did in the past.

** As a rule, real names of persons and congregations are not used.

tion of the masses. When Azalee Jefferson exchanges the white cook's uniform she wears in Judge McCormick's kitchen for the equally white crisply starched one she wears on "the Mothers' Board," Azalee is at home in Mount Moriah. There she is in the company of Amos Tulson, a chef for the State University; William Evans, an accountant for the state; deacons Towner and Bell, the local barber and tailor, respectively; custodians Harris, White, Mound and Jordan; housekeepers and maids in the persons of the Misses Green, Dryer, Coleman, Jones, Davis, and Mesdames Turner, Taylor, Donaldson, Matthews, Carter, Gentry, Thompson, Singleton, Dexter, Trotter, and Benjamin. In addition to being a center for these stalwarts who can be counted upon the years around, Mount Moriah is the home of their children, relatives, and friends, and of the graduate students from Negro colleges in the South studying at the University. The church is the only local organization these residents support, feeling unwelcome in the organizations sponsored by the larger community.

The striking character of this lower-class fellowship is the lack of education above the eighth-grade level for all but a few of the adults and many of their children, the manual and mechanical labor of the male members, and the large number of mother-dominated families. Whether the male is divorced, in another city working, in prison, or unknown, few of the children have the benefit of the male image. Familial and personal disorganization, illegitimacy, and juvenile delinquency abound in homes where the children are reared by their mothers or maternal relatives, and more often than not they are under the guidance of the eldest child while the mother earns the living. The absence of the care and encouragement of both parents, and of incentive and support for upward mobility via positions of status and education, as well as the lack of security in the matriarchy leads to an unbearable amount of intra-family and inter-

group strife. The relatively few families distinguished by
the presence of both parents, public morality, and education
of the children are impotent to balance the families on dead
center, or spur them forward.

Azalee Jefferson illustrates the pattern of the Negro
community in the Mount Moriah church. She lives alone
in a two-family house purchased with the $10,000 settle-
ment for personal damages in an auto accident, the father
of her only daughter having not appeared during the twenty-
odd years she has lived in Prairieville. When Azalee returns
home after a long day in the Judge's kitchen she is fond of
telephoning her friends. Inadvertently, the conversation
gets around to a subject dear to her, her grandson Buddy
Baker, whom she frequently harbors after his fights with one
or more of his several wives, street brawls, altercations with
the law, or during recuperation following his routine hospitalization for chronic alcoholism. When Azalee's friend ventures a suggestion which seems to bear unfavorably upon
the condition of Buddy Baker, Azalee breaks into a rage
which develops into a defense of Buddy and a personal attack upon her friend. Seething with venom, these "friends"
begin telephoning around the community, quickly dividing
it. Eventually, they each call their minister, the Reverend
Howard Corson, placing him squarely in the middle of what
by this time is a congregation split down the middle. When
this occurs, as it has intermittently during the thirty-plus
years of his ministry, Pastor Corson braces himself for the
inevitable. By the time this self-educated, trustworthy,
honest man of manual labor enters the pulpit, his ear is filled
to capacity. During the week he has already been excused
several times from his custodial duties in the Western Union
office to meet some crisis in the Negro community. Arbitrat-
ing the dispute between Azalee and her adversary on this
occasion is but one among many problems: rushing at midnight to console Margie Taylor who has just been beaten to

within an inch of her life by her husband who had ignored a court order forbidding him to enter the state after an untold number of previous attacks; accepting the responsibility of and opening a room in his home for such parolees as Charlie Johnson who has been imprisoned for ensnaring minors in a sexual crime, or Felix Turner for non-support, or Clarence Chapman for murder; visiting Sarah Guy in the Winnebago home for unwed mothers, Bill Allshouse in the narcotics ward of the State hospital, Jeff Stewart in the home for the aged at Monona, Joe Andrews in the Waupun State Prison, Isaac Fields in the City Jail, Joan Moncrief in the General Hospital; aiding Leola Smith to find employment after being deserted with her eight children by her common-law husband; burying Tom Trotter, who has been felled by "Big Bill" Jones in an argument over a baseball statistic; and unofficially adopting as his own the latest in the long line of children born to lovers out of wedlock or abandoned.

When Pastor Corson mounts the pulpit before a congregation divided over repetitious and petty disputes, he is concerned with the whole community of diseases which he seeks to eradicate in the only way he knows—by citing precepts and pointing to concrete examples. Sensitive ears hear what they will, and his parishioners imagine he condones one side or the other in the dispute instead of admonishing each to seek a common solution for the health of all. Pastor Corson holds the mirror before the people once too often and for too long a time:

You feeble, burr-head excuses for manhood are too lazy to earn a living.

Where are our Negro men? You know where they can be found during the day—in Dickson's poolroom, and at night they are spending the women folks' hard earned money on whiskey in a bedroom where they are creating another family they will not support.

I don't know what the Negroes of Prairieville are coming to. They have no self-respect left at all, leaving our children to grow up wild in the streets and subjecting them in the home to foul-mouth talk, fights, brutality and ignorance. Some of our women lie down mad and get up mad. We ought to stop this fussing, feuding and cursing around our children all the time.

There ain't no sense in shouting for Jesus here and forgetting all about him in your homes. We are always singing and praying about living for Jesus in Mount Moriah, but we need to live for Him in our homes. You know it's the truth. If we are ever going to remedy the situation we'll start right in our home life. Charity begins at home and then spreads abroad.

We need love and respect for each other as well as for Jesus. Let's covenant together as we sing 'This little light of mine, I'm going to let it shine, everywhere I go.' Let this be the theme in our homes.

Pastor Corson is no politician. In his sincere but direct and uncompromising way he intends to meet the needs of the people in the pulpit as he does during the week. He is a good man with a sixth-grade education who has worked hard to be an example for the community in his personal and family life, on the strength of the conviction that all problems are spiritual ones, created by the failure of individuals to live the good life. Pastor Corson is unable to penetrate to the underlying socio-economic causes which lead to frustration and degeneration and to which he is unequipped to bring to bear the larger forces of the community. His parishioners do not understand the conditions provoking their violence, but they do feel that their pastor is unsympathetic.

Prompted by the tangible rift between parties to the Azalee Jefferson quarrel and by the intangible malaise eating away at the heart of the community, together with the moral strictures uttered by Pastor Corson, Mount Moriah explodes into one of its periodic political upheavals.

Instead of aiding the pastor to heal the breaches and draw the congregation together to work at the real problems of the community, Deacon Towner and Deacon Bell take advantage of this tension to seize the power they have been denied over the past few years. They immediately call a special meeting of the congregation, making sure that the old-timers who have long since been inactive are present to insure the outcome they desire. Pastor Corson is voted out of "the pulpit" without a hearing. Having relieved their anxieties by making the Pastor the scapegoat, the people are in a state of confusion and look to Deacon Towner and Deacon Bell. With the pulpit declared vacant they are free to politic. For several Sundays they enjoy their favorite preachers from neighboring cities and Chicago. During the next months they are visited by various unattached preachers in the vicinity, with whom the deacons craftily exchange a preaching opportunity or two for assurances of deference in the event of a call to Mount Moriah. The public contest in which each candidate, or potential candidate, attempts to outpreach the others permits the congregation to oscillate between contestants week after week; at the same time, the deacons are leaning toward a favorite on the basis of his ability to place the largest amount of money in their pockets. These conflicting judgments terminate in a stalemate and none of the candidates are called. Moreover, the faction in Mount Moriah continues in a subdued form, and added to it is the split between the officers following Deacon Towner and those for Deacon Bell, who have committed themselves to different candidates totally unacceptable to each other.

Into this wave of petty politics rides the Reverend Eugene Sanders from Birmingham, Alabama, by way of Chicago and Milwaukee, where he has been unsuccessful in his attempt to gain a large metropolitan fellowship. He is an experienced politician and a master at turning difficult situations to personal gain. Deacons Towner and Bell capitulate to his eloquence and manipulative ability, and Pastor Sanders emerges, without compromise, as the leader of the Mount Moriah Baptist Church. Promptly he overwhelms the congregation with his oratory and enables them to put aside their petty differences by concentrating their efforts upon erecting a new church.

Sanders is successful in gaining pledges from the congregation and donations from the white congregations in the city, appealing to their "home mission" spirit and benevolence. His selling point with the white congregations is the same as that with the business concerns,

. . . an investment in Prairieville as a whole through erecting for the Negro people a church center of which all can be proud to point to as a symbol of Negro and white relations. If you will aid me to build it, my people will come to this church. Through this concrete structure, the real needs can be met in an effective way which will relieve the community's recreational and social services. Dollar for dollar, this is the best investment possible in the Negro people.

On one occasion when Pastor Sanders notices some influential white citizens at the Sunday evening musicale he boldly directs attention to them during the offertory:

You all know Mr. P. T. Gardner who owns the leading cafeterias in town. He has been a good friend to us over the years. Mr. Gardner is here tonight because he feels it is important to contribute a significant amount to our building fund. I want Mr. Gardner to come up here and bring his friends with him. We are going to ask them to make the first contributions. Now, ushers, pass the baskets to these good friends. . . . Mr. Piper, your generous response to an important work will not only generate a similar spirit in others, but it will enable us to develop healthy minds and bodies that will create a new community out of this end of town. I think I can safely say you are making it possible to alleviate the fears which shadow us all.

Sanders receives substantial financial support from the civic groups of the city and obtains permission from the City Council to station young people at strategic corners on the Capitol Square to solicit funds from shoppers. Within two years there are sufficient funds to begin construction. But prior to the execution of these plans Sanders withdraws the funds and departs from Prairieville with a young maiden, leaving behind his own family, and Mount Moriah is again in a most precarious position.

In the light of this experience the people of Mount Moriah demand that the deacons request the Reverend Howard Corson to return as interim pastor, which he does for a number of years. The deacons again withhold full support and over the years build up sufficient tension and backing to force Pastor Corson to resign in favor of the Reverend Charles Cunningham. Cunningham is a traveling evangelist from Austin, Texas who in two weeks of preaching and consorting with the deacons manages to secure Mount Moriah as a permanent base of operation, which he then uses to obtain a larger church in Milwaukee, Wisconsin, within a year.

Once again the Reverend Howard Corson is asked to assume the duties of pastor to Mount Moriah, although he has been unofficially ministering to the people all the while, being the most stable, honest, and dependable force in the community. Despite the persistent resentment of Pastor Corson by an articulate minority, the need for a more adequate building is so obvious that the people as a whole back the pastor in his pursuit of this goal. With a limited constituency and a previous record of financial instability, Mount Moriah is dependent upon the personal prestige of Pastor Corson as a reputable citizen and minister. The choice before the congregation is between erecting a new building on land purchased by the congregation in the recently developed ghetto on the South Side or buying a

building midway between this site and the old church which
has been abandoned by a white congregation. Before the
decision can be made, a business session of the church is
called. The funds for purchase of the now dilapidated building had originally been borrowed from the American Baptist
State Convention. The Secretary of the Convention is present to point out that the balance due on the old church has
been neglected for some years and must be paid before any
more money can be borrowed toward building or buying a
new structure. He is blunt and to the point:

I am here tonight to remind you of your debt to the Board of
Missions. As you know, several of your deacons visited me this
week to request a loan for the building of your proposed church.
I just had to remind them of the interest we have had in you for
a long time. The evidence of this is the $2,000 we loaned you
for repairs several years ago. When the old bill is paid, you can
be sure there will be no question at all about negotiating a new
loan. I would not feel compelled to be here tonight if an attempt
had been made to pay the old debt.

The reminder gives the forces for independence and
the building of a structure without assistance the opportunity to speak out against both the purchasing of an old
building and the representative of the white Baptist Convention. Deacon Towner then speaks for the party which
desires the least expensive way out of the crisis:

When are we Negroes going to become independent? Is there any
good reason why we cannot be responsible for erecting a building
which is for our purposes and which we claim will benefit us all
directly? The time has come for us to stand upon our own two
feet. I have just been thinking about what we could do if we set
our minds to it and pulled together. White people have doled out
conscience money in the past. But it is time that we mind our own
business and the white people their business. We can purchase

the South Side Methodist Church for a mere $5,000; why go in debt for a ridiculous sum to build a new church? Let us pay the whites what we owe them, then purchase our own building.

The atmosphere is tense. Pastor Corson had originally aided the people of Mount Moriah to affiliate with the American Baptist Convention (white) and Deacon Towner had held out for the National Baptist Convention of the U.S.A. Pastor Corson is uneasy and the white Secretary is embarrassed. Deacon Golightly arises to defend the building of a new church and to continue relations with the white convention. In his humorous way he restores an atmosphere of good will and at the same time calls upon racial pride:

Brother Towner, I am not ready to bite the hand which feeds me. If you think about it, you are not either. Certainly this is the case with most of us here tonight. What is wrong with tapping an available resource? I am for accepting all the white people are willing to freely give us, and then ask for more. Good white folks have always helped good Negro folks—let's keep the tradition alive.

Negroes are on the lower end of the totem pole in this town. Good jobs and all the money belong to those on the other end. However, we can be rich in spirit. While it is true that several of our fellowship are in a position to contribute liberally, there is no question in my mind but that the good women folk of this congregation can be relied upon to pull us over the goal.

We have done enough airing. Let's act! We can pay this $2,000 according to Treasurer Harris. There is no reason under the sun why this should not be done. I so move. Moreover, I pledge ten per cent of this amount to replenish our bank account. It is my plea that you all join me in this pledge of honesty to the past in order to build with integrity in the future. Let us show this community we have confidence in ourselves; they will then have confidence in us.

Deacon Towner is on the spot at this point. Though visibly shaken, he calls for the vote. It is unanimous. The Secretary of the Home Mission Board is assured that the Convention will be paid in full within two weeks with additional pledges made prior to the vote. Deacon Golightly continues:

For the first time in my life I am proud to be a member of this congregation. You have all shown me tonight that given a clear-cut situation you are able to rise to the occasion. It is now clear that we are on our way. The question still has to be resolved between purchasing an inexpensive but inadequate abandoned church or building a new one. The sense of pride we will develop in a new building, together with the contribution we will be making to the future well-being of our children while they reside with us, weighs heavy in the balance.

Prior to this business meeting, Deacon Towner had control of one segment of Mount Moriah which would vote only for acquiring the abandoned property, and Deacon Golightly of the other body which is convinced that a new structure with recreational and social service facilities is the answer. The deadlock persists for several months until Deacon Harris proposes a compromise. He introduces to the congregation the Reverend Charles Winter, an experienced builder, who will design and construct a building with his own hands if he is named the pastor. Pastor Corson agrees to retire in favor of Winter and the majority vote to continue their relations with the American Baptist Convention and give the new pastor permission to build on the South Side.

But the Deacon Towner faction refuses to go along with the majority. They split from Mount Moriah and call the Reverend Thomas Halley of Milwaukee to be their pastor, forming the Second Baptist Church in the building vacated by the white Methodists, affiliated with the National Baptist Convention of the U.S.A. The result of this split over non-ecclesiastical and non-theological issues is two very weak congregations—neither of which have any impact upon the community and both of which spend their political energies on in-church questions, rather than combining their political power at the polls for the health of the whole community.

The political struggle which led to the split of the small Mount Moriah congregation into two, preventing the community involvement of these people for several decades, is an example of a familiar pattern. In both North and South, in urban and rural areas, the details vary but the results are similar: psychological, social, and economic insecurity create a larger number of Negro churches than white ones in proportion to population. These factors are used for the political advantage of some Negro leaders who gain personal power by starting new congregations regardless of the number already existing in the same neighborhoods. This pointless duplication is common knowledge, and is the subject of ridicule and amusement for both Negroes and whites. "Overchurching" is not a unique problem among Negroes. It is its political origin which sets the Negro apart, most conspicuously among the National Baptists, whose constituents comprise the majority of Negroes.[7]

The significance of these seemingly pitiful struggles for power and control in local congregations must not be underestimated. Insofar as the folk religion is misdirected toward spirited politics in independent Negro Baptist circles, the local church is the primary base of operations. The Baptist preacher, who is also a politician, begins by an apprenticeship as an associate in a well-established congregation. He rises to leadership of his home church, or branches out in smaller ones, either by promotion on the basis of ability or by starting his own, if not by taking advantage of a rift which he has encouraged. By whatever route, honorable or not, the aim of the Baptist preacher-politician is to pastor a congregation. Once in control as leader, he is in a position of power within the local National Baptist Association. Depending upon his astuteness, he can become influential in community politics, as well as county, state and national Baptist politics. Particularly in the South and the large urban areas of the North there is a parallel between the political machinery and the mechanics of the preacher-politicians in the national conventions.

For more than a decade now, in New Orleans, the Reverend A. L. Davis has been the man to deal with vis-à-vis the vote of Negroes in the City's elections. In addition to being the pastor of the large New Zion Baptist Church, A. L. Davis is the political boss of the Interdenominational Ministerial Alliance—the Negro counterpart of the Crescent City Democratic Organization in New Orleans. A. L. Davis is the acknowledged leader of the Negro community with respect to politics, without being subject to review or censure, as long as he is the pastor of New Zion. In the regularly scheduled meetings of the Interdenominational Alliance, composed of the majority of the reputable Negro ministers of New Orleans, Davis selects the protests the group will support, as well as the candidate at election time.

While A. L. Davis was formally recognized as the Negro leader by the previous mayor of New Orleans, Chet Morrison, who created a post for Negro affairs, paying Davis $300 per month, this gesture was eliminated by the incoming mayor, Victor Schiro, whom Davis did not support. In comparison with his personal gain, there has been no commensurate increase in the well-being of the Negroes of New Orleans throughout the decade of the Davis machine. This failure of a Baptist political structure is due not only to the image of Davis as a politician, but also to the inability of Negroes to coordinate their limited political voice, fractured by the Roman Catholic-Protestant tension. In this religious split of the Negro community, Davis is able to develop and control a majority of Negro votes for the purposes he deems best. Through conquering in the midst of a division, Davis keeps faith with the white power structures, though not I think with the "genius" of the American Negro folk religion.

An even more blatant use of the folk religion for political expediency is seen in the strategies of the Reverend Joseph H. Jackson, boss of the National Baptist Convention of the U.S.A. However ineffectively, Davis in New Orleans seeks token relief for the Negro in the larger community via a religion-based politics. It is difficult to estimate the influence of Dr. Jackson and the Olivet Baptist Church in the life of the Chicago community. By and large, Jackson uses his political talents to maintain his position as head of his Baptist Convention.

To understand the excessive amount of political energy which is drained from community politics for the purposes of maintaining a national Baptist political structure, it is necessary to compare the National Baptist Convention with the parent body from which it bolted, the American Baptist Convention. The American Baptist Convention (A.B.C.) is not free of church politics.[8] Yet there is a loyalty to this Convention which transcends the compromises made by both the conservative and liberal elements.

The real issues, and petty grievances, which are deliberated on the floor of the annual American Baptist Convention do not focus upon the leadership of the body. There is a duly elected and permanent General Secretary with a staff and there are equally permanent Boards and Secretaries of Missions, Education, and other concerns, responsible to but not controlled by the General Secretary. Moreover, each year a president of the Convention is elected, alternately a layman and a clergyman. The Convention proceeds, however indirectly, according to the Convention schedule which is well-publicized in advance of the meeting. There are pressure and interest groups, though it is assumed that "pure democracy" is possible in this large denomination. In effect:

A small elite makes policy, and delegates strive to vote as intelligently as possible under conditions which do not favor an intelligent response to issues. Nonetheless, Baptists insist that the policies of the Convention "are subject to the will of the churches as expressed by democractically chosen delegates from the churches of the convention." [9]

Autonomy, freedom, and democracy are the ideals or slogans which hold Baptists together so that the work of the denomination can be carried out, but the actual power lies with state and national executives, who claim to use it benevolently. Moreover, experience and personality are the keys to the kingdom of Baptist power:

The Baptists may have been wise when they removed the bishops from their places; but when they also eliminated the ecclesiastical authority of their own associations the bishops returned in business suits to direct affairs from behind the curtain of the center stage. Since their responsibilities are prodigious their presence is acknowledged. But paradoxically, their power is unrestricted because their authority is so limited. When Baptists recognize that authority is more than a grant to power and that it also defines and therefore limits the uses of power they may sustain the proximate harmony which they are seeking.[10]

National Baptists do not differ from their white counterparts in the free church dilemma of the proper disposition of power and authority. The difference is in degree, rather than in kind. Negro and white Baptists believe their organizations are indispensable to the tradition and program adhered to. White Baptists maintain church order via an ecclesiastical bureaucracy committed to approximate democracy.

Negro Baptists maintain church chaos via a dictatorship perpetuated for personal gain.

The blatant, naked use of power at the National Baptist Conventions reaches a climax when the delegates are preparing to vote for their officers. The power of Dr. Jackson is so entrenched that he is able to maintain his strangle hold on the Convention year after year through the simple declaration that challenging him would be tantamount to breaking up the Convention. This appeal is sufficient to hold the majority in line, believing as they do that the Convention must be maintained. But a minority dedicated to reform gather each year, literally fighting their way to the platform to make speeches and to nominate candidates other than Jackson and his slate. In the 1961 meeting in Kansas City, the tension was so high that one delegate seeking to curb the powers of the president was jostled off the platform, required hospitalization, and died on the same day.

In 1962, with the support of the Reverend Gardner Taylor, pastor of the Concord Baptist Church in Brooklyn, a sufficient body of dissenters formed to split off from Jackson's National Baptist Convention. However, this new National Baptist Progressive Convention hardly disturbed the parent body.

It is apparent that the way out of the Baptist dilemma is for the local churches, associations, and state conventions to rejuvenate along the lines of three principles of democratic procedure:

The principle of free discussion; the principle that no member be excluded from ecclesiastical office unless he lacks natural ability or formal training; and the principle that legislation and policy making be executed in accord with methods of representative government.[11]

Unfortunately, leaders in the American Baptist Convention who may recognize the need for realignment in order to

increase the reality of democracy cannot do so, for to confess
to undemocratic procedures would be to belie democratic
polity. National Baptists will not realign because they are
committed to one-man rule on every level, necessitating a
perpetual rear guard action that stifles the progress of the
people no less than the denomination.

The epitome of Baptist politicians, above the local-state-
county-national-denominational divisions, is the first Negro
congressman from New York City, the senior pastor of the
enormous Abyssinian Baptist Church in Harlem, Adam Clayton Powell, Jr.:

I am what I am because of the Abyssinian Church. I believe
that Harlem is what it is mainly because of the efforts of that
institution. I know that many of the gains that have been made
in Harlem would have been made with or without the support
of the church, but I am sure that the time table for those gains
was speeded up and many of the victories more permanently
secured because underwriting every step of the way was the
oldest Negro Baptist Church in the North, the largest Protestant
church in America, and one of the most financially independent
institutions anywhere in the Negro world.[12]

Congressman Powell first learned the craft of politics in
his home church, and he is a living example of the suggestion that rising on the ladder of Negro Baptist politics is the
best experience for the practice of politics on any level in
America. Adam Clayton Powell, Sr. became the pastor of
this historic congregation in 1908, when it was dominated by
Negro aristocrats, and he built a $400,000 structure in the
middle of Harlem with a membership that reached 11,000.
He resigned three times in favor of his son, who was finally
elected unanimously as a result of manipulating the younger
members and outlasting the Old Guard. Young Powell
turned the congregation into what he called a "social gospel
institution of Marching Blacks":

This is what I am a product of—the sustained indignation of a branded grandfather, the militant protest of my grandmother, the disciplined resentment of my father and mother, and the power of mass action of the church. I am a new Negro—a marching black.[13]

From the beginning he has asserted: "My father was a radical and a prophet—I am a radical and a fighter." [14]

As pastor of this huge congregation, Powell had a ready-made base of support for his future political aspirations. Early in the 1940's he had already begun cooperating with the Greater New York Coordinating Committee, which began in his office and developed the technique of forcing open doors for Negroes "through the power of nonviolent direct social action." Powell was among the first of those who nearly a quarter of a century ago opened opportunities for Negroes in New York City unmatched in any other area in the United States. He walked the streets of Harlem carrying such signs as the following:

WE STAYED OFF THESE BUSES FOR 12 DAYS THAT WHITE
MEN MIGHT HAVE A DECENT STANDARD OF LIVING—STAY
OFF THEM NOW FOR BLACK MEN.

Four years of sustained effort resulted in thousands of jobs for Negroes in Harlem. With the economic breakthrough, there was every reason to expect even greater things through the power of politics. Adam Clayton Powell, Jr. and the Abyssinian Baptist Church early exemplified the "genius" of the American Negro folk religion. The minister spent the majority of his hours, in and out of the pulpit, advancing the cause of the people of Harlem with the lever of his congregation. The slogan was, "The Negro wants social equality but not social-intercourse equality." Marching Negroes were proud, religious, and convinced as they sang on the way to political rallies the Negro spiritual:

On my Journey now, Mount Zion
On my Journey now, Mount Zion
And I won't take nothing, Mount Zion
On my Journey now!

Supported by the Abyssinian Baptist Church, the mass or-
ganization of The People's Committee, the American Labor
Party, the Democratic County Committee, Republicans, and
Democrats, Powell was elected to Congress in 1944.

Pastor Powell understood the intent and dynamic of
the American Negro folk religion. Because he marched,
fought, bargained, and worked with the people of Harlem
he received their response in the form of a tremendous congregation, second to none in size among Negroes, and their
vote at the polls. Those who remember the fighting Adam,
a quarter of a century ahead of the present nonviolent movement, are convinced that he can do no wrong. His personal
life is considered his own. Having done all in his power not
only to identify with the common black man but also to advance his cause, Adam Clayton Powell, Jr. has met the acid
test of the Negro. His primary image in the minds of the
Abyssinian people, and of many others too, is that of neither
a clergyman nor a congressman but a "race man," and a
giant among them. Powell is mocked by white semi-liberals
as a dishonest minister and congressman. There are many
Negroes, too, who have nothing but contempt for him. Both
groups have ignored the wretched economic conditions of
Harlem which Powell literally devoted his life for years to
eradicating, after which he turned to politics in the hope
that this avenue would hasten socio-economic equality of
the Negro.

Powell began as a young idealist, a social gospeler. At
the age of twenty-two he was an experienced protest leader.
While many of his white counterparts were preaching a
social gospel which ignored the insufferable position of the

Negro, it was Powell and other Negro leaders who fought on this front. Thus Powell, in the tradition of the folk religion, disconnected himself from the mainstream of Protestantism, and no less from an affiliation with National Baptists:

The great wedge that keeps America split is the hypocrisy of the Christian Church. The fundamental postulate of Christianity is equality and brotherhood. We have perverted this glorious doctrine to exclude interracial love. Religion has lost its ethical integrity and, there, its moral dynamic. It has not only become static but it represents the status quo.[15]

Powell reflects the pessimism of many Negro leaders today, vis-à-vis Protestantism, the Christian Church, and the Negro. On the one hand he affirms that "no one can say that Christianity has failed. It has never been tried." On the other hand he states that "the first duty of the blacks therefore is to Christianize religion." In both these positions he demands a religion which will accept the Negro without equivocation and he calls for the Negro to provide the balance:

It doesn't matter a tinker's damn what faith or denomination one's brother belongs to. The paramount standard is, "Is he going my way?" To establish this standard is, therefore, one of the major tasks confronting the Negro in the postwar period.[16]

But Powell has long since lost his commitment to religion as a force for change. His failure in this area is the failure of America and the Protestant churches in the field of race religions.

Presently, Powell has "waxed fat and kicked." Nearly twenty years of being both a minister and a Congressman have taken their toll. The dynamic of his religion has subsided and with it his early idealism. Powell has become a realist and a politician, no longer convinced that anything less than power can improve the lot of the Negro. After twenty years of working in noble ways against the perennial foes of the Negro, often brilliant in his offensive on behalf of his people, Powell has tended to rest upon his laurels. Although he has been persistent in his interest in the equal rights of the Negro, the very facts of his race, flamboyancy, and directness made it impossible for him to gain a committee chairmanship in Congress until the 1960's. His seniority notwithstanding, the very forces against which he contended on behalf of the Negro people combined to block any chance that Powell might become a statesman.

Between frustration and temptation Powell was driven to the brink of choice between integrity of character or demagogism. Increasingly, he has chosen to repudiate character and to become a demagogue. In this way he has broken faith with the best in the folk religion of the Negro, following the mediocrity of so many Baptist preacher-politicians. Because he has reached a higher level of influence than all but a few of his cohorts, substantially bolstered by a religiously oriented political constituency, Powell's choice was more notable. His degeneration into a daring playboy with a foreign villa who has had three marriages and been faced with charges of income tax evasion and government-financed European trips with two secretaries all add up to a serious challenge to his clerical collar and his Congressional ethics. Nevertheless, this disparity has been more disconcerting to white Americans than to Powell's loyal Negro supporters. The contributions Powell has made to the Negro people and his willingness to identify with their aspirations are the factors which endear him to them. He is their leader in the primary question of race; his private and public life are considered irrelevant to this issue. The moral weight of the majority of Negroes, who do not look toward Powell as a hero, stands with that of white Americans against him, because he had a clear choice of taking the more noble route of integrity.

In spite of his personal disintegration, Powell clearly remains a dedicated religionist in the American Negro folk tradition. Under his leadership, the Abyssinian congregation has striven to meet the economic, political, recreational, and social needs of its Harlem constituency. It is difficult to measure the qualitative value of this extension into the community. One fact is beyond question: there has been no split in this congregation—a reflection of both the dictatorial rule from the top and the satisfaction of the people that Powell has continued in the line of those who have "advanced the race."

It is widely held that the Abyssinian church represents the pinnacle of independent Negro folk religion. For many it has stood as a tower of strength in an age of disenchantment with respect to the religion of the Negro folk. There is truth in the claim that if all independent Negro fellowships were as enmeshed in the fight for justice and equality as the Abyssinian the Negro would be less impoverished. Nevertheless, the equation of the Negro folk religion with politics for the sole purpose of increasing the number of Negroes in the socio-economic mainstream of American life is more than an indictment of the free enterprise system and the democratic process in the United States. It is also a revelation of how perverted religion is forced to be among Negroes and of the limited if indispensable value of secular success as its ultimate criterion.

While Baptist institutions are products and reflections of the masses, their Methodist counterparts differ noticeably in values and direction. The ecclesiastical system of independent Negro Methodists inhibits the emergence of both extremely competent and incompetent leaders in the folk

religion of the Negro. The political power of Methodists is
limited within the system, with its intense pressure and
competition to effect a smooth operation. There are occasional ministers who engage in the political structures of the
larger community, who are also involved in the practical
politics of their ecclesiastical system for the sake of the
wider community, such as the Reverend Archibald Carey,
Jr., of Chicago, but he is a rarity among Methodists. Each
Baptist preacher is a potential bishop with all the power
and privileges pertaining thereto. This independent power
and authority develops a higher percentage of real leaders
in the Negro community, varying in integrity and quality,
among Baptists than among Methodists. By and large, deference to the Methodist hierarchy and the work of the
institutional machinery means the Methodists inspire mediocrity. With the exception of the rare Methodist minister
of a large and influential congregation who is able to act
according to the dictates of his own conscience, Methodist
ministers are dictated to by the presiding elder (district
superintendent) and the bishop, who are dedicated to one
thing—the Methodist system.

Power politics is no less real in this communion. Splits
have occurred in Methodist bodies, too, notably when the
Independent African Methodist Episcopal Church bolted
from the African Methodist Episcopal Church in 1907, following a power struggle with the district superintendents.
As far back as 1869, the Reverend James R. Howell of
the African Methodist Episcopal Church in New York organized the Zion Union Apostolic Church in protest against
white discrimination and the ecclesiasticism of many Negro
Methodist churches. Personal and political friction led to
the disruption of the Z.U.A. Church until its reorganization
in 1881-1882 as the Reformed Zion Union Apostolic Church.
Still another body left the Ashbury Methodist Church in

Wilmington, Delaware, in 1805, to form the Union Church of Africans, in response to the lack of full acceptance by the white-controlled congregation. Internal struggles for power led to the formation out of the U.C.A. of the Union American Methodist Episcopal Church, the parent body, as well as the disgruntled body incorporated as the African Union Church. On the whole, the two historically independent Methodist organizations (African Methodist Episcopal Church and the African Methodist Episcopal Zion Church) are stronger than the Christian Methodist Episcopal Church (formerly the Colored Methodist Episcopal Church which in 1870 grew out of the old white-controlled Methodist Episcopal Church South), and no less stable than the two National Baptist Conventions.

Fear of further disorganization has led Methodists to invest dictatorial powers in their bishops, whose consuming interest has been the organizational life. On the whole, regimentation and the hierarchy have systematic priority and the energy dedicated to the organization has resulted in fewer prima donnas than among Baptists. Even more, Methodists have betrayed the intent of the American Negro folk religion. Organizational politics have taken precedence over participation in the struggle for socio-politico-economic justice and equality, at the same time that the independence of Methodists has not either led to attunement with the historic spirit of Methodism or contributed a unique innovation. In the case of independent Methodists, the original intent of the folk religion has clearly been suppressed in favor of organizational concerns. This is clear when it is recalled that Methodists have generated neither a congregation comparable to the Abyssinian Church nor a leader such as Martin Luther King, Jr. Moreover, in communities across the nation, it is the exceptional Methodist minister and congregation who are in the forefront with the host of

Baptist ministers and congregations in the march to insure justice and equality for all Americans through dramatization of the Negro's disfranchisement.

Organ for Recognition, Leadership and Worship

Although Methodists and Baptists have varied in their faithfulness to the spirit of the religion inherited from the Negro folk, all but dead among the former and only sporadically revived among the latter, they hardly vary in their current use of this historic stream. The once noble work of independent Negro religious institutions in the area of freedom and equality is only verbalized, now, in times of tension to keep the people involved in congregational activity. Maintaining the tradition of freedom and equality is no longer the express purpose of those who gather in the meeting house. Rather, community fellowship, leadership development, and worship comprise the dominant (originally subordinate) interests of a people estranged from both the intent of their unique beginnings and the mainstream of the communion whose name they assume.

The question is frequently asked, referring to camp sites, national parks, community swimming pools, and public facilities in general: "Why is it that Negroes are conspicuous by their absence?" It is more than a matter of economics, just as the fact that generations of native Negroes have congregated in the Roxbury area of Boston while Negro newcomers search for housing outside the ghetto is not altogether a matter of economics. Even in this era of rapid transition Negroes are inclined not to frequent public accommodations in many areas of America for substantially the same reason natives of Boston tend to accept housing in "the colored section"—it is a matter of habit based on the past experience of being unwelcome in, though legally entitled to, other facilities. Any Negro who has traveled across the length and breadth of the United States, taking advantage of the normal hotel and restaurant accommodations available to the conventional traveler, discovers that in the wake of the protests in the South (Houston, Atlanta, Greensboro, New Orleans, El Paso, Nashville) he is as much of a surprise to the personnel and clientele as he is a topic for conversation in comparable Northern facilities. It will take a number of decades and a concerted effort on behalf of Negroes to frequent these establishments on occasions other than conventions and sit-ins.

In the meantime, the traditional Negro, who is a creature of habit, will continue to function as if America is a closed society. Following the pattern of those before him who have turned the thrust of the American Negro folk religion as community action into community insulation, he will operate within the confines of the local meeting house as the disguised but acceptable form of Black Nationalism. The shackles of the past may be broken, but their psychological effect is no less tangible in the present. For the local congregation continues to be the community center for an appreciable portion of Negroes. While this centrality of the folk religion as the organ for communication continues to be a forced option in the South and in the metropolitan areas of the North where the Negro is left to reside unto himself, the response is as much habitual as it is necessary. That is, whether it is the case or not, the Negro member of a congregation acts as though the religious fellowship is his primary means for social acceptance and recognition.

The rise of the Negro in the political and economic spheres may occur, though almost imperceptibly, but his lack of social status is unchanging. Historically, the political

and economic handicaps were insurmountable even by the
spirited drive of the folk religion. The failure to accept the
Negro fully in the political and economic areas was rooted
in his complete unacceptableness in the social area, burden-
ing the American Negro folk religion with the task of being
the social organ, in addition to being the amusement center
and political arena. In fact, the role of the American Negro
folk religion as a community center is its most important
one in the life of the Negro, although it no longer functions
as *the center* of the Negro community. Given the failure of
the folk religion to be a missionary force in the achievement
of freedom and equality for the Negro, compared with the
primary mission of Protestant and Christian denominations
to extend the gospel of Jesus Christ, the result has been the
emergence of the meeting house as the focal point of the
community for the sake of sociability.

As social centers Negro fellowships function in the
same way as their white counterparts, with the exception
that they are more important in the lives of Negroes who
are, or at least feel they are, excluded from community
organizations. The masses who belong to Negro congregations in institutions separate from whites gain a sense of
identity through organized groups. The leisure time of persons with limited education and means is not uncommonly
spent in an inordinate worship of and participation in religious activities.

The custodian who is ordered about the office building
in his daily routine of delivering freight, mopping up floors
and emptying wastebaskets gains a sense of self-importance
in his role as superintendent of the Sunday School. The
housekeeper for an industrial manager who spends all day
with "the madam" deftly arranging and ordering, retreating
to the kitchen or her quarters upon the arrival of guests, can
display her talents and be publicly credited for her initiative
as director of the Baptist Training Union. The secretary to

the president of the college for Negroes is in league with the professionals in status as the president of the Women's Society for Christian Service and financial secretary of the leading Methodist church. The college graduate who is unable to earn a living with his gifted voice and therefore works as a porter at the air terminal wins applause and acclaim as the soloist in the Metropolitan Baptist Church. The enterprising local grocer whose political awareness and popularity are insufficient to elect him an alderman increases his prestige, circumscribed though it may be, through his election as chairman of the board of trustees. The saleslady obscured in the downtown department store adds recognition and influence to her life as the chairman of the pastoral relations committee. The construction worker who receives an adequate financial reward for his endeavors gains prestige and control as the senior deacon. The waitress whose shrilling voice places orders all day enters the limelight as the leader of the gospel chorus.

Precisely because the local congregations sponsor many activities which require leaders, they provide opportunities for recognition and fulfillment. Occasionally, grotesque methods are used to spark a sense of competition. St. Clair Drake and Horace R. Cayton in *Black Metropolis* give a classic example of such methods by one minister who said:

One thing we plan to do is to get out a weekly reminder, and we will mention all the good work done by all the good people. We know that this will stir the people who don't work so hard as others to do more, because we feel that our people are jealous of one another and will work hard to keep others from getting ahead of them.

Artificial stimulants are unnecessary in the smaller congregations which are often created or joined for purposes of having a "finger in things," as one member put it. Once again, from *Black Metropolis*:

In a little church there is something for everybody to do. Every
man in the church, as well as every woman, can have an office.
You know people like to be called on so they can do things.

Leadership positions are only as significant as the quality of
persons attracted to them. Training in leadership begins
with attendance at the church school where children who
are able to read may have an opportunity to make the report for their class before the whole session. Adult members of Sunday school classes and the pastor support these
budding leaders with their enthusiastic encouragement, and
in this atmosphere of approval young people discover in
early adolescence that regardless of their rejection by society they can achieve acceptance as a leader in the religious
fellowship. Those who fail to complete high school but are
church-oriented may look forward to recognition as a church
school officer, licensed preacher, or functionary on one of the
boards. Often the ability to speak persuasively, sing effectively, and record minutes reasonably well are as important
as education and experience in a specific field to the attainment of a leadership position. Those who have aspirations
can look forward to service as officials of numerous women's
auxiliaries and men's groups, members of trustee and deacon
boards, and delegates to associations and conventions.

There are far more faithful workers than leaders, of
course, who are satisfied to belong to the various groups
within the congregation, delighted with whatever occasions
they have to meet the quotas and enjoy the fellowship.
What is taken to be love for the fellowship, chiefly among
the women, is expressed through spending a high proportion
of their leisure hours in its activities. It is not unusual to
find the women of the congregation idolizing their fellowship and minister, sharing a substantial proportion of their
income with each. In many ways the organized groups of
the congregation serve as substitutes for social clubs:

The only social outlet I have is the Mount Zion Methodist Church. I belong to the Women's Society for Christian Service which is a vital part of the church with all of its various activities. I spend most of my time in group meetings and the activities which develop around them. I spend most of my time there, giving all I can to the work of the Lord and His spokesman. This is the least I can do for my God and His church. What could be more rewarding than a full life within the church?

The matriarchal pattern among Negroes places the burden of supporting the family upon the women, who seek to keep the children in a spirit of harmony and to sustain themselves through the fellowship of the congregation. Adults who cling to the religious societies as the means of obtaining refreshment and pleasure in the fellowship of the disinherited, no less than as a way of serving God, are not being imitated by their children. Membership and activity in congregations is increasingly peripheral for the younger generation. The aspirations of youth are expressed through attendance at the religious exercises on Sundays out of deference to their upbringing, but even this activity is participated in with less of a sense of indispensability than in previous generations. The psychological needs of youth are singularly and often unwholesomely met by the attractions of theaters, nightclubs, ball games, poolrooms, gambling, and sex. The religious society as a community organization for fellowship and recognition, substituting for the "genius" of the American Negro folk religion, is limited by its design for a stable and segregated society. The response of one adult "faithful" indicates a certain perception, reflecting a general awareness that congregations are unequipped to meet the social needs of youth:

Our children are in need of a wholesome environment in which to express themselves creatively. This church was built as a recreational center, as well as a house of worship. Each year the activities of the church decrease. The children are spending their time in the streets without supervision. My children don't seem to find anything of interest in the church. It seems to me that Pastor Barr ought to work at this problem, if not make it his number-one responsibility. After all, the future of our fellowship is at stake. Teen-age clubs are lacking in spiritual teachings, and they are not well directed, which is foremost in my mind; what they do can better be done in the churches.

Methodist and Baptist congregations are dominated by the preacher, few of whom resemble, in stature or interest, their predecessors who personified the religion of the Negro folk. The dictatorial structure of Baptist congregations militates against a cooperative ministry of associate and assistant ministers, regardless of the size of the congregation. Each pastor is committed only to the tradition he creates, which is maintained by personal magnetism coupled with ingenuity. This system of empire-building is saturated with jealousy and leaves little room for sharing the work with persons other than those who have come under the spell of the cult. Baptist preachers are surrounded instead by "jack-leg" preachers or "chair-backers," who are doled out responsibilities when they are not in other churches preaching to win congregations of their own. Usually they are not in in-service training. They are lesser men who have not been so fortunate as to obtain a church commensurate with their ambition. It is not unusual to view on the platform of a church older men who have lost whatever chance they had to pastor their home church, or another, but who cherish the prestige of being called "Reverend." A guest minister who spoke in the worship service at the Greater Galilee Baptist Temple in Los Angeles observed the following:

The Reverend J. C. Wieman, widely respected in the city for his service to and influence within the Negro community, is a graduate of a local Baptist seminary and the recipient of an honorary doctoral degree from an equally provincial college. During the major portion of the service, Mr. Wieman stood at the centered pulpit. He was dressed in a long black formal coat with gray and black striped pants and a matching tie. Behind him sat one young and two older preachers. From his central position Mr. Wieman called for the chorus to sing "a special number," whispered to various deacons at frequent intervals, clicked his fingers as he hummed the tunes and waved his arms leading the congregation in the chorus. In between times he turned to one pulpiteer and asked him to read the scripture, another to give the pastoral prayer, and the third to "bless the offering." Then he introduced me as the preacher of the morning. Following my sermon he gave a resumé of equal length and then proceeded to call for the missionary collection. When this was completed a third offering was taken and turned over to me for my services. Leaving the three pulpiteers in the background, Mr. Wieman pronounced the benediction and introduced me to the parishioners. Afterwards we chatted in his office where he pointed out pictures of his various trips around the world made possible by his parishioners. He then drove me to the day-care nursery building he developed with the public welfare, turning on his forty-five inch record player and playing some gospel music he had recorded on the way. Confident of my interest in his person and accomplishments he remarked: "I find myself involved in all kinds of community affairs, the load is tremendous. I have been inquiring about, seeking a young man who would be my assistant. I can't find the right man. In your work among college students you might come across the kind of person who would fit in here. If you do, let me know."

Baptists are noted for their prestige pastors, shadowed by ambitious preachers desperately looking for a fellowship to lead. There are always more "jack-legs" than pulpits among Baptists, despite the frequent division of congregations. Baptist preachers do more than aggravate and capitalize upon splits. Their surplus serves to provide Methodists with preachers, for the order among Methodists tends to mitigate the number of clergy available. Methodists are also plagued with preachers on the sidelines who wish to have a charge, or congregation. An ambitious Methodist preacher without one knows his system closes ranks against splits. He also knows that a presiding elder (district superintendent) is receptive to three things: "grit, grace and greenbacks." One untrained Methodist preacher without the third essential could speak only in contempt of what he called "the system":

Ever since I came up here from Arkansas I have worked hard in the St. Paul A.M.E. Church. My wife faithfully sings in the choir and both of us have contributed a lot, financially as well as spiritually. Some years ago, I made my intentions known to the pastor and to the presiding elder. I am an ordained deacon, now, after long study, but I am unable to get a charge through the conference. For years I have been a member of the conference, attending its annual sessions. Do you know there are men who have less education than I, and I am sure, less integrity, who have no trouble being assigned to a pastorate. It would be no trouble for me either if I would take the hard-earned money my wife and I both receive and slip it to the presiding elder. But I refuse to do that.

Baptist and Methodist congregations, conferences, and associations are, more and more, demanding college- and seminary-trained ministers. It is still the case and to a great extent that a man with a good voice, an attractive personality, a sense of humor, and sufficient desire can find a church to serve without formal training. It is apparent, however, that the larger the congregation the more the minister without credentials must excel in organizational ability and preaching power. As the congregations increase in sophistication and numbers there is a comparable increase in the quality of ministers, and there are less of those who have only "the Call" to rely upon:

Brothers, the day is past for untrained preachers. You can't hop around, whoop and holler and spit-at-a-bubble these days. You have to deliver the goods. Some of these preachers are ordained for a mere five-dollar bill. Some of you deacons get notions you ought to preach, so you go to your pastors and pay a few dollars and you are ordained. I remember an incident in Philadelphia. A huckster used to sell vegetables; he used to go down the alley shouting his wares. And one day his wife said to him, "You sound just like a preacher." He got the idea, and decided if he sounded that good to his wife he could preach; so he started a church.[17]

Independent Methodists and Baptists encourage their future ministers to attend an institution of higher learning. Those who respond usually choose a Negro college or university. A small proportion of these pre-ministerial students attend a first-rate college like Morehouse in Atlanta, or a solid university like Howard in Washington, D.C. Some pre-theological students who complete their undergraduate work at Morehouse or Howard go on to seminaries like Yale, Harvard, Chicago, Boston University, Andover Newton Theological School (Massachusetts), Colgate Rochester Divinity School (New York), and Princeton. A larger proportion attend state institutions for Negroes in the South or denominational and private colleges associated with the United Negro College Fund. Among the latter are such second-rate institutions as Morris Brown College in Atlanta; Bishop College in Dallas; Benedict College in Columbia, South Carolin; Huston Tillotson College in Austin, Texas; Wilberforce University in Ohio; and Wiley College in Marshall, Texas. These and other Negro colleges are second-rate in comparison with Fisk University, Nashville, Tennessee, and Morehouse College. They are at least second-rate by comparison with any national or even regional norms, or by the criterion of the small number of graduates who achieve one of the

following distinctions: election to Phi Beta Kappa, a Woodrow Wilson fellowship, a Danforth grant, or a Fulbright or
Rhodes Scholarship. The reasons for the lack of quality in
these colleges are obvious today, but are no less detrimental
to the value of the educational process in general and pre-
ministerial students in particular. The following view by a
former member of the faculty of a private college for Negroes in the mid-South, which we will call Seymour, reflects
what many others have said about their experience in similar
Negro institutions:

Seymour College exists for about two dozen students, at a liberal
estimate. In any given year, at least during my years as a member of the faculty, there were less than twenty-four students with
the ability to enter a reputable graduate school, or in comparable
ways to compete with their peers across the nation. With the
desegregation of the inexpensive and excellent neighboring State
University, the best Negro high school graduates are enrolled
there (and better than 50 per cent of Seymour students are
commuters), and the once noble function of Seymour is no longer
necessary, at least as long as it continues to be a segregated college for Negroes (it has no white students but it does have a
faculty which is one-third white).

Seymour does not encourage white students; its two or three
white graduates were separated by a number of years, although
some of us advocated this openness as a way out of being among
the segregating if not segregated institutions in the area, as well
as providing a sense of competition among the students. Students attend Seymour knowing they will be protected; having
paid their tuition, they assume the teachers are obligated to see
them through. There are good reasons why they come to Seymour. There they have a sense of belonging; they can develop
the social life which is denied to them in white institutions, and
perhaps even discover a marriage partner. But these are not
"the best of reasons." We were told that Seymour had graduated
some distinguished persons but the illustrations were usually a
generation old. We are also informed that Seymour has a "spe-

cial role" to play in the education of students who would not otherwise have had the opportunity to attend college. It is nearer the mark to say that students come to Seymour who would be unacceptable in the State University, or at least would be readily dismissed. There are an insufficient number of good students to pull the institution above the level of a social affair. It is a serious question—are not the students at Seymour, trained as they are in a segregated community for a segregated society, adding to the number of those who will be unemployed in the future? Is this really the way to insure equality with justice for the Negro?

Graduates of colleges like Seymour, who are interested in the ministry, may attend such institutes as Turner Theological Seminary in Atlanta; Payne Theological Seminary in Wilberforce, Ohio; and J. J. Starks School of Theology in Columbia, South Carolina; none of which is accredited by the American Theological Association. Negroes interested in institutions predominantly attended by Negro seminarians can choose the Interdenominational Theological Center in Atlanta, a new co-operative venture (Baptists, Methodists, Christian Methodist Episcopalians and African Methodist Episcopalians) which is in the process of becoming second to none, ideally situated in the environs of the Atlanta University System. The Center has stirred some concern as to its seeming duplication of existing institutions, and one official of the Board of Education of the Methodist Church commented about its future:

The reports are that I.T.C. has an excellent faculty, with some question about the quality and quantity of the student body. It appears to be on the move. The rumor that it is a monument to Benjamin Mays (President of Morehouse College, former Dean of the Howard School of Religion) is to be doubted. However, with the desegregation of the neighboring Candler School of Theology at Emory University it will need to be certain of its responsibility.

The School of Religion at Virginia Union University in Richmond is comparable with the School of Religion at Howard University, about which a Dean of an Eastern seminary remarked: "Howard's School of Religion once had a sparkling faculty and earned the respect of educators in our profession. It has gone downhill in recent years."

Regardless of the quality of the institution, there is a widespread consensus among Negro seminarians about the peculiarity of pastoring a Negro fellowship. It is assumed that their theological education must not interfere with the primary task of "spiritualizing" the congregation of whatever socio-economic orientation:

In classical cultural terms, there is no difference between the Negro Baptist Church and the Baptist Church proper. In folk terms, however, there is. Not only do we Negro Baptists have a way of preaching and singing, but there is a meaning to our imagery that is peculiar to us.[18]

This image was held before a class in preaching by one instructor at a School of Religion in the Southeastern section of the United States:

Aunt Jane is not interested in theological understanding, although you must convey a certain amount of *savoir faire*. She expects to be relieved of thinking and inspired by the sacred Word, vividly portrayed. You will be successful to the extent you are commanding, articulate, clear, convivial, illustrative, and dramatic. Remember, Aunt Jane is impressed less by what is said than by the enthusiasm with which it is said.

A chapel hour followed this class and the instruction of the teacher was reinforced by a lay member of the University's faculty, the guest speaker for the morning:

Young men, I was asked to speak to you as a layman. I don't know anything about theology, except that the average member in the pew hasn't the slightest interest in it. The church is the house of worship and I expect to enjoy a good service. After all, the task of the minister is to be soul-stirring.

By the time he is graduated, the young seminarian knows the importance of the oratorical stimulus. He has learned, as well, that the effectiveness of his leadership is judged by his "verbal commitment" to the problems of discrimination, employment, and housing. The Negro pastor is expected to be intensely loyal to Negro enterprises on all class levels. The successful leader, in terms of his following, gives evidence of his versatility in interests if not in ability, as one astute pastor summarized it:

I have no illusions about my limitations in ability, time, and energy. I have never been solely interested in seeing that my people get into heaven, and more and more they are not interested in this hope either. They demand that I be "all things to all men" and this means a consuming secular interest in my preaching, as well as weekday activities. In the eyes of my people I am qualified to carry out these functions: race and civic leader, moral instructor, preacher, church builder, labor arbiter, organizational official, promoter of businesses, social and welfare agent, denominational spokesman and educator.

The leadership of Negro religious societies is highly secular. Often ministers are frustrated social workers in religious garb with little of the social worker's professional competence or the insight of a theologian. Moreover, the majority of Negro ministers who have degrees received them from colleges and seminaries which leave much to be desired. For the most part, professional social workers are more skillful in their chosen work, receiving their graduate degrees from accredited graduate schools, than are the ministers who are evaluated according to the number of community activities in which they directly participate.

The prestige of a pastoral ministry is unquestionable, and its financial rewards are supplemented by the women who so idolize the pastor that they frequently buy him an automobile, send him abroad, and present him with "purses" on his anniversary, birthday, and at Christmas time. But the gifts which are lavished upon the minister who is "worshiped" do not compensate for his frustration, insofar as he maintains his perspective. Fortunately, there are ministers who rise above the mediocre in response to the social service expectations of the ministry, refusing to allow the allurements to harness their creative powers.

Orientation as a pastor and social worker in this transitional era, particularly in urban areas, presents a challenge to Negroes ministering to Negroes. A good many have been cut off from both a theological heritage and the religion of the Negro folk, leaving them with the urge to do something but without a perspective from which to work meaningfully. There have been a few who have not capitulated to the secular perspective or pretended to provide some special "spiritual" power. But the combination of social concern and Christian depth is a dimension of the most demanding order, escaping those who are not rooted in a theological tradition and frustrating those who are.

Perhaps the most successful pastor-social worker among Negroes is the Reverend Dr. James H. Robinson of New York City, a Presbyterian who upon graduating from Union Theological Seminary in New York founded the Church of the Master, on the fringe of Harlem. A wise pastor and an eloquent preacher, Mr. Robinson developed a dynamic congregation which has held the respect of the community and his alma mater for over thirty years. Through his able leadership his congregation has joined with him in active engagement within the United Presbyterian Church in the U.S.A. (white). Measuring his achievements would be a difficult task. Dr. Robinson has raised his assistants and associates to the level of a cooperative ministry, one that is both interracial and intercultural, complementing his congregation. He has been one of the distinguished preachers of England and America who has delivered the Lyman Beecher Lectures on Preaching at Yale University, one of the most famous series of lectures delivered in this country. The General Synod of the United Presbyterian Church in the U.S.A. sent him as its ambassador around the world. Yet his ministry has not been without its trying hours, even within his own presbytery. A graduate of Union Seminary who joined the Church of the Master with his wife pointed out a memorable occasion in Dr. Robinson's career:

When Jim held an ordination service in our church for one of the first women to be ordained in the New York presbytery, the ministers and representative elders in each congregation were invited. Not one of them appeared. This sparked Jim to comment: "I guess they are afraid to come down here."

In addition to his denominational loyalty and pastoral effectiveness, Robinson has a keen social conscience, differing from Adam Clayton Powell in depth with respect to denominational loyalty and in direction with respect to social consciousness. Robinson is primarily a social welfare promoter, and much less a politician and social protester. He developed the Morningside Community Center as an outreach of the Church of the Master, and has sponsored summer camps for the children of Harlem in Northfield, Massachusetts. As an institutional worker and organizer, Robinson is unmatched by other preacher-social workers. He and Powell have gone by different routes to the same end: both have forsaken the pastoral ministry at the height of their careers—Powell for politics and leisure, Robinson for a mission to Africa. These two former pastors, like Martin Luther King, Jr., used the local congregation as a base for larger

operations within the tradition of the American Negro folk
religion. For the tradition has seen the meeting house as a
way to equality and justice for the Negro, irrespective of his
less urgent spiritual requirements. Robinson's Operation
Crossroads Africa is a national organization, which works
with colleges and universities all across the country to sponsor students who will spend a summer working and living
with Africans, sharing each other's worlds, and informing
their representative communities of their experience upon
the completion of a summer's work. This magnificently conceived and instituted operation is a million-dollar enterprise.

As a pastor, Robinson was well within the Presbyterian
tradition, but the severity of life for the Negro of Harlem
claimed his creativity and energy. Rooted more deeply in
the Negro folk than in the Presbyterian tradition, Robinson
faced the choice of being a superior pastor or an unexcelled
leader. He chose to become a leader on the international
level.

The Negro leader whose background is ecclesiastical
and limited by education, interest, and experience to the
milieu of the Negro is without a historical theological perspective and lacks the dynamic of the folk ingenuity. In
their attempt to be "all things to all men" Negro pastors
lack the wherewithal to lead and, therefore, are ineffective
in community problems. There are exceptions, but the trustee who reflected upon the work of his ministers over the
years is essentially accurate:

The average minister is not a teacher instructing his congregation in how to face the moral, social and economic problems
plaguing them, either because he is inadequate before or worn
down by the problems. What he does is to rely upon exhortation
and make a show of doing good. Instead of concentrating upon
current issues he concentrates upon current expenses. The real
truth is that the ministers of today serve the organization instead
of the people. They all preach about equality and fraternity, but

the emphasis is upon increasing the budget and the size of the church. Comfort, security and activity comprise the trinity in the midst of a social revolution.

By and large, Negro ministerial leadership deals with the symptoms of the socio-politico-economic unrest and fails to be significant in an ecclesiastical or folk tradition:

Furthermore, the Negro clergy has yielded a considerable amount of its influence in recent years to business and to other professions. Only lately are there some indications of a renaissance in clerical leadership; and even now, the most significant social leadership is offered by those denominations that lack institutionalized hierarchy. "For the most part, Negro churches have contributed to the reinforcement of the extant mores." In spite of its estimated 10 million members, the Negro church has sponsored comparatively few programs against the discrimination it exemplifies.[19]

Worship

Excessive emotionalism, dubbed "escapism," characterizes the popular image of the Negro and his religion. Actually, this exuberance is a vestige of the white Baptist and Methodist evangelists, and to a lesser extent the other evangelists, and remains the bond of kinship between Negro and white Protestants, along with organizational procedures. American Negro folk religion committed itself to freedom and equality for the folk through the structures of independent Negro religious organizations. Their hopes dashed by the reality of a segregated society, Negroes took refuge in institutional maintenance and emotional fervor as a substitute for militant and direct action. Thus, there is nothing

96

unique in the worship life of the Negro. What is taken for uniqueness is but the extreme of what may be found in comparable white congregations. The son of a conventional pastor, recalling his childhood religious experience, noted that it was not noticeably different from that of kindred white Protestants in his community:

We used to go to our own church (Negro) on Sunday morning and in the afternoons we had cottage prayer meetings in our home or the home of one of the other members of the prayer circle (white). This was a weekly ritual in which the adults called each other "brother" and "sister" and the children joined in the service of song and prayer. My father and mother used the same expressions in their prayers ("gift of the Holy Ghost," "tarry," "precious ones," "free from sin," "Down at the Cross," "Jesus keep me Near the Cross"), as their white friends. There was a real spiritual harmony which obviated all racial differences. Father served as a pastor to nearly as many whites as Negroes. His counseling and participation in the life of white friends was made possible by their pietistic orientation. Even, now, when I go home for a visit these old friends continue their round of prayer and conversation each morning by telephone. Recently, one wealthy old friend willed father a substantial sum of money as a part of her estate, undoubtedly an expression of appreciation for his spiritual fellowship over a span of twenty-five years.

The "arousements" featured at worship services are enjoyed by old and young alike, of various socio-economic levels. There are no innovations in their claim of "justification by faith," "restoration of the backslider," "the fruits of the spirit as joy, peace, and a clear conscience," "the sweet by-and-by," "determination to press on in the face of trials and tribulations." Testimonial services may dwell upon how the individual overcame "weakness of the flesh," or his dramatic conversion: "I remember the day, I remember the hour, when I was saved by the blood of Jesus. It was on July the

16th, 1938, at high noon. I was walking down the road to
Birmingham, looking for the way. Thank you Jesus, thank
you, I found the way and I never will turn away."

The eschatological emphasis on sin, worldliness, and repentance expressed by one enthusiast is on a par with all
those who take the Bible literally:

What is sin? It is in plain words dancing, drinking, card playing,
gambling, lying, and stealing. These are the things God sent
his Son in the world to free us of. His plan for us through the
ages does not include these wicked sicknesses. You had better
wake up to this; you cannot depend upon a death-bed salvation.
We are living in the last dispensation and God's about to close
the books. The millennium is upon us. How do I know? The
Bible says Jesus will return "in clouds of glory" when there are
"wars and rumors of wars." This is the time, this is the end, for
all about us are the hoofbeats of the Four Horsemen of the
Apocalypse. I tell you, Armageddon is upon us. The sheep and
the goats will soon be separated and the "last trumpet will sound"
waking up the dead. Whosoever is not "found written in the
book of life" will be "cast into the lake of fire."

If there is a "native touch" in the worship of Negroes
it is in the spontaneity of their prayers. Drawing upon a
common stockpile of phrases, interspersed with congregational Amens, Hallelujahs, the true believer may "line a
hymn" and then begin to pray:

O Lord, we come this morning knee-bowed and body bent
before thy throne of grace. We come this morning, Lord, like
empty pitchers before a full fountain, realizing that many who are
better by nature than we are by practice have passed into the
great beyond, and yet you have allowed us, your humble servants,
to plod along just a few days longer here in this waste-howling
wilderness. We thank thee, Lord, that when we 'woke this
morning, our bed was not a cooling board, and our sheet was not
a winding shroud. We are not gathered here for form or fashion

or for an outside show unto the world, but we come in our humble way to serve thee. We bring no merit of our own, and are nothing but filthy rags in thy sight. We thank thee, Lord, that we are clothed in our right mind and are not racked upon a bed of pain. Bless the sick and the afflicted and those who are absent through no fault of their own. And when I've done prayed my last prayer and done sung my last song; when I'm done climbing the rough side of the mountain; when I come down to tread the steep and prickly banks of Jordan, meet me with thy rod and staff and bear me safely over to the other side. All these things we ask in Jesus' name, world without end, *Amen* [from *Black Metropolis* by St. Clair Drake and Horace R. Cayton].

Such a prayer may lead a sister to lead the gathered in singing a familiar hymn among Negroes:

> This little light of mine,
> I'm going to let it shine;
> This little light of mine,
> I'm going to let it shine,
> let it shine, let it shine,
> let it shine.
>
> Everywhere I go,
> I'm going to let it shine;
> Everywhere I go,
> I'm going to let it shine,
> let it shine, let it shine,
> let it shine.

Set off by this hymn, some of "the faithful" may "get happy" and begin "shouting," flinging their arms, jumping and running down the aisles, and screaming at the top of their lungs, "Yes, yes, yes!" The excitement of these " 'rousements" is joined in by some, enjoyed by others, and accepted by still others.

A typical worship service will last about two hours, depending upon the length of the singing, prayers, Bible lessons, sermon, collections, announcements, and introduction of guests. The heart of the service is the singing of gospel songs, but never Negro spirituals, by a soloist, quartet, or the gospel chorus. Only the "saints" and the "saved" are permitted to "feel the spirit" by breaking out in "shouts of joy," but the less extroverted and ecstatic enjoy a good preacher. The text and subject of the sermon seldom bear any relationship to each other. The Bible serves as a springboard for a highly imaginative improvisation to chide the "worldly wise," to remind the people of financial needs, for "the Lord loves a cheerful giver," or to denounce "sin and the devil." It is to the minister's credit if he applies his sermon to contemporary situations, calling the people to "march on Washington," to stop being "adult delinquents" and to "pray for peace." Above all else, the sermon must make alive Bible stories and religious tales which parallel the life of the Negro: Moses and the Egyptian Queen, Lazarus and the Rich Man, The Three Hebrew Children in the Fiery Furnace, The Prodigal Son, and the adventures of Job, Jeremiah, Ezekiel, Hosea, Jonathan, David, Esther, Ruth, and other familiar passages from the Bible. That preacher who is able to preach the whole Bible and not miss a single high point from the Creation through the Crucifixion to the Last Judgment "will be around for a while."

An illuminating sermon-in-illustration by a popular minister, let us call him the Reverend T. Anderson Brown, is his interpretation of "Let My People Go." A retired prizefighter, who by his own proud admission was converted "to battling for the Lord instead of the devil sometime between the last trip to the canvas and the descent to drudgery as a bootblack," preacher Brown is an impressive figure of ebony hue. He is preaching in a large Methodist church: "We are an enslaved race, cut off from our past and at the mercy of the present. But our Lord has spoken to Pharaoh's heart through a prophet: 'Let my people go, that they may serve me.'" Sensing that the people are with him, he moves to the edge of rostrum and leans in the direction of the people: "We have endured hard trials! They seem to be getting worse. Do you believe the Lord will redeem us 'with a stretched-out arm, and with great judgments'? Will He deliver us? (Congregational response: "Yes, He will!") Have you ever doubted it? (Congregational response: "No! Never!") The Lord your God is at work in these hard trials." Brown takes out a white handkerchief to wipe his face as he stalks across the platform declaring: "I will rid you of their bondage. You shall know it is the Lord our God who bringeth us out from under the bondage. But you must trust Him. The way will be filled with pain and disappointments. There will be setbacks and heartaches. But He has promised. Our God has never broken a promise." Bending over and pointing his long finger knowingly, he describes the trial by tribulation as a test of their faithfulness: "You will need to face rivers of blood, wars of nerves, the loss of your first-born, plagues of all kinds. But you can trust the promises of the Lord and lean upon His everlasting arms."

Brown then jumps behind the centered pulpit, and with outstretched arms, shouts: "He will make a way out of no way for His people. To be His people does not mean feuding, fussing, and fighting. It does not mean love of whoredom, wine, waggery, wallowing, wantonness, whimpering and wishful thinking. It means letting go and letting God. There will be a land flowing with milk and honey. There will be no pain in that land, no sorrow there—nothing but joy in that land." Cries of "Take us to that land" are heard as Brown paces to and fro across the platform with his arms pointing ceilingward as if God were perched on the chandeliers. He stops abruptly, turns to the choir behind him, and in a pleading tone says: "Let my people go." And turning back to the congregation, declares, obviously imitating

Moses: "Let my people go. But old Pharaoh has a hard heart. He cannot be persuaded. He refuses to acknowledge and obey the Lord above all gods." Brown then drops to his knees and in perfect mime dramatizes the plagues of frogs, lice, flies, locusts, beasts, and hail, claiming each time that Pharaoh hardened his heart and "would not let the people go." The preacher then rises and begins to relate the plagues which the present-day Pharaohs face: "We begin with a statement describing the conditions of our bondage, but Pharaoh hardens his heart. We call for negotiations, but the heart is hardened. We protest, march, sit-in, and call for negotiations again. The heart is still hard against us. We are suffering, but thank God we are no longer alone. Like the people of Israel, the battle is being fought for us. Finally, the day will come."

With great vigor he steps down out of the pulpit and into the pit where the junior choir is seated; reaching out, he gathers three youngsters and ties their stoles together, binding them as one into a chariot team, placing a fourth youngster behind as the driver. Brown, walking in front as if leading the people of Israel through the Red Sea, declares: "The Lord shall fight for you, and ye shall hold your peace." He takes the pose of Moses, and stretching out his hand, he says: "My, look at the sea become dry land. But the Egyptians will follow." Then the preacher turns quickly, grabs a table and places it between himself and the youngsters of the chariot, at the same time that he stretches out his hand "so that the waters may come again upon the Egyptians." He declares: "Thus the Lord saved Israel that day; and one day He will deliver us. One day Pharaoh will let my people go. But then it will be too late for him. My God and my Lord."

"The Lord is our strength and song, and He has become my salvation," he screams at the top of his lungs. With this triumphant note people arise throughout the congregation, clapping and shouting, "Preach! preach!" He continues:

"The Lord is a man of war. Names can't hurt you. Jails can't hold you. Setbacks can't deter you. Laws can't break you. Dogs can't harm you. Mighty men can't bend you. The right hand of the Lord will become glorious in power. Just hold onto Him and trust His name. Who is like unto thee, o Lord, among the gods of men? Thou art glorious in holiness, fearful in praises. Thou art our redeemer and in Thy strength we shall go forward." As he closes, a gesture is made to one of the ushers, who brings his coat, which he puts on, apparently to minimize the possibility of chilling his profusely perspiring body, and, wiping his brow, he begins to sing: "I sing because I'm happy. I sing because I'm free. His eye is on the sparrow, and I know He watches me." One woman, overcome, runs up and down the aisle, gasping, "My, my, my." A man on the other side responds, "Go right on. Don't stop now." A choir member speaks the mind of all: "He's a preaching," and the congregation joins with an "Amen."

The Reverend T. Anderson Brown, like many of his white contemporaries, is a showman of the first order.

Worship as " 'rousements" is often set in a pattern emphasizing "the great beyond." The theme of heaven and the "afterlife" may be sounded by the singing of

> Nothing but joy in that land,
> Where I am bound, where I am bound,

or a sermon illustrating the great white way:

Heaven is my home and I am homesick. There I will meet all the saints who have gone on before me. My mother and father will be there in that great host. I want to see them again. I want to look into the eyes of Abraham, take a long walk with Moses, talk with Ruth, feel the arms of Esau, and shake Jacob by the hand. There I will have the chance to ask Job about his suffering, thank the prophets for their courage, and sit beside Lazarus. Above all, I want to be with Jesus of Galilee: my Lord and my God. There will be no more crying up there, no pain up there, no second-class citizenship up there. There will be nothing but peace in God's kingdom. Up there, I will have a time.

The color, enthusiasm, and imagery in the worship of Negroes varies from class level to class level, as does its quality. Independent Negro congregations are pointed out as examples *par excellence* of the special brand of worship which is native to the Negro. In reality, this stereotype is but a variation on the evangelical theme introduced and sustained by white evangelists.

It is understandable that the Negro might be expected to add something of his own to his worship after generations of spiritual ferment. But the fact that he has chosen to place his experience and faith in God within the forms inherited from a severed past, if at times stretching them to their limits, is irrefutable. The obvious response to this situation is that the Negro is characteristically emotional. Yet a more profound reason is that worship is but a means to the end of equality and justice. The eschatological theme in worship is but the expression of frustration in this world, worship being the means of deployment during an era of helplessness. In the meantime, clergy and laity alike have tended to equate worship with the "genius" of the folk religion, often substituting an inherited religion for personal gain— in this world as well as in the other. What has been taken for the heartbeat of the Negro people is the concentration of Negroes at worship services. This is misleading, because Sunday morning is the one occasion when Negroes gather in conspicuous numbers, on any regular basis. Moreover, even this gathering of Negroes for worship is not representative of the people as a whole since historically the formal praise of God has claimed a minority of Negroes at best.[20] Freedom with opportunity has been the central concern of the Negro, entangled, to be sure, with evangelical relics and

frustrated by persistent opposition. But as the great bulk of
Jews attend the synagogue only on high holy days as a
pledge of family loyalty to a heritage which transcends individual beliefs, so the Negro characteristically gives his
support to the American Negro folk religion—the possibility
of the recurrence of World War II Germany has bound together the Jews as the possibility of the militant nonviolent
movement has given unity in hope to Negroes. The authentic hallmark of the Negro folk in religion is the demand for
full and civil rights. In effect, the Negro who has turned to
the medium of worship as an antidote for melancholy dese-
crates the folk religion and the evangelical spirit.

The condition of the American Negro has forced him
to be individualistic even in the matter of worship. As a result, there have been no creative contributions of the Negro
people to worship, but there have been creative individuals
within the context of worship. Negroes have produced great
preachers, but few intellectual leaders. The gap between
spiritual depth and social action has never quite been
bridged. This contrast is visible in the divergent paths of
two notable Negro preachers of extraordinary influence.

Dr. Benjamin E. Mays, president of Morehouse College
in Atlanta, is a national figure held in high esteem as an educator by his colleagues. As both a preacher and a spokesman for the Negro, he has been respected and admired for
several decades. *The Negro's God* and *The Negro's Church*
are two of his books which gained him recognition as an
authority on the spiritual life of Negroes. In his sermons,
speeches, and weekly articles in the *Pittsburgh Courier* Mays
has consistently wedded his primary interest in "the race"
with social action. On this level he has consistently been
akin to the American Negro folk religion, seeking to attune
the good will of white Americans to the Negro's will to the
good. Mays has been no less persistent in his advocacy of
the qualities of intelligence, directness, and independence

among Negroes. His primary image as a preacher among both white and Negro Americans is that of a traditional Baptist preacher distinguished by his wisdom, wit, and witness. Affinity with evangelism and the social issues of the people have not rooted Mays in any major theological tradition which could be tapped as a means of contributing value to the worship expression of the Negro. In this way, Mays is typical of the preachers produced by the Negro folk.

On the other hand, Dr. Howard Thurman is without question the most provocative innovator in the spiritual realm yet produced by the folk. He has rejected both the evangelism of white Protestants and the social action dimension of the American Negro folk religion. Howard Thurman is one of the dozen or so leading preachers in the United States today. He is the leading preacher among Negroes and their most creative spiritual leader. A specialist in the realm of the spirit, the epitome of spiritual leadership evoked by a segregated society, and a minister who stands in sharp contrast to the traditional Negro preacher, Howard Thurman merits our careful attention.

After graduating from Morehouse College, to which he later returned to teach, Thurman was rejected on the basis of race at the Andover Newton Theological School in Newton Centre, Massachusetts, but was accepted at the Rochester Theological Seminary in Rochester, New York. His graduation was followed by a pastorate in Oberlin, Ohio. While in Oberlin he studied as a special student for a year with Rufus Jones, the renowned Quaker, at Haverford College. With this background he went on to teach in the School of Religion at Morehouse College, and several years later accepted the appointment of Professor of Theology in the Howard University School of Religion and was Chairman of the University's Committee. As Dean of the Chapel at Howard, he achieved a national reputation as a preacher among white and Negro students, ministers, congregations and religious conferences from coast to coast. In 1935, he led a delegation of Negro Christians to Asia where they met with the members of the Student Christian Movement in India, Burma, and Ceylon as an experiment in confronting non-white Asians with American non-whites to counteract the usual pattern of white students meeting with colored students.

Three significant factors in the life of Howard Thurman have profoundly shaped his spirit. First, there was the limitation of being a Negro, which restricted not only his theological education but also the sphere of his ministry throughout his life. His welcome as a speaker at white conferences and churches, but exclusion from an integral life within the organizations of white Christians, as well as their local and institutional commitment to segregation, led this "apostle of sensitiveness" to be suspicious of the whole Christian enterprise, while embracing Jesus: "The concept of denominationalism seems to me to be in itself a violation of what I am delineating as the Jesus idea." [21] His reaction to "the witness of the church in our society" early led him to oppose, on racial and spiritual grounds, denominationalism and institutionalism:

Whatever may be the delimiting character of the historical development of the church, the simple fact remains that at the present moment in our society, as an institution, the church is divisive and discriminating, even within its fellowship. This would indicate that it is essentially sectarian in character. As an institution there is no such thing as the church. There has to be some kind of church.[22]

The second factor influencing Thurman was the period in which he developed and the liberal spirits to which he attuned his own. Thurman received his formal theological education in the liberal 1930's at Rochester Theological Seminary where Walter Rauschenbusch, the exponent and interpreter of the Social Gospel Movement, had been an influential teacher. But the Social Gospel was oblivious to the question of the Negro, except insofar as he was a victim, like all other Americans, of the socio-politico-economic system. Thurman perceived that those Protestants whose voices were the loudest in protest against the inadequacies of the capitalistic system were conversely indifferent to the Negro. He never lost his social consciousness, but remained a non-social actionist. It was this inclination which led him to study with the Quaker Rufus Jones in the 1930's. This was a period of liberal thinking throughout the Protestant world, of disillusionment with Biblical or confessional theology within the Christian Church, and of intense belief in the universality of all men centered upon some kind of religious experience common to all. The Quaker emphasis upon the "inner light" and personal religious affirmations outside the community of faith met the needs of Thurman. In the very years when the mainstream of Protestantism was moving away from a social conscience, specifically away from the social gospel, toward a theological revival which laid the basis for the present ecumenical dynamic and its call for a universal Church without racial apartheid—Thurman was outside this mainstream, moving toward a Unitarian theological structure built on the foundations of a Quaker or mystical religious awareness.

In this movement away from the currents of Protestant thinking, Thurman did not differ theologically from many of the leading churchmen of the 1930's. But the added factor of dislike of racial hypocrisy prevailed, and prevented his reception of the Protestant revival of Pauline theology and reinforced his distrust of Protestantism. In truth, Thurman's dissent was rooted in his childhood days when his grandmother, to whom he regularly read the Bible, would not allow him to read any of the Pauline letters for this reason:

"During the days of slavery," she said, "the master's minister would occasionally hold services for the slaves. Old man McGhee was so mean that he would not let a Negro minister preach to his slaves. Always the white minister used as his text something from Paul. At least three or four times a year he used as a text: 'Slaves, be obedient to them that are your masters . . . , as unto Christ.' Then he would go on to show how it was God's will that we were slaves and how, if we were good and happy slaves, God would bless us. I promised my Maker that if I ever learned to read and if freedom ever came, I would not read that part of the Bible." [23]

Christians in the liberal tradition who joined Thurman in opposition to mainstream Protestant theology attacked the Pauline letters on theological and philosophical grounds. Thurman, representative of the disregard for theology among Negroes, dismisses Paul on psychological grounds. This difference is typical of that between white and Negro liberals, who are otherwise kindred spirits:

It cannot be denied that too often the weight of the Christian movement has been on the side of the strong and the powerful and against the weak and oppressed—this, despite the gospel. A part of the responsibility seems to me to rest upon a peculiar twist in the psychology of Paul, whose wide and universal concern certainly included all men, bond and free.[24]

Paul is a representative of all Christian theology, in the mind of Thurman, and is contrasted with the person of Jesus: "Unless one actually lives day by day without a sense of security, he cannot understand what worlds separated Jesus from Paul at this point." [25] Insofar as Protestants extol Paul as the greatest theologian and spokesman for the mind of Christ, the position of Thurman is illuminating:

It would be grossly misleading and inaccurate to say that there are not to be found in the Pauline letters utterances of a deeply different quality—utterances which reveal how his conception transcended all barriers of race and class and condition. But this other side is there, always available to those who wish to oppress and humiliate their fellows. The point is that this aspect of Paul's teaching is understandable against the background of this Roman citizenship. It influenced his philosophy of history and resulted in a major frustration that has borne fruit in the history of the movement which he, Paul, did so much to project on the conscience of the human race.[26]

The crowning experience on Thurman's way to being a spiritual leader was his trip to Asia, where his mystical tendencies were fulfilled and his thought was crystallized. The people of India and the Negro people were one in the inspiration of the spiritual "Were you there when they crucified my Lord?":

Some time ago when a group of Negroes from the United States visited Mahatma Gandhi, it was the song that he requested them to sing for him. The insight here revealed is profound and touching. At last there is worked out the kind of identification in suffering that makes the cross universal in its deepest meaning. It cuts across differences of religion, race, class, and language, and dares to affirm that the key to the mystery of the cross is found deep within the heart of the experience itself.[27]

These three factors led Thurman and his wife to the point of decision:

We knew that we must test whether a religious fellowship could be developed in America that was capable of cutting across all racial barriers, with a carry-over into the common life, a fellowship that would alter the behavior patterns of those involved. It became imperative now to find out if experiences of spiritual unity among people could be more compelling than the experiences which divide them.[28]

His great experiment was The Church for the Fellowship of All Peoples in San Francisco. This interracial, intercultural, interdenominational fellowship began with Presbyterian financial and spiritual support, with some "Protestant Christian" understanding in its initial commitment:

In this commitment I am pledged to the growing understanding of all men as sons of God and seek after a vital interpretation of the highest manifestation of God—Jesus Christ—in all my relationships.[29]

In this beginning, which did not reflect the true perspective of Thurman, the fellowship began. It soon reached the point of deciding whether it would become a Presbyterian mission church of interracial character or an independent communion oriented toward the Judeo-Christian heritage which "affirms the validity of spiritual insight wherever found and seeks to recognize, understand, and appreciate every aspect of truth whatever the channel through which it comes." [30] The latter course was chosen, and with it a commitment which varied from the initial one:

I affirm my need for a growing understanding of all men as sons of God, and seek after a vital interpretation of God as revealed in Jesus of Nazareth whose fellowship with God was the foundation of his fellowship with men.[31]

The point of this detail is that Thurman created a truly remarkable fellowship, based considerably on his personality, outside the mainstream of Protestantism:

I had known theoretically that Christianity as a religion is *adjectival* in character; that is, there is no such thing as a church, as such, without denominational description—it has to be some kind of church—Methodist, Baptist, Congregational or what not. In other words, the organizational genius of Christianity is sectarian. If we were to continue as an independent religious fellowship, our greatest temptation would be to multiply ourselves on the basis of program and commitment and thereby become another denomination. Again and again, people would raise the question, "When you join Fellowship Church, what do you join?" The only answer we could give was that they were joining The Church for the Fellowship of All Peoples. We were a religious fellowship dedicated to the worship of God and the kind of common life that worship inspired.[32]

The success of Thurman's interracial fellowship in San Francisco, like his later success as Dean of the Chapel at Boston University, testified to the response of the community to the magnetism of his person which communicated a religious experience—yet Thurman's experience in both places suggests that he was essentially outside the Protestant stream. In his noble ventures on both coasts he endeavored to create a non-segregated community of worship, perhaps even a prototype, but he failed to change the patterns within the denominations he opposed, where Negroes and whites worship in numbers.

Although Thurman's sophisticated syncretism in religion and middle-class orientation in religious fellowship failed to impress America as a whole, he has been most effective as a religious mystic. A dramatic preacher, Thurman is known for his undertone, pointing finger, and mystifying presence embodied in this affirmation:

It is my belief that in the Presence of God there is neither male nor female, white nor black, Gentile nor Jew, Protestant nor Catholic, Hindu, Buddhist, nor Moslem, but a human spirit stripped to the literal substance of itself before God.[33]

Thurman has come as close as any Negro to being a theologian, exerting his powers in the area of "spiritual disciplines." To be in his presence during a sermon is an experience. The participant-observer is impressed with the man, the mind, and the message. Aware that this creativity has been lost to the Christian Church, one wonders how many other equally imaginative and provocative spirits have been the victims of a discriminating Church.

Certainly, as a creative spiritual leader Thurman is in a class by himself. His ten published books bear out this critique. A philosophical poet of the spirit, Thurman is a deeply sensitive individualist whose route to the universal man is via the simple path of recognizing spiritual unity and ignoring differences of form:

Brooding over all of life is a Presence that no single event or experience can possibly exhaust. This truth is not peculiar to any one religion but is shared by many; and it is through religion that this universal insight may be made available to the believer.[34]

Jesus is not Jesus Christ the Son of God, but a man everyone meets who seeks God: "Men come to God through nature; it has been said, men may come to God through other good men; but he who seeks God with all of his heart will someday on his way meet Jesus." [35]

It is an error to proclaim creativity in the life of the Negro and his worship. Such ingenuity is to be found in the folk religion. But the possibility for creativity is clear in the person of Howard Thurman:

There is in every person an inward sea, and in that sea there is an island and on that island there is an altar and standing guard before that altar is the "angel with the flaming sword." Nothing can get by that angel to be placed upon that altar unless it has the mark of your inner authority. Nothing passes "the angel with the flaming sword" to be placed upon your altar unless it be a part of "the fluid area of your consent." This is your crucial link with the Eternal.[36]

The Negro Cults

The genius of Negro or black religion is in this Negro spiritual:

> Freedom at last!
> Freedom at last!
> Great God-a-mighty,
> Freedom at last!

But with rare exceptions since the turn of the century, notably the current Negro protest movement, the religious life of the Negro has developed counter to this authentic spirit of freedom. Particularly, the independent Negro congregations and institutions (African Methodists and Baptists) which were the bearers of the tradition have more often than not served as obstructionists. Within their communities the fire of black religion has been at best smouldering.

Negro independents, as we have seen, and dependents as we shall see, both differ significantly from Negro cults. Negroes in cults, the separated brethren, are for the most part on a lower socio-economic rung in the world of the Negro. Indeed, there is some basis for the oft-repeated claim that cults were created out of the failure of independents and dependents to keep alive concern for the well-being of all Negroes, regardless of their education and station.

The distinctive fact about the Negro cults is their origin outside the dynamics of black religion. The cults are a twentieth-century Negro phenomenon that has ignored the orthodoxy of both black religion and white Protestant evangelism. Developed in response to the migration of the Negro from the rural South to the urban South and North, the cults are the only new religious group the Negro has created. These separated brethren have no tradition and therefore cannot be helpfully viewed as a distortion of either Negro or white religious traditions. These Negro cults came into existence in the very years when the folk religion was in its deepest depression.

The cults have a wide variety of names, including African Orthodox Church, Christian Catholics, Temple Moorish Science, Black Muslims, Liberal Catholic, Spiritual and Spiritualists, I.A.M.E. Spiritual, Church of Christ, Church of God in Christ, Church of the Living God, Church of God, Church of God and Saints of Christ, Apostolic and Pentecostal, Pentecostal Assemblies of the World, Old-Time Methodist and Holiness. Several factors were instrumental in their spread over urban areas.

In the South the cults have been created by the constant movement of rural people into the cities where they find more opportunity for employment. Accustomed to Baptist and Methodist churches of intimate size, insecure and without recognition in the urban churches of their persuasion, these migrants tend to form religious communities in their homes—moving later to the first empty store or building they can afford to rent or buy.

The flow of Negroes from the rural to the urban South is more than matched by the flow of Negroes from the rural and urban South to the cities of the North. The big wave began in 1914 and continued through 1920. The flow is still heavy to cities such as Detroit, Chicago, Cleveland, Pittsburgh, Los Angeles, and New York. This continuing migration from the South is based on the wider opportunity for employment, the call of friends and relatives, and the hope of dignity.

The first great surge, 1914-1920, was in response to recruitment efforts by northern industrialists who were in need of workers, having depended up to that time on European migrants. Those forces at work in the creation of cults in the cities of the South were no less present in the North.

The needs of these Negroes for recognition and community life, as well as conflicts of leadership within the established denominations, resulted in the twentieth-century phenomenon of an unprecedented number of congregations formed in abandoned theaters, garages, stores, and halls which were vacated before the tide of the Negro mass movement.

As in the past, many of today's cults include a membership that is less than lower-class in status, with untrained charlatans for leaders, and worshippers who not only "shout" but speak in strange "tongues."

The shadow of charlatans and ugliness is far-reaching in the separated Negro cult movement. By and large, these cults are imitative and exhibit little or no ability to contribute to the religous dimension of the Negro.

There are cults which adopt for their own peculiar use the rituals, liturgies, colorful processions, and robes of a major religious body. A good example is the Liberal Catholic cult. Samuel Taylor, a student at the Harvard Divinity School, volunteered this observation:

My barber is a priest of the Liberal Catholic cult. He is no charlatan. Oddly enough, he does not exhibit the crudities usually associated with the "jumping-jack" religion of racketeers. His name is William Smith Jones and he is called Father Jones by his parishioners. His customers and co-workers call him "Smitty." Often there is conversation around the topic of religion in the shop. The owner of the shop works at the far end and vigorously defends his local Baptist church, in which he is a deacon, against the jibes of the barber in the middle chair who is often drunk, unkempt, foul-mouthed and fixated on sex. All three barbers bet with the policy men who frequent the shop. On one occasion, after "Smitty" returned to cut my hair from the back room where he had placed a bet, we began conversing

about religion. It was then that he discovered my involvement
as a theological student. Aware of my interest in religion, and
as it turned out one who was totally ignorant of his communion,
he began to inform me of his ministry. As a result of several conversations and his request that I contribute to his religious work, I
visited his assembly hall, located within a few blocks of the barber
shop. He always appeared pompous in a dignified way, but I was
amazed by how well his personality fit with clerical dress—replete with vestments, cap, stole and cassock. The dignity with
which he read the psalter, the smoothness with which the liturgy
flowed and the sacraments were administered made it difficult for
me to realize that I was not at a Roman Catholic Low Mass.

On the whole, separated Negro cults are not liturgical.
The great majority are variants of the United Pentecostal
Union or Holiness bodies but there are considerable differences among these cults, depending to a great extent upon
the personal interests of the cult leader. However, the tendency of cults to flourish, because of the continuing influx of
Negroes to urban areas, has led to some common elements.
Various cults have state and national meeting places, where
members may hold forth when the convocations coincide
with their vacation periods to present reports and enjoy a
wider fellowship for worship. These cult centers in every
city are communities for the renewal of friendships and
resting places for "brothers" and "sisters" traveling across
the country—without them members might not find a place
to rest and refresh themselves.

The older ministers of these separated cults are generally without a high school education, attracting persons of
the same educational level. Since World War I and especially since World War II the mass movement of Negroes
to urban areas has been so constant that even the cults have
gained in stability. Along with this tendency toward per-
manence, there has been a marked increase in the education

of the ministers and the people. A number of young preachers are traveling evangelists who make their living by holding revivals. Other young men, trained in Bible Schools, begin in a local situation and with an understanding of procedures and the opportunity for a new fellowship go out on their own. Usually the neophytes hold down outside full-time jobs.

These young men are dedicated, serious, and articulate. One such "elder" leads a group at a Negro college in the South. Here are the comments of the teacher in charge of the religious activities of the college:

An increasing number of the Holiness students attending our college are interested in a religious student organization comparable to the Methodist, Baptist, Congregational and Episcopal campus fellowships. Last fall Agnes Broadfield, the most eager of the students expressing an interest, succeeded in gaining sufficient support to organize officially. Agnes was granted permission to call in her pastor as the liaison between the fellowship and the local congregations. The liaison, Elder Jones, is an amiable young dynamo who has real rapport with the students. The United Pentecostal Student Union, composed of students from varying Holiness persuasions, is unable to agree on basic beliefs.

At one of the meetings, Elder Jones brought along a well-edited and attractively bound discipline upon which he proceeded to expound in the hope of providing an authoritative basis for discussion of religious questions. The discipline was filled with scriptural passages which he interpreted in a manner comparable with the Jehovah's Witnesses. The students had previously disagreed with each other and with Elder Jones concerning various interpretations of the Bible, but when he finished no questions were raised with respect to his Biblical exegesis. This was a little surprising to me since each of them had completed a course in the Old Testament taught by a very able liberal graduate of the Union Theological Seminary in New York, William Stovall, who really "shook them up." (Bill and I had conversed on numerous occasions about the reaction of the students to his

course and their tendency to dismiss him as an excellent example
of the comfortable illusion that northern white people do not understand southern Negroes.) The questions of these Holiness
students reflected the existential situation of contact with non-
cultic students and centered about the use of cosmetics, smoking, dancing, hair styles, length of dresses, dating, drinking and
pre-marital sexual relations. Elder Jones was as flexible in his
response as his rigid orientation would allow, but his condemnation of these "worldly" interests was per usual. The fact that
these restricted students, in behavioral patterns, dared to raise
these questions indicated that while the course in Old Testament
did not make an impression upon them, the student culture was
making an impact. I have wondered ever since if these students
will be like their peers in the next decade. It is apparent that
leaders like Elder Jones will have to change tactics or change
with the rising expectations of the more educated younger generation.

Young adults who are attracted to separated brethren
in cults are nurtured from childhood in the movement, for
the most part. Many of these young people have diplomas
from high schools and others from professional schools; a
more limited number are college graduates. A friend who
teaches at a Baptist Training Institute reports the following
about mature young Pentecostal men and women:

This year, during the Christmas holidays, my family and I
were the guests in the home of a high school classmate for two
weeks. His father was a Holiness preacher who died some years
ago and Ronny decided to join his mother in Los Angeles. He is
married to a very intelligent gal, employed as a stenographer for
the State of California. My classmate, Ronny, is a stock boy during the week in a dress manufacturing shop. In the Negro community he is known as the Reverend Mr. Turner, assistant minister of the Thirty-second Street Temple Church of God in
Christ. Since I was an old friend, a member of the "brotherhood," and a minister, Ronny took it upon himself to schedule
me for two preaching engagements. One was in a large institu-

tional Baptist Church. The other was in Temple Church. I had not previously preached in a Holiness service of worship and was anxious about what would happen. It did! Although the people were gracious and kind, I left even the young people cold. Prior to the worship service there was a Sunday school period which consisted of adults and children separated by a few feet in small class sessions. Reading the Bible, prayers, hymns, an offering, and personal expressions of the Biblical passage describes the period. Worship began with a long testimonial warm-up. Each adult member testified around the theme "I know the blessings" and recited the highlights in which these blessings were realized throughout the previous week. A favorite scriptural passage, or song, preceded each testimony. This was followed by the recitation of the week's events, including congregational participation: "Amen," "Tell it, Sister," "Oh yes," "I know what it means," "Take it to the Lord," and "Jesus, Jesus, Jesus." Each testimony ended with a final affirmation which took the form of a confession and seemed to give release. My sermon was anti-climactic on this occasion, but the minister followed with a sermonette, topped off by a full length off-the-cuff sermon by Ronny's brother-in-law, a Holiness evangelist who was visiting on that Sunday.

On New Year's eve my family and I were expected to join our host and hostess in their annual celebration. There were not many young adults at Temple Church that Sunday. But all the youth from the various congregations of this semi-organized Holiness cult gathered for the New Year's party. None of the women wore lipstick, but very low-cut and flashy dresses were everywhere. It appeared from the conversations that these young people were employed as secretaries, typists, clerks, beauticians, domestics, mechanics, gardeners and postmen. The party consisted of telling "clean" stories, drinking non-spiked punch with a variety of good foods, and playing such interesting games as "Musical Chairs." Apparently it was the fellowship that made the party.

Old-timers and young adults do not seriously vary in their response to religious enthusiasm, strict moral rules, seriousness about their beliefs, and literal interpretation of the scriptures. The quality of these cults varies with the imagination and exploitative interests of the leaders. Neither freedom, in the sense of equality, nor flight from the condition of the disinherited are high on the priority list, but there is evidence of "creeping social consciousness." The life and times of the cults are variations on the theme of withdrawal or diversion. The intensification of their rituals is not for or against the future or the present—it is to blot out time. The religious sessions are a time of carelessness, like that which comes over participants in a jazz session who are caught up in the rhythm until the spectators become participants and are uplifted to a level of sheer feeling. Cults are without theology, though they use Biblically-interpreted terminology; without a style of worship, though they are demonstrative; without ethical emphasis, though they conform to an expected code of morality; and they are highly individualistic in their organizational structures.

The separated brethren in Negro cults do not contribute to the eradication of the underlying problems facing the tide of Negroes surging up from the rural areas of the country. Leaders who take advantage of their need for identification and desire for exhibition are often native urbanites who have split off from an established congregation and prey upon the newcomers. The new serfs do not know what the going values of life are and therefore do not attempt to achieve them. They are at the whim and mercy of religious pimps whose prostitution of a simple people is possible by reason of their socio-economic pain—the pill of togetherness and ecstatic rituals gives instant if temporary relief. Exploitation feeds upon the poverty of body and spirit. Those separated cults which are the extension of plundering sharks and unconscionable greed quickly pass out of existence as the Negro peasant gains a foothold in the ghetto.

The socio-economic conditions make these cults a live option. Negroes are attracted because of their easy access and service of relief from a life of boredom. The fact that Negroes seek out cults as well as other forms of relief may be due to their early experience, which has usually involved some supernatural setting, when no other forms of wholesome activity were present. From this perspective, what is called the dispossessed Negro's compulsion to be attuned to supernatural power is well within the mark—be that supernatural power God, Jesus, Allah, or the Holy Ghost. This supernatural orientation is part of the rural life and earlier training of isolated Negroes, making the task of a personable leader in a depersonalized city a simple matter of psychology. Added to this supernatural inclination is the emotional strain due to economic insecurity, loss of familiar surroundings, and face-to-face contacts with friends, neighbors, and relatives. In the early days of adjustment such crises as illness and death cannot be handled through the familar ways of the folk culture. One of the ways to meet these crises and construct a new meaning for existence is the ever-present cult.

The "faith healing" cults provide a "cure" for mental and physical disarrangements. A combination of folk piety and urban sophistication equips the "faith healer" with magnetic pulling power. Sanctified or "Holiness" cults restore a sense of balance for the Negro who is torn between the mores of the folk environment and their absence in the "free and easy ways of the city." The fundamental pulling power of all cults is racial identification, in the absence of other alternatives.[37]

To the extent the separated cults swing away from exploitation and toward aiding those who need help they are in the spirit of the religious relief agencies Negroes sponsored through congregations following Reconstruction. The difference between Negro independent congregations and the separated cults is that the militant push for redress of many problems of the Negro people was central to the original intent of Baptists and Methodists of the independent variety. Now, the cults have taken over only what was originally a peripheral concern and made it central—providing the Negro in a changing society with relief, while the independents have withdrawn from both areas of social concern. As communities for healing cults burst the boils, they do not prevent the spreading of the disease. Because they exist, suffering is bearable. On the other hand, there are as many or more Negroes who adjust in ways which are no less questionable from the point of view of moral realism, but far more destructive. The hoodlums, gangsters, thieves, pimps, and prostitutes are often persons without religious affiliation and the sense of family ties which even a cult tends to strengthen.

The Father Divine Peace Movement is the best example of a combination "faith healing" and "Holiness" cult which has been ineffective through ignoring the basic socio-politico-economic issues, but of real value to the Negro in the area of service. There is no question concerning the perversion of religion if the "Father's Messages" published in his newspaper, *The New Day,* are the standard:

I need not do a thing PERSONALLY especially, but the very Spirit of My EVER-PRESENCE will dethrone everything that tries to ascend the Throne for a selfish purpose. That is the mystery! My SPIRIT will dethrone it! My PRESENCE will dethrone it! Now just look at the happy faces sitting and standing in this dining room this evening (Banquet Table, Stone Ridge Extension, The Promised Land, Saturday, May 1, 1937 A.D.F.D., 2:05 A.M.). Just a week or so, a couple of weeks or so ago, there were some of whom thought you would be clinging to them in opposition to Me . . . because you had been led erroneously by them, causing you to think that they were Me and I was them!

Now, PEACE shall flow like a river, and shall continue to extend this way, and sorrow and misery shall no longer be, when you all whole-heartedly accept ME and live exactly according to MY teaching universally ("God's Kingdom is a Principle, a Standard, a Law and a Government Within," a message given at the Banquet Table, 1887-1889 Madison Avenue, New York City, Tuesday, July 11, 1939, A.D.F.D., 3:45 P.M.).

You cannot be unified together unless you first harmonize with Me. You have to harmonize with Me in opposition to your sense of feeling, in opposition to your ideas and your opinions, especially when they are not with Me. I mean, when your ideas and your opinions are not with Me! You have to harmonize in opposition to yourself! That is the mystery of FASTING ("Produce the Desirableness of the Desirable Within You and You will be Desired," a message given at the Banquet Table, Madison Ave. Mansion, New York City, Friday, January 20, 1939, A.D.F.D., 2:15 P.M.).

(Song)

Oh, my beautiful FATHER, how we love YOU!
Oh, my beautiful FATHER, how we love YOU!
You are so kind and so true,
You are so beautiful too,
Oh, my beautiful FATHER, how we love YOU!

(FATHER speaks as follows:)

PEACE, EVERYONE: Good Health, Good Will and a Good Appetite for everyone! Manners and Good Behavior, All Success and All Prosperity—these and all other blessings to you I bring, with All Wisdom, Knowledge and with All Understanding ("Man With All His Prejudicial Ideas and Opinions, I Use as Praises For Me," a message given at the Banquet Table, 152-160 W. 126th Street, New York City, Sunday Evening and Monday morning, July 9-10, 1939 A.D.F.D., 1:50 A.M.).

(Remarks of "Our Beloved MOTHER DIVINE":)

Oh FATHER, I thank YOU! I thank YOU for this Victorious Spirit!
I thank YOU that YOU have come and turned the light on and the
darkness has no power over us! Oh I thank YOU FATHER that we
can be held securely in YOUR heart, because we are YOURS! ("We
Are the Daughters of Virtue and Not of the Sons of Perdition,"
Gladwyne, Pa., Saturday, July 13th, 1963, A.D.F.D., 9:40 P.M.).

It is a wonderful day, FATHER, A WONDERFUL day when YOU are
drawing YOUR Children from the far corners of the earth to step
out on their faith and knowledge that YOU are GOD. (Gladwyne,
Pa., Tuesday, July 16, 1963, A.D.F.D., 3:30 P.M.).[38]

This movement began in Long Island, New York, and
attracted Negroes from Harlem who made so much noise
that Father Divine was arrested. This event was a momentous one, for the prosecution of the Father and the death of
the judge who tried him led to the belief that this was an
act of divine punishment. Father Divine was hailed by his
followers as the Messiah (his Caucasian widow continues
his work as "Mother Divine"), and, they believe, in his death
leads all others "that call *you* and know *you* as God." In
1932 he entered the depressed area of Harlem and fed the
hungry, "cured" the sick and "healed" mental ailments of
his followers by their thinking of him and repeating "Thank
you, Father." Father Divine may have been possessed by vi-
sions of grandeur, a judgment which the creed of the Rose-
buds (virgins dedicated to denying themselves and conse-
crating their hearts, minds, souls and bodies to the "Cause")
supports:

FATHER DIVINE, GOD ALMIGHTY,
WE PLEDGE OUR HEARTS TO LOVE YOU,
OUR STRENGTH TO SERVE YOU,
OUR MINDS TO BE FOCUSED DIRECTLY UPON YOU,
OUR LIPS TO PRAISE YOU,
OUR LIVES TO BE SACRIFICED UNTO YOU,

OUR SACRED HONOR TO ACKNOWLEDGE YOU IN ALL OUR WAYS,
THAT WE MAY BE WITH YOU THROUGHOUT ALL ETERNITY,
ONE SPIRIT, ONE MIND AND ONE BODY,
LOST AND ABSORBED, ONCE AND FOREVER, IN YOUR HOLY WILL!

He did possess economic wealth. However perverted his means and ends, Father Divine faithfully led his flock in the direction of being interracially-minded, literate, moral, and good citizens:

One must refrain from stealing, refusing to pay just debts, indulging in liquor in any form, smoking, obscene language, gambling, playing numbers, racial prejudice or hate of any kind, greed, bigotry, selfishness, and lusting after the opposite sex.[39]

Father Divine exhibited, and his movement perpetuates, the worst in the worship of the Negro cults and the best in their social concern, a marked contrast to racial chauvinism and racial exclusiveness expressed through the cults committed to Black Nationalism.

The Black Muslims are the product of Negroes being cut off from the mainstream of American Protestantism and the frustration of the militant drive within the American Negro folk religion. They exemplify the final catastrophe of a religion without authentic roots, and action without social conscience.

The Black Muslims represent a cult that is more distinctly this-worldly in its concern than many other religious "missions." The movement began with the spirit of W. D. Fard, the Detroit prophet from Mecca who "came to restore the true language, nation, literature, and religion" of the lost tribe of Shebazz.[40]

Black Muslims are negative in their aggresive attack upon the racial problem. They capitalize upon race and in an alienating way spotlight the racial essential in all facets

of Negro religion. Their growth is possible because they
dramatize the deprivation of the Negro, thereby attracting
disillusioned members from other cults and congregations.
The interesting and honest approach of these avowed ex-
Christians is the conscious rejection of the Christian faith,
instead of simply ignoring it in the usual manner of Negro religion. In this way, Black Muslims are distinguished from
their cultic brethren and independent cousins who use Christian terminology as a means of diversion.

The positive expression of this cult is in the approach
to self-dsicipline, industriousness and independence. Black
Muslims are required to reform their old socio-economic
habits. Prostitutes, dope addicts, alcoholics and ex-convicts
are rehabilitated by them in a way that no other "respectable" Negro religious group can claim.

Seriousness of purpose distinguishes this cult. Their
leaders are not exploitative, nor are they fanatics who ring
the changes in an appeal for emotional religiosity. The un-
adulterated and direct appeal is racial unity. Like all cults,
the Black Muslim Movement is dominated by individual personalities who are "worshipped" in the place of God or as
God, even though Allah ostensibly authorized the Honorable
Elijah Mohammad as His messenger, priest and prophet.[41]
The Muslims really constitute another in the long line of
personality cults, but one which intends "to wake the sleep-
ing Black Nation and rid . . . [it] of the white man's age-
old domination." [42]

Black Muslims have, in common with other cults and
the independent Negro bodies (Methodists and Baptists),
a general misconception of the Christian faith. This is understandable as we shall see, since all Negroes have been
forced outside the Christian community, but Black Muslims
perceive the Christian faith as the exclusiveness of white
laymen and clergy. In their consciousness, and in the un-
consciousness of many Negroes who are not Muslims, Chris-

tianity equals white and white spells oppression and deprivation for the Negro. In this way, Christianity and white people are rejected. Life in America is realistically seen as black and white, but this reality is distorted and exploited for the purposes of a separate Negro civilization.

Black Muslims are representative of Negro cults and Negro independents in being bound by color, in being arrested in racial conflict, in being ineffective in breaking through the socio-economic barriers and in existing primarily as a sympathetic fellowship. Black Muslims, however, dismiss both the hope and the objective of the American Negro folk religion—full acculturation. Religion is manipulated by Black Muslims to motivate a community of hate ("cultural despisers") for outsiders and one of love for insiders. Cults have a tendency to defend their existence on the grounds that congregations (Negro and white) are not doing an adequate job of evangelization. This is twisted by the Black Muslims in the claim that churches are not supporting the Negro in his socio-economic need. James Baldwin has said that Black Muslims make only one contribution, they "scare" white people. This much is certain, Black Muslims are, as Louis Lomax has pointed out,

. . . an extreme reaction to the problem of being a Negro in America today. Instead of working to improve conditions within the framework of American society, as do other Negro leadership organizations, the Black Muslims react by turning their backs on that society entirely. Their one positive aspect is that they work to make Negroes proud of being Negro.[43]

Dependent Negro Communions

Dependent communions consist of Negroes in racially separate congregations affiliated with the dominant white denominations (Episcopal, Congregational, American Baptist, Methodist, Presbyterian, and Roman Catholic). Historically, this is an alignment of middle-class Negroes running parallel with the independent congregations and institutions of the masses. A generous estimate of 800,000 middle-class Negroes distinguish themselves by their segregated life within white religious structures. Middle-class Negro congregations are identical with their white counterparts in the flight from emotionalism, in organizational procedures and operations, in educational standards for the clergy, in the formation of associational (occasional gathering for worship only) and primary (basic social fellowship) religious groups along the lines of class identity, made visible in the members' styles of life, and in the consciousness of social status. Dependents are loyal to their own congregations, whereas Negro independents are prone to visiting other congregations, seeking variety. The black *bourgeoisie* independent congregations believe in the "committee process," central administration, the democratic process, and the function of the minister as a "pastoral-director." Their congregations are centers of wholesome activity: youth fellowships, Girl and Boy Scout troops, clubs, bands, and organizations for the various needs of the community, including groups for adults. A distinction between white and Negro middle-class worship does not exist in any significant way:

The visitor to an average Negro church will see much the same type of service—with choir singing, hymns by the congregation, organ music (in the larger churches), prayer, sermon, collection —and hear the same theological terms he does in the average white Protestant church. Except for a slight slant in the direction of "race," there is nothing in the formal content of the sermon to indicate that the church is a Negro church.[44]

It is equally apparent that these dependent congregations are continually being replenished through withdrawals from independent Negro congregations. Following the white pattern of moving up the religious scale along with status ascension, Negroes who look to religion as a way of integrating primary emotions with a sense of solidity become involved in middle-class congregations.

Precisely because middle-class congregations manifest the same strengths and weaknesses, whether Negro or white, it is generally assumed that the racial distinction is of no significance. Herein lies the great delusion of white and Negro Americans.

As we have suggested, the injection of Negro folk religion into independent organizations was intended as a means of moving the masses toward freedom and equality with dignity. Frustrated, this militant movement was diverted and the religious house assumed the burden of being the community center for the people—replete with amusements, politics, fellowship, leadership, and emotional release. The inner dynamic of the folk religion gave way to evangelism as a means of diversion, severed from any sense of traditional theological direction. The severance of the masses from the folk religion and the evangelical tradition was paralled by the serverance of the middle-class communions from the roots of Protestantism. Mechanically, in their attempt to escape the stigma of lower class religious life, the black *bourgeoisie* have succeeded—they are ghetto replicas of the white middle class. But the very fact of their imitation, necessary since they have been prevented by racial barriers from identification with the central Christian tradition, is indicative of their failure. These middle-class congregations are one with the folk fellowships in being partial participants in the culture; like them, they are forced to create their own religous societies. The characteristics of organization among the black *bourgeoisie* who are religiously inclined exists because its participants cannot find rapport with the lower classes nor opportunity for identity with the intimate life of their white peers. The same forces which frustrated the American Negro folk religion have arrested the Negro middle class and prevented any possibility of their contributing to the Christian faith and Church. However disguised are their feelings by outward sophistication or suppressed in controlled activity, middle-class Negroes share with the Negro masses the experience of exclusion from mainstream participation. Dependent communions may be the height to which the Negro may advance on his own, but he is nevertheless far from his objective.

Religious Deficiencies of Negro Fellowships

There are a limited number of books about the Negro and religion, but those which are of real significance are those which measure the worth of religion among Negroes by the extent of its movement away from otherworldly themes and toward relating religion to life.[45] Perhaps the most provocative work in this area, *The Development of Negro Religion*, by Ruby F. Johnston, identifies the religious position commonly held by Negroes as: empiricism (or liberalism), transcendentalism (or traditionalism), and the road of moderation between these two extremes:

"The empiricist" concentrates upon experimental values; "the moderate religionist" considers spiritual and temporal values; "the transcendentalist" feels the need of overt emotional expression while some experimental ends are pursued.[46]

Regardless of the difference in the socio-economic status of these three religious types, as individuals and as congregations, and despite the variation in response to the religious society as an organization, there is a definite common link among all Negro Protestants—"either subordination or elimination of pronounced action accompanying religious sentiment." That is, a tendency is developing to suppress or extinguish emotionalism proportionately as Negro communions become program-centered:

At one time, manifestation of sentiment in overt emotional action enjoyed moral authority in religion. Motivation by transcendental values was expected of churchmen. In the established religion, uniformities of action in terms of non-experimental ends were inculcated. However, as religion becomes more highly organized, there is a decrease in the intensity of emotion. Though the manifestation of emotion has remained relatively constant for a few church members, the wane of emotional behavior is conspicuous at present. The tendency to impose uniformity of conduct by defining appropriate standards of behavior while pursuing ends is applied in terms of unemotionalism and rationality as a norm in Negro religion.[47]

This functional-dysfunctional sociological analysis of the Negro in religion tends to assert that the majority of Negroes in Protestantism are moving away from otherworldly or emotional emphases to the assumption of their functional role in society. The validity of Johnston's functional-dysfunctional approach is its support of the obvious fact that Negroes variously reflect in their religious activities the normative objectives and standards determined by the forces operative in society—and in this are hardly distinguishable from white congregations:

As a unit, churchmen believe that religion should prompt man to act to attain the ideal in society as there is regulation of action in correspondence with the Christian norm. Man should integrate religion with life and coordinate the church with other social institutions as he seeks to act in compliance with a standard of rationality. There should be extirpation of extreme manifestations from religious action. Emotionalism is a barrier to rational action. Man should actively identify himself with society and cease contemplating the Day of Reckoning. However, man must not lose sight of spiritual values in the pursuit of empirical ends.[48]

This clarification of the trends in religion among Negroes is helpful in undermining the prejudices which assert that in the sphere of religion the Negro proves his inferiority. While the movement from emotionalism and otherworldly concentration upon the "Day of Reckoning" toward the integration of religion with life may be encouraging to the sociologists who stand outside the Christian faith, it is not particularly encouraging to one who contemplates its source from within the faith.

The hallmark of religion among Negroes has been emotionalism and otherworldliness. This pattern resulted from a combination of factors—the frustration of the militant concern for equality in the folk religion, the response of the Negro to the emotionalism of the missionaries, the tendency to use religion as an escape valve from insufferable conditions, the failure to accept the Negro within the mainstream churches, to identify a few. Religion is always a means to an end, always functional in the context of the situation. So that when the socio-economic situation changed for some Negroes, when they found life worth living through gaining responsible economic positions and diversion in social life, it follows that, like all other disinherited groups, they gradually began to orient their religious life to their new-found selfhood. This is all the de-emphasis of the "otherworldly" points to—the Negro considers himself a real person, a typical American.

The basic question which the Negro has yet to face is not, "What is the function of the churches?" This is a secondary question which finds its proper answer in the knowledge of what the Church is. The Negro has been forced to use the meeting house for purposes which are peculiar to the socially and economically distressed. The religious center has always been a racial center—for the needs of race, whether the needs were freedom, justice, equality, or social status.

Another traditional criticism of Negro religion is directed toward its *leadership*. Those who view the Protestant tradition as one which is primarily charismatic do not understand the role of Protestantism in America, and although the Negro religion began in response to charismatic leadership it too has gone the way of all religious institutions in the United States.

The majority of Negroes belong to the independent Negro communions. Here in the congregations of the masses, or folk, there is virtually total dependence upon the leaders. Particularly among the Baptist congregations, where the great masses congregate, though no less among some Methodist ones, leaders have exploited their power. Such exploitation is possible among the masses, though even here the minister may no longer be the most intelligent participant in the society, because the minister is considered to have a sacred calling which allows him latitude not permitted the laity. There is some support for this view in the response of the New York Abyssinian Baptist congregation to its senior minister, Adam Clayton Powell, Jr. And speaking about a nationally known Baptist minister in Atlanta, a former member of his congregation remarked:

There is something spurious about the fact this present-day Baptist minister of the independent variety can personally hold the deed to our local house of worship, though this further evidence of the extraordinary power which the minister still holds in congregations of the masses is not surprising when it is recalled that a single Baptist preacher can begin a religious society, because the idea is still common which holds the local fellowship to be the work of human endeavor, often that of an individual minister.

Though such a pastor still tends to be autocratic in his programming, dictatorial in carrying out procedures, and paternalistic in withholding information from the laity, it is generally assumed that as the Negro minister increases in *educational* attainment his approach will be more democratic. There are signs which support this view.[49] Even among the congregations of the masses, there is an upgrading of quality of ministerial training, orderly worship, and programs which take into account responsibility in the surrounding community. It seems only natural, then, to look to the minister as the key to a responsible congregation since he "plays an important role in shaping the policy of the church and in directing the interest of communicants." [50] Yet, the irresponsibility of too many Negro ministers persists as a conscious effort to maintain personal prestige and power. The lucrative occasions of birthdays, anniversaries, and conventions are still tempting and the willingness of members to deny themselves in order to boast of their minister's obvious economic success may be more nearly correct than the view which holds that

. . . some ministers seem unaware of their potential strength in regard to diverting changes which are occurring in the Protestant church. Indeed some do not grasp the full import of change in various directions.[51]

It would be a mistake to underestimate the awareness of the minister. It is quite possible that he is alert to the changes which challenge his dominant position.

In fact, the dependence upon leadership to be the primary means of a breakthrough to an effective and creative independent Negro religious society may very well be a disappointment. As long as the economic division between lower-class white and Negro blue-collar workers remains as sharp as it is, the minister will maintain a lofty position, unchallenged by those who wish him to be all they cannot be. Moreover, this dominant and dictatorial role is enhanced when the minister becomes a spokesman in civic affairs, especially in race relations. Particularly as a spokesman for race relations, it continues to be the case

. . . that the Negro pastor is one of the freest, as well as most influential, men on the American platform today. This is due to various causes, but chief among them is the factor of the long-time prestige of the Negro minister, the respect for him and for religion; and the poverty and the financial freedom of the Negro church.[52]

What is often overlooked is that the freedom of the Negro minister is limited in the very area which ought to be his real concern—the Christian faith. In this reversal his area of freedom is a direct opposite to that of his white brethren. Free to say whatever he chooses in every generally accepted area of controversy, the Negro minister is not free to preach and teach the great questions of faith, theological insights, and the movements of renewal and reform within the Protestant tradition. In matters of faith, the Negro minister is a prisoner.

Ministerial leadership in the economically lower- and middle-class congregations such as the dependent Central Jurisdiction of the Methodist Church and the less organized Congregational communions is far less exploitative than its counterparts in the independent organizations. Negro Episcopalians, Presbyterians, and other Negro congregations within white religious denominations tend to pattern their religious life after their models. Even here the minister is given far more freedom and independence in non-theological matters of controversy than comparable white ministers receive from their congregations.

Negro middle-class dependent congregations tend to respond to the emerging conception "of the minister as a pastoral director." [53] The movement of integration includes the religious life, though in these congregations there is a pronounced tendency to perpetuate "separate but equal" integration. Their membership has an increasing number of participants who are middle class in their over-all orientation, including college graduates, although the intellectual edge has yet to come into its own.[54] The critical element alive in white Protestantism, however spotty and dispersed, is not evident among Negroes who participate in religious conformity. So that while dependent Negro communions may be indistinguishable from their white standard-bearers in many areas where measurement is possible, they are in a very different category with regard to the nature and purpose of the Christian fellowship. If white congregations tend to err and stray from the nature and purpose of the Christian community, their Negro neighbors tend to ignore them, and in this context of ignorance are free to continue without a sense of guilt. The real gulf between these two is the tragic sequel of segregated communions. Regardless of their class position, Negroes are free to use the sphere of religion as the primary base for racial identity and social justice; all else is secondary and in some measure irrelevant.

This kind of a commitment to racial barriers erected by white communions and class walls against lower-class Negroes does not prevent but rather increases their desire to be models of external correctness in form and appearance. Though the individual interpretation of religion as the rhythm of respectability, order, and beauty remains rooted, middle-class Negro congregations are indistinguishable from white ones even in the growing activity and initiative of laymen.

The growing Negro middle class, at least in aspiration, is not composed of advocates of overt social action. Thus, rising from the ranks of the masses and no longer able to identify with procedures of protest movements (however delighted they are that some others do so), enamored of respectability and orderliness, Negroes who cannot discard religion join the dependent, segregated congregations. Basically white-collar workers without knowledge of theology but with a great feeling for religion, the new Negro middle class shapes its religious life, as all other life, after the white pacesetters. Their pastors, graduates of mainstream seminaries, tend to reflect the patterns they have learned, which continue to be reinforced through participation in the denominational program. Therein lies the hope for the continuance of lay development and conformity to the mainstream congregations. Herein also will develop increasing concern for institutional congregations which serve the community and provide programs for delinquents and other social programs. But no comparative leadership has yet appeared to include Negroes in the community of faith, for even the middle-class congregations are limited by segregation from participation in the Protestant tradition.

Typical critics of Negro leadership further assert that with education and economic advantages Negroes can produce, as they have not, a body of Negro Christians equal to white Christians in involvement in all facets of the Christian faith. But the reality of segregation means that the masses feel no need to move in this direction, and the middle class will be unable to do so. And although the middle-class leadership can aid lay development and imitate patterns of white congregations, it is fallacious to assume that, by this natural middle-class alignment, equality is achieved.

It is impossible to produce a separate body of Negro Christians which are equal in faith to their separated brethren, however equal they may be in function. To assume further that equality in function will mysteriously overcome the inequality in heritage is naïveté of the first order. What has occurred and will continue to occur is a predisposition to or toleration of religious practices without the chastisement of faith.

The traditional criticisms of Negro religion have included otherworldly emphases, lack of leadership, and primary interest in racial considerations and political life. The optimistic and prevalent view has urged support of segregated Christianity as not only realistic but possible, based on the false premise that Negro congregations may become equal to their white brethren. Instead of conscious participants in the Christian faith there is a climbing body of middle-class Negroes seeking a "religious experience more in accord with developed religious sentiment"—sentiment not only divorced from the old ways of righteous causes, but sentiment steeped in congregations rooted in nothing less superficial than "social paraphernalia."

The Negro middle class serves as the best, though not the only, hope for development of a responsible society of Christians. Middle-class Negroes who remain within the religious fold do so with their traditional religious perspectives, modified as they curb emotions and streamline organizational procedures. As long as they remain segregated from their fellows, the hope that they will become responsible participants in the breadth and depth of faith is illusory.

In the inclination to start religious groups at the drop of a hat, Negroes did not differ from their white fellows who split over political, evangelical, and social differences. Within such communions as the Lutheran, Presbyterian, and Congregational-Unitarian there have been theological conflicts. Negro congregations have been divided on every conceivable issue except that of theology—within the Negro communions virtually no theology has existed.

That the absence of theology is vital to the understanding of the deficiencies among Negro communicants is sharply revealed at the point of Protestant reunion. There is a deep mood of repentance and considerable endeavor to bring separated bodies together in Protestantism today (e.g., Presbyterians, Episcopalians, Methodists and members of the United Church of Christ are seeking to repair their broken relations). It is not necessary to deny that elements of strategy and other less noble considerations have contributed to the surge toward unity. But the fact that these bodies can rejoin is in no small measure due to a common faith and theology which stands in judgment over their separation. One of the reasons why there is a dearth of such stirrings among Negro religious bodies is the dire absence of a common faith and theology. The causes of the splits among Negroes were not theological, nor did congregations have in the first place a sense of theological unity, though they did have a sense of racial unity. Personality and class differences were the basic points of contention. There is no need to reunite on a racial basis; one racial institution is as good as another, or as bad as another. It is doubtful whether the National Baptist Convention of America and the National Baptist Convention of the U.S.A. have any sense of theological guilt about their separation—without a sense of faith, moreover, it is doubtful whether they can be joined on other than purely practical grounds, a rather dubious basis for these irrational bodies. The same general judgment holds true for the African Methodist Episcopal Church, the African Methodist Episcopal Zion Church, the African Union First Colored Methodist Protestant Church, and the Christian Methodist Episcopal Church.

Perhaps no organization has provoked unification among

Protestants so vigorously as the World Council of Churches. This ecumenical movement has laid bare the division and sense of guilt among Protestants in their denominational separation from each other, as well as between Protestants and Roman Catholics. That there are cultural and missionary pressures which have served the cause of unity among Protestants does not detract from the fact that unity is principally possible because there is a common Lord, faith, tradition, and mission which faithful men discover to be of far more significance than their denominational interests. Yet, this world-wide movement has caused little more than a wrinkle among Negroes. Negro Christians certainly affirm with other Christians the Lordship of Jesus Christ, but that this affirmation has little of the binding significance it holds for white Christians is indisputable; it is also *prima facie* evidence of theological poverty and the destitute state of faith among Negro Christians.

It is possible to state with some authority that the middle-class Negroes in dependent, segregated congregations are beyond the state of schism over any issue. Yet, having risen from the ranks of independent Negro organizations, or having always been segregated in separate congregations, there is the same general indifference to theology, faith and the ecumenical movement. Racially separated from their white brethren, they have no sense of guilt or even remorse about the scandalous division of the Church— this is not nearly as disgraceful to the Negro as his own social separation. This problem of the Church is utterly unreal to them.

Whether speaking of independent or dependent Negro congregations, if Protestantism implies identification with the Christian faith and tradition and the unique contributions of the Reformation, along with the post-Reformation interpreters, it is not helpful to call Negroes Protestants, in this historical and theological sense. The fact that Negroes form congregations called by the same denominational names as white ones, and carry out similar organizational programs, exhausts the extent of their common ground. Segregation in religion is so disparaging that the insensitivity to it on the part of Negroes who are content to remain separated and on the part of whites who are delighted to have them do so is incomprehensible.

It is most difficult to understand the dissipated state of religion among Negroes if it is viewed as a temporary sickness resulting from the abuse of parasitic and intentionally exploitative leaders with limited educational background. No amount of trained, dedicated, and perceptive Negro clergymen can solve the real difficulty—any more than the World Council of Churches can bring about a unity of Christendom without the receptivity of Roman Catholics. The Negro has too long been considered a full-fledged Protestant because his middle-class congregations are so similar to white churches. Rarely is it admitted that Negro communities do not constitute churches by any stretch of the theological imagination, but religious congregations. Religion initiated and perpetuated in racial fellowship can persist in response to whatever social, economic, or political needs are dominant. Concern with the ultimate in the Christian faith and what God requires of those who are called to live responsibly in His world may easily be less than primary for a segregated minority without a theology. It is evident that a crass materialism pervades Negro congregations, overlaid with a few theological generalizations, a terminology, and a feeling for religion which when analyzed may now be more this-worldly than otherworldly.[55] But a firm theological basis for a responsible perspective is missing, and Negro congregations are finally forced to seek purpose from the twin stimuli of social dictates and class values. In the process of becoming effective functional institutions, Negro congregations remain dysfunctional communities of faith—through lack of experience rather than lack of obedience.

In the perversion of the religious community for purposes of ostentation, personal gratification, and social security, the Negro religious community takes its cue from the white community. White Protestant congregations are to some extent status symbols and social clubs, existing in conformity in a state of exclusiveness. But the white community knows better. Insofar as white churches are exclusive societies rather than centers of mission, they are in defiance of the Christian faith. White Protestantism can ignore but cannot eradicate the judgment of theology which declares a need for more tension between faith and culture. Although faith must live its life out in culture, it must not capitulate to that which it is called to be—a mission. There is clearly a conflict between religio-social paraphernalia and the Christian faith. However disobedient white Protestants may be, the possibility of renewal and reform persists even in the most decadent communities. Whether the call to reform is heard in the witness of non-Christian communities of faith wherein the works of inclusion and reconciliation are dynamic, or in the words of prophetic lay and professional theologians, the very call produces guilt—the necessary pre-condition for renewal. In seeking economic and social status under the guise of religious affiliation and class congregations, the Negro knows no theology, and therefore has no feeling of condemnation in making of the communions whatever seems practical. White Christians have damned Negro congregations to existence in a religion without faith and therefore without theology—where racial concerns, economic status, and class symbols are the final sanctions.

The judgment that the absence of theology prevents Negro congregations from bearing a corrective which distinguishes between participation in economic well-being

and seeking economic values as ends in themselves is corroborated in E. Franklin Frazier's sociological research,
which discloses the Negro community as the most materialistic religious group in America. The truth that this absence of a theological undergirding was not the result of
intentional failure on the part of the Negro does not alter
the fact. Those who join a religious community in search of
meaning and relevance are thwarted in this quest, not because there is no ultimate belief in God, but because there
are no middle guide-lines for the faithful in this world. In
this perspective, Negro congregations are not churches but
religious societies—religion can choose to worship whatever
gods are pleasing. But a church without theology, the interpretation of and response to the will of God for the faithful,
is a contradiction in terms.

Whether Negro societies are meaningfully understood as
either Protestant or churches is debatable; what is beyond
debate is the fact that these segregated communities have
been denied access to the very faith from which they take
their name. Christians there can be; segregated Negro communities of faith there cannot be. It is possible to create, as
we have done, an American Negro folk religion and racially
separate congregations of Christian persons, but it is not possible, as we are desirous of doing, to create a Negro Christian
faith.

The absence of theology in Negro religious communities
and the opposition to all forms of intellectual endeavor
within the sphere of religion have not provided a place for
creative, independent thinkers. Unlike white communions
which continue to attract brilliant laymen and clergy as
spokesmen for the faith, Negro communions can only boast
of leaders in the field of race relations. There are no first-
rate Negro theologians, and a limited number of Negro
scholars and teachers of repute are to be found in non-Negro
institutions. A clear indication of the future is the very diffi-

cult task the Protestant Fellowship Program has in attracting young men who are qualified to spend the funds allotted specifically for Negro seminarians, not to mention the sparsity of college graduates who are awarded the Rockefeller Brothers Theological Fellowship, which provides an opportunity to obtain a theological education without cost for a single year. Seminary students are not really at a premium among white communions, but a much lower percentage of Negro students with high potential apply to seminaries. This fact is substantiated by concessions made at the Lutheran Missouri Synod, where Negro students are rushed through with less academic preparation than their white peers.[56]

The disproportion of Negroes who are able thinkers in the theological field is obvious in the area of mainstream Protestantism to which the dependent congregations pay their token respects. Evangelical Protestantism of the fundamentalist or orthodox variety, the closest frame of reference for independents, has produced no Negroes who advance "orthodoxy." Factors which have led to the dismissal of religion by intellectual Negroes includes the lack of admirable Negro images in mainstream white religious organizations, and the presence of distinguished Negroes in assorted fields not restrictive of Negro clientele. One prominent Negro clergyman of no mean ability indicated that his colleagues in a Negro university frankly regarded his role as dated. Several of them are presently distinguished by their contributions to the United States and to the world in nonacademic pursuits.[57] The several Negro professors in mainstream seminaries, primarily Methodist institutions, are not pure theologians, but work in disciplines such as social ethics and religious education. The absence of topflight Negro theologians not only indicates that this area has been restrictive in its numbers and discouraging in its support of

Negro candidates, but has been regarded by the Negro as a field for others. Whatever other contributions Negroes can point to, they "have made no innovations in theology or in the general character of the church service." [58]

It is possible to see in many Negro congregations around academic centers with a large percentage of faculty members, particularly in the South, evidence of some intellectual attainment, though often such persons reserve their critical faculties for more academic work, seeking in religious communities inspiration and fellowship.

A general attitude of indifference to critical interpretation of the Christian faith prevails with the Negro who has been nurtured in an atmosphere of pious religion and matured in an environment which first asks, "What is the evidence?" The Negro professionals, government workers, and technicians who compose the bulk of the middle class which dot the religious rolls, have developed sophisticated forms of worship and made their meeting houses into social and institutional centers. Religion is basically a personal affair, not a community of faith, for these participants. That these centers are communities other than communities of faith is unquestionable:

The ambivalence of the Negro middle class is manifest in their churches, which underwent marked changes with the emergence of the bourgeoisie. An organizational style appeared, the emotionality of the folk religion rejected, services became formal and dignified; congregational life was elaborated in various activities and recreational groups; moreover, the committees, children's groups, men's and women's activities, and recreational interests of the organ-church appeared full blown within the churches of the Negro middle class.[59]

Rather than participation in the historic faith, "the middle-class Negro wants a religious style which insulates him

against his Negro identity and yet acknowledges formally
his bond with the people upon whom he depends financially
and to some extent emotionally." [60]

The perceptive participant in a Negro congregation of
whatever class hears common theological terms but discovers no sense of theology in the preached word, the study
group, or the general discussion. Instead of experiencing a
sense of participation in the Cross, the Crucifixion, and the
Resurrection, the Negro relates singularly to the life and
ministry of Jesus:

> He is a man who found the answer to life's riddle, and out of
> profound gratitude he becomes the Man most worthy of honor
> and praise. For such his answer becomes humanity's answer and
> his life the common claim. In him the miracle of the working pa-
> per is writ large, for what he did all men may do. Thus inter-
> preted, he belongs to no age, no race, no creed. When men look
> into his face, they see etched the glory of their own possibilities
> and their hearts whisper, "thank you and thank God!" [61]

Jesus is widely regarded as a kind of trailblazer through the
thicket of human experience, a belief which has no necessary
connection with the Crucifixion or the Resurrection, the focal
points of faith:

> Jesus was himself the subject of religious experience and . . .
> he, born out of the womb of Israel, felt that in himself the true
> meaning of Judaism blossomed and flowered. What he did with
> life, others can do—if they are willing to use the tools that are at
> hand. When the emphasis is given to Jesus, he becomes the
> source of inspiration and humiliation. Inspiration—because those
> who come after him have so much of him and make so little of it.
> In a man's confusion and frustration, it may be easier to worship
> Jesus than to walk in his steps. [62]

Christianity is not only seen as primarily a matter of
moral concern; it is a kind of Jesus ideology. The imitation

of Jesus would be, understandably, a part of faith if Jesus' way were intended: "Not my will, but thine be done." But another point is being made which is simply portrayed in the common speech of Negro laymen, who have the happy faculty of saying what they mean. An African Methodist Episcopal layman put it this way: "All there is to Christianity is obeying the Ten Commandments and living the Sermon on the Mount." In conversation with one of America's most articulate interpreters of theology concerning a controversy over creating a central pulpit or a divided chancel in a chapel, a Congregational layman boasted of the fact that the decision for the latter was based upon its providing aesthetic beauty, dismissing theological concerns as trivial compared with the main criterion of good taste: "These questions of theology are recent innovations." A notable layman in the Central Jurisdiction of The Methodist Church voiced his disgust with a noted theologian because he failed to emphasize "Jesus, the master teacher."

Perhaps a more significant commentary on this "Jesus-ology" is the selection of scriptures. The visitor in Negro services of worship is impressed by the infrequent use of New Testament scriptures beyond the four gospels, with the exception of I Corinthians 13. The significant theological writings of Paul are ignored. It is apparent that the lack of theology in the past is determining the present—the preference for the uncritical equation of Christian living with the Sermon on the Mount, as well as with the life and ministry of Jesus. The question is not one of denying their indispensability but of refusing to relate these vital concerns to contemporary life. No distinction is made between Christian principles and the Christian faith. Changing mores and attitudes toward life find no theological counterpart.

It is not surprising to discover that the reduction of Jesus to the role of exemplar goes hand-in-hand with the belief that Christian principles and the Christian faith are interchangeable. Among Negro Christians, generally, Christian principles serve as a shorthand for the teachings of Jesus, without considering the myriad liberties which may be taken with Jesus and the Christian faith by theological interpretation. It is one thing to shape Jesus into whatever form is convincing; it is another to consider this the mainstream of Christian understanding and thought. The attempts to pattern contemporary life after the Sermon on the Mount are unassailable—Jesus meant exactly what he said, but what he said is not best understood by the proof-text method. What is vulnerable is the blind spot which seeks to equate the Sermon on the Mount with static laws and rules.

Further, the whole mood of the present Church has bypassed Negro congregations. There is no understanding of the Church as people—faithful in some circumstances, failing in others; gathered in worship or mission on some occasions, but usually dispersed amid their responsibilities. The Church is not approached as primarily a community of persons differing in ability, perspective, and degree of commitment to the love and purpose of God revealed in Jesus Christ; persons who are aware of their principal calling to communicate the love of God in relations with their neighbors whom they meet in the daily market place. Nor is the Church seen as an extension of the Christian faith which it endeavors to clarify and make relevant in the world. It is simply not declared in Negro congregations that the function of the Church is to point toward the faith that God acts in Jesus Christ through the Holy Spirit, declaring His purpose as response to Him through reconciliation between man and man. Unfortunately, the white community bears no witness to this ministry of the Church, but the Negro has yet to be conscious of the fact that the failure of the white community does not deny the truth that the foregoing understanding of the Church provides meaning in life and direction in existence. The Negro community has yet to see that meaning and direction are as absent in their religious life together as racial acceptance is within the framework of the white congregations—to know this denial by the white community is not to deny the truth to which they are committed. From this view of the Christian tradition, the Negro community can learn to disentangle the Church from the congregations where people wear their holy airs under the cover of the latest fashion in hats and are kept busy in routines which could have relevance to life's meaning—but not as long as they exist in segregated bodies.

A final mark of the missing theological link between white and Negro Christians is in the matter of symbols. Symbols in Negro congregations are so much beautiful furniture or ornaments which are placed or hung as signs of style and correct form. The power of symbols in white centers of worship is unmistakable and they reflect a movement toward unity which has not touched the Negro communities, excluded as they are from the mainstream of Protestantism.

The tragedy is that the socio-economically disinherited and undernourished Negro becomes the most materialistic of religious men—turning even the religious community into a status symbol of racial-class identity because he has no basis on which to judge it as other than a means of security, prestige, and identification. The means and ends are one; materialistic values serve to build the economic kingdom—an interesting substitute for the kingdom of God.

The failure of the Negro's religion is inherent in the dichotomy of the Church, which cannot be *one* when in reality it is always at least *two* in America—custom says there can be Negro and white Protestants, and Negro and white Catholics in separate and distinct bodies, while the faith and the Church militate against all barriers. The religion of the Negro was limited from the start—not by lack of leadership and educational and economic well-being, but by lack of participation in the faith and in the Church, which were reserved for the superior race. As in the public toilets in the South, there is a sign over many houses of worship, both North and South, blocking out the symbol of the cross, which is everywhere the same: "Colored."

In its disregard of theology and mission, the Negro's religion allows for the toleration of peripheral interests. Both of these movements in Protestantism are at the heart of the renewal of the Church, but, being separated from the Church, the Negro has not participated in its various forms of renewal.

There is a growing awareness among Christians that the life of the Church is mission. This overarching view is but a few decades old, but it has already proven to be the most significant foundation upon which a sense of unity is being built. Negatively speaking, where there is no real mission, there is no life. We measure the dynamics, intent, integrity, and quality of a Christian community by its vitality in mission. To be sure, the old, smug, image of "I have the truth" has fortunately given way to something like D. T. Niles' simile of one beggar aiding another beggar to find a piece of bread—or meaningful existence in a world of confusion. However radically the forms of mission change, the will to share the depths of meaning and relevance remains a Christian constant.

Among the factors which have served to revive the idea and practice of mission several may profitably be mentioned. First, theology has been recognized as an imperative for the critical and interpretive renewal of faith in the laity and clergy. Moreover, as lesser developed nations have emerged, they have insisted that primary emphasis be given to the cultivation of indigenous leadership for the carrying out of their own mission. Further, various communions have become attuned to the ecumenical movement. Finally, there has arisen a tension between faith and culture, with an accompanying insight into the mission need within local situations at home. These emphases, along with a good many others, effect and support the judgment that the quality of a Christian community is reflected in its extension through mission, overseas or at home.

Protestant communities may discover their mission program to be in a state of considerable disrepair, but these four emphases in the life of their denominations at least provide the local communities with a starting point.

It is this widespread absence of a sense of mission among Negro religious societies which provides such a sharp contrast between them and their fellow Protestants. The very heart of the Christian faith is missing in these communities, be they segregated independent or dependent religious societies. The obvious absence of mission among Negro religious organizations is a phenomenon which deserves more serious attention than it has received, for it discloses the death knell of segregation. Though the results may not be happy ones, it is time that the situation be in the open so that the virility in this area of the Christian faith may provide a standard by which to gauge the Negro in religious life and mission.

It is clear that Negroes are fantastically difficult to recruit in any endeavor which includes sustained sacrifice for the well-being of others. Historically, the independent Negro religious bodies were the direct result of the Negro missionary. Unlike the white missionaries who had been his teachers, the Negro missionary came not to keep the slave in his place but to offer him a way of freedom. Following the Emancipation Proclamation, the Negro missionaries offered the Freedmen an opportunity to join a movement independent of the white communities. To these two calls of freedom and status the Negro responded with great enthusiasm. As these independent bodies grew they became embroiled in problems of growth and internal affairs. Their sense of mission included some concern for Liberia, Panama, Jamaica, and Haiti, but it has been backed by few dollars and even fewer persons. From the earliest days to the present, Negro missionary work has been directed only at people of color, and the quality of mission continues to be inferior to that accomplished by "mainstream" denominations. The only study yet made of the expenditures of Negro congregations shows a mere 6.3 per cent of the budget for "missions, education, repairs, and upkeep." [63]

Where there has been missionary fervor, it has been racially oriented, being concerned not with mission of the Church but with the work of the denominations. Action tends to be based on doing good works rather than being faithful to the Church. While Negro religious groups are engaged in political, social, and other endeavors, including providing recreation for juvenile delinquents, the fundamental basis of this is the secular hope of racial improvement.

The sit-in movement and other forms of social protest do not contradict but support this situation. The valid Negro sacrifices in the area of civil liberties are a form of mission related to the earliest Negro missions. Negro leaders were able to involve their fellows in the flight for freedom and membership in independent racial congregations. Present-day Negro leaders are able to involve masses of Negro students and adults from lower economic levels in drives for basic participation in public life. These sacrifices are in the best interest of the entire nation and the world, as well as of the Negro, but they, too, are motivated and sustained by the desperate needs of this racial minority. Aside from racial interests, the Negro is not well-represented in missionary work. Within the confines of religious societies he has only concerned himself with limited interest in Colored People, in contrast with white bodies which have striven for the betterment of all peoples.

But in spheres other than that of local religious congregations Negroes are less than prominent in mission. To put the matter succinctly, the Peace Corps, the Ecumenical Voluntary Projects sponsored by the National Council of Churches of Christ in the U.S.A., the American Friends Voluntary International Service Assignments and even Crossroads Africa are each extremely hard-pressed to enlist Negro volunteers. The search of these organizations proves what the mainstream churches have known for a very long time. Whether the mission be overseas or in the inner city, Negroes are few and far between—though mainstream white institutions have yet to awaken to the fact that by the very process of segregation they defeat their ultimate purpose of mission, through providing no indigenous life and increasing opportunities for work where Negroes are concerned. If the Negro has not involved himself in the mission of the Church, the white Christians have not been involved in the mission of including the Negro within the Church.

Certainly it is true that mainstream organizations eagerly seek out Negroes who are easily accepted, especially in these days of acute sensitivity and increasing guilt. Few missionary organizations or church boards, would not welcome a roster of competent Negro men and women to bolster their effectiveness in the mission of extension. It is to be expected that few Negroes will be involved in white missions when even the predominant Negro institutions are near total defection in the realm of missionary endeavor.

This situation is the result of two related factors. First, there is a defensive attitude on the part of Negroes, whose concern with their own racial life is so overwhelming that to direct their energies in other channels would be to condone the status quo. Second, there is the illiberal attitude of white Protestants who continue to ignore the reality of Protestantism as distinctly black and white in America. In these extremes there abide no seeds of renewal.

Historically, the Negro has been the object of prey for the life and mission of various black and white communions for totally different purposes, particularly those of Protestantism. In partial repudiation of inequality in the white communions, following the Revolutionary War, Negroes formed their religious societies as a means of achieving status, though this status has proved to be segregated so that there exist two status systems in the United States, black and white, within the congregations as without. Nevertheless, even the socio-economic forces which forced the separation of Negro and white Protestants were unable to remove the Negro as a mission field. In the immediate aftermath of the Civil War the Negro was in need of education, a vacuum not filled by Negro religious organizations but by white Protestant organizations, overwhelmingly. The white contributions in religion and education have been heroic. The products have often been splendid. But the anticipation that this education would lead the Negro into the full stream of American life was ill-founded—the Negro was not accepted in the North by the same societies who worked for his acceptance in the South. North or South, the white spirit was unwilling to include numbers of black men and women except as exceptions to various rules. But the fact remains that generally in the fields of religion and education the accomplished Negro has traditionally been the flower of some Protestant mission. Denied access to the roots of Protestantism, as well as ties to its European tradition, the Negro race was unable to immerse itself in its genius for emitting new and relevant patterns.

Religion and education among Negroes were born of and are sustained by the mission spirit of an age now past. In a real sense, they still live off the capital and interest of this past. Negro bodies have broken no new ground nor contributed uniquely to the culture, apart from this past inheritance (the very fact that the Negro is criticized for not making new contributions is a singular reminder of the fact that he is unconsciously expected to have a different breed of religion, whereas if he had been thought of as a part of the mainstream he would be seen as sharing in the new patterns).

Thoroughly Negro religious and academic communities are so completely mission products that they find it strange, at best, to be expected to be a mission beyond the Negro community—the source of mission which sends out persons with a mission.

The non-commitment to mission finds its corollary in theology. Without communication with the white community and their source of direction the Negro has been without theology, except that of the severely limited eschatology in the spirituals. There are Negro religious congregations which are predominantly this-worldly as surely as there are Negro colleges which are directed toward the end of being good colleges, but this is not the same as saying Negro congregations are within the household of faith. The real weakness in the mission of Negro religious groups is the lack of theology. To expect Negro religious groups to have enthusiastic and numerable participants in mission work without a faith is to force the Negro to be inferior indeed.

These historical caveats identify the lack of mission in Negro religious societies. But these caveats do not pinpoint one fundamental reason why Negro fellowships look so much like mainstream Protestantism and act so differently in response to mission.

It is widely agreed that while mainstream or middle-class Protestantism often pioneers in mission, the responses they receive are usually less than those of evangelical and lower-class Protestantism. While Negroes are increasingly partaking of middle-class values and are anxious to move in this direction out of the lower-class values which predominate among them, their production of persons with a mission does not compare with their white models on either level.

There is a provocative factor here which needs far more consideration than it is usually given. A sense of mission or sharing, the sacrifice of personal advancement for a meaningful and authentic life of inspiring others to realize what they otherwise would not, is not fundamentally the result of an inferiority or superiority complex. In the first place, it is a sense of having something which the whole world needs, and such a sense of uniqueness can inspire purpose and meaning which no amount of money can purchase. Certainly the Negro's religion of racial identity by forced segregation is not considered by him or anyone else as something needed, but rather as something from which to be delivered. Fundamentally, the message and mission of the Negro folk religion must always be negative and not positive, a denial of something and not its affirmation.

In the second place, a sense of mission or sharing is the consciousness that though the material fruits of society are available for the asking, they are powerless to attract. In some instances, persons who decline economic well-being and give themselves to mission work have often had the material advantages of life through their own efforts or those of their parents and found them wanting. Not sufficiently motivated or fulfilled by status-seeking, these persons do not have any sense of being fundamentally denied opportunities for a prosperous life should they so desire. Certainly the qualitative standards in all mission areas today mean that these participants have made or could make their way in the world of success. Where the mission fervor is, two birds in the bush are worth more than one in the hand. Biblically stated, the ninety-nine sheep can be counted upon to be there while attention is given to the single outsider.

It is precisely at this point that the Negro finds it most difficult to imitate the white Protestant of any class where mission is involved. The Negro has never really tasted the economic fruits and is not certain that they are within his grasp. Denied so long, the Negro now believes that economic rewards are the ultimate values, which he is psychologically unprepared to forgo. In this frame of mind, without the Christian faith and its theological interpretation of the depths of meaning, relevance, and purpose, it would be less than realistic to expect him to sacrifice that which he so desperately wishes and is not sure he can receive, for a life which appears to be woefully near the deprivation he is running hard to leave behind. The Negro cannot be appealed to at the point of, "What is the purpose and meaning of life for you?" He has been so completely divorced from the full life within the community of faith until he cannot really listen to or rightly hear the message which is basic to the faith he has been denied: without a mission, economic values are mere pottage. Perhaps he will have to be a full member of the whole of life before he can experience, as some of his white peers have, an encounter with reality.

There are those who regret the limited number of Negroes available for mission, since their engagement would make for good public relations overseas, as well as because the metropolitan areas are fast becoming predominantly Negro: "What could be more honorable than for the Negro to minister to his own!" It is this very appeal which reinforces segregation within the denominations and forces the Negro out of the sphere of interest in missionary work. Why should the Negro sacrifice himself on behalf of a segregated institution, white or black, which will perpetuate this segregation? The Negro will never be able to minister to others until it is seen that everyone is "his own." Until he is brought into the inner circle and groomed for tasks based upon his competence and not his color—until many Negroes find their mission in middle-class suburban and urban centers now dominated by white Americans—we should expect that the Negro will have no special sense of responsibility

for the Negro rejected by white communions. Not until the
Negro has been freely accepted by the whole of society
should we expect to see him in missions to Negroes, not because they are Negroes, but because they are in need of mission. We should expect that the heroic negation of economic
rewards will continue to emerge very slowly among Negroes.

Denominational executives in places of influence, who
in their boot-strap philosophy wish the Negro to be a race
man, are tied to the past, even as the Negro who is thus
blinded. The new stirrings of revolt are not for "separate
but equal." It cannot be assumed that the Negro can be
appealed to at the point of racial pride to do for Negroes
what white people are unwilling to do for him. For the future motivation of the Negro is not to deny that he is a Negro but to affirm that he is an American, seeking to participate and contribute to the whole and not the part. One real
measure of being in step with the future is having a sense
of mission. This may come only as he knows himself to be
not simply respected as a Negro but accepted as a person—
politically, economically, socially, and sexually. Realization
of this mission may come in the decades ahead, but not unless there is an endeavor in the present to be aware of and
prepare for relevance, the responsible mission under God.

The role of the laity has become increasingly significant with the development of the organizational fellowship
among Negroes. Where once the deacons and deaconnesses,
stewards and stewardesses were simply foils for the minister,
they are now engaged in activities which are considered the
measure of a going concern. That the minister is still looked
to as the basis for hope or despair with regard to a particular Negro communion is seen in the fact that the major works
dealing with the Negro's religion center on the minister and
ignore the layman.[64] In addition to the fact that these writers are biased toward effective ministerial leadership, they

reflect accurately the dominant trend of Negro congregations toward personality-controlled pulpit centers, supporting the judgment that Negro congregations stand outside the central concern of Protestantism.

It is often the case that the religious societies pioneer in voluntary groups and undertake a task which has been neglected by the agencies of the larger community. Often, too, the voluntary organizations relinquish this initiating role when they have sufficiently impressed the larger community with their responsibility in this area. Because they have not understood this function, as well as what it means to be the people of God, Negro laymen and their institutions continue to busy themselves with tasks which may be more capably administered by other organizations.

In an attempt to rediscover the role of Christian laymen, in a period when many of the traditional functions seem marked by duplication or irrelevance, laymen have begun to think through their area of responsibility. Where laymen have become interested in their responsibility they have become engaged in the study of theology as a way of clarifying who they are and what they are called to do. Here and there have arisen lay academies with intense interest in study. Another mark of these lay communities is experimentalism. Not satisfied with past forms of the life they have lived in the churches they are attempting to blaze new trails.

Released from past rigidity and traditions which do not provide the flexibility that the times require, laymen-centered experiments have been conducted with small groups meeting for the discovery of the meaning of the Christian faith. Out of this has grown the awareness that laymen are daily involved with fellow specialists or routine workers who are puzzled about the meaning and purpose of their existence. It is these persons, with whom they rub shoulders each weekday, who are rarely reached by the minister, or, if reached, have a sense that he understands their frustrations.

Thus in addition to theological study and personal renewal in small groups, there has come about action in the form of discussions with their colleagues on a deeper level.

This lay movement, expressing itself not only in industries but also in the form of the Faculty Christian Fellowship, is no less than a sign of renewal, re-vision. Negroes are not caught up in this new movement. Where one attends a Faculty Christian Fellowship meeting which includes a few Negroes, he is impressed by the completely different orientation with which they come to this occasion, no less than with their lack of real awareness about what is going on. As the Negro becomes involved in organizational patterns he tends to become more rigid and punctilious, less flexible. Without any affinity for vocation *per se,* the Negro layman attunes himself to the functional aspects of the organization. Few are perceptive of their call to the responsible throughout the daily round.

As laymen, Negroes relate religion to life in terms of institutional and organizational matters. But when it comes to the living of their lives at the edge of faith there persists the traditional insistence that religion has nothing to do "with my life."

The measure of a congregation is not the smooth, methodical way in which it functions as social institution, though such a congregation is in a position to further the work of the denomination. The measure of a congregation is the quality of the laity in its awareness of and response to the theological side of study, reconciliation, and action. Negro congregations understand what it means to be functional, but what it means to minister is an alien concept. The need for more well-trained Negro clergymen is real. But the assumption that there is a responsible community only where there is a dynamic minister tends to undercut the role and effectiveness of lay development. Where lay movements are effective, their mission may be set forth by professional theologians and ministers, though their dynamic is lay-inspired. The underdevelopment of Negro laymen encourages their association in congregations for social functions and acceptance alone, insensitive to the need for awareness, purpose, meaning, fullness, and freedom from conformity and for mission. Negro laymen have yet to awaken to the difference in function, but identity in mission, between themselves and the ordained clergy, wherein they together are ministers of a community called to minister to themselves and the larger community.

Religion for the Negro is inherited and changed by the contemporary mood without reference to the theological dimension of faith. His religious institutions exist without any meaningful goals, with the sole exception of providing refuge for the disinherited. The only possible change is from the status of disinheritance to that of inheritance. But this change is not completely within the power of the Negro. Though he is involved in a separated religion he cannot create a separate faith, nor enter into this faith by his merits as a functional and respectable fashioner of a small-scale model of white denominations. Those who assume that change is possible from within the Negro religious life are either seeking to perpetuate personal rewards or to exclude him from the Christian faith as it finds its life in the Christian community. To separate the Negro out is to force him to be imitative. To exclude him from the Church and to permit him to be set adrift places a burden upon the Negro of creating what is not within his province. In producing a substitute for the Christian community, the Negro has done his job well. Within his religious life there are no seeds for renewal of the Christian Church and faith, but his participation in the Christian faith may well bring a renewed Church.

Like the Ethiopian eunuch, in charge of treasures, the Negro will never lose sight of religion as a source of diversion until he is of such real concern to the white community

that it will take time to ask him if he understands what the
faith demands, to which he may then reply: "How can I
understand unless someone will give me the clue?" But this
understanding can only come when the entire white community, not just the benevolent and paternalistic missionary, is
willing "to get in and sit beside him."

Chapter 3

RESPONSE TO PROTESTANT PATERNALISM: NEGRO FRATERNALISM

White and Negro Americans take exception to the evidence and its inescapable conclusion that the religion of Negro Protestants is different because Negroes have never been included in the mainstream of American Protestantism.

In part Negroes fear that the admission of the difference between Negro and white Protestant religion and life would be equal to declaring the Negro inferior and unequal. Also, Negroes want to protect the prestige and interests which have been built up over three centuries.

White semi-liberals disregard the differences by simply pointing to a counterpart among white Protestants for every identifiable deviation or mutation exhibited by Negroes. In so doing, they dismiss the real issue which persists beneath the surface and also escape involvement on the spiritual level. Magnanimity of this kind is no more helpful than the white illusion of empathy with the Negro, or the delusion that Negroes prefer, as a matter of choice, racial compartmentalization in religion.

The old liberal white American has yet to awaken to the fact that Negroes represent a peculiar breed of Protestantism, different from his own. Not only does the fact escape him, but its serious implications as well. The white liberal camp is divided into two parts. One division is headed by those professional people and scholars who have been intellectually on the side of the Negro but who have remained emotionally aloof. They honestly believe the problem is too tough, and consequently they spend their non-

scholarly energies in areas where their efforts produce meas-
urable results. The other division is emotionally involved
with the Negro and is comprised of those liberals who wish
to dismiss the past as only a prologue and to concentrate
upon progress. These liberals will be the first to point out
that in their local congregation or offices they have token
desegregation. Neither the realism which ignores the American dilemma nor the idealism which repudiates it helps cure
the malaise. Indeed, realism is dangerously near conservatism and idealism borders on tokenism masquerading as
moderation.

However, there is a new group of liberals, passionately
and intellectually committed to the visible unity of Negro
and white Protestants. They are dissatisfied both with token
integration in geographical and spiritually isolated communities and with stargazing into some distant future. They
are aware that pronouncements are only helpful if they
bring concrete action throughout the length and breadth
of Protestantism. But if this emerging spirit is to create an
unprecedented and deliberate Protestantism which is moving spiritually and physically toward a racially inclusive fellowship, white and Negro participants will do well to reflect
upon the historical conditions producing white and Negro
Protestantism. Prior to this decade, white and Negro persons and institutions never had a chance to participate in
an inclusive milieu. To brush over this truth may result in
the failure to provide not only the necessary catharsis, but
also the forces for reformation.

1 Colonial Religion and the Negro

The equation of the Negro with American Protestantism
is as misleading as the equation of the founding of the Colo-

nies with religion. Both are half-truths which foster a nearly complete misconception.

African natives accompanied the New World explorers seeking an expanded trade route. The first permanent settlement, in Jamestown, Virginia, in 1607, was an economic enterprise. In 1619 a Dutch slave ship sold twenty Africans as indentured servants to supplement the labor supplied by white indentured servants. Jamestown was not an experiment in religious freedom, but in free enterprise.

Priests of the Church of England settled with these English entrepreneurs, establishing the Church of England in Jamestown and the other Southern colonies. These priests were not missionary-minded, since the settlers were communicants of the Church, including the indentured white servants. Moreover, the missionary zeal of Protestantism at large and the Church of England in particular was not aroused until more than a century after the Jamestown settlement. There was no effort to convert the Indians, because they were outside the bounds of the Colony.

The first religious excitement in the Colonies centered about the Africans. By 1640 they were the only labor force without the benefit of indentured servitude or contracts.[1] At first the Virginians felt that they could reap the harvest of the New World without slaves, but their abundance, low cost, and utility presented an irresistible temptation. Unlike the white indentured servants, slaves were without exposure to Christianity. Their presence was increasingly felt, causing some real stirrings among the limited number of priests.

Slaves were everywhere, in the fields and in the households of the planters. Priests, too, found slaves readily available and the ever-growing number of slaves prompted the priests to consider depaganizing them. Unlike the Roman Catholic priests who followed the explorers to extend the domain of the Roman Catholic Church, and unlike the evangelicals who swept through the colonies and extended the

frontier in the eighteenth century, the Anglican priests did
not endeavor to advance any cause. They thought that the
slaves ought, as a matter of course, to be baptized Christians,
without regard to their being introduced to the rudiments
of education or doctrine.

Anglican priests did not oppose the institution of slavery. No more were they interested in swelling the number
of Anglican communicants. Clearly, the slaves were to be
treated in a different manner from that of the white Christians. In their view, priests were merely expressing a pastoral concern, without political, economic, or even social
implications.

What appeared a matter of pastoral procedure to the
priests was seen as a threat to economic enterprise by the
planters. Ordinarily, the planters took the functional role of
the clergy for granted. But the idea of baptizing slaves met
with full and vigorous opposition from the masters. The
planters considered slaves to be at their disposal, in the
same manner as the other animals and tools which were used
to work the land.

This understanding of the role of the slaves was in conflict with the European tradition of Christianity inherited
by the planters. In the sixteenth and early seventeenth centuries Europeans believed that a baptized Christian was to
be recognized as a free man, or on the way to being a free
man (as in the case of indentured white servants). The
doctrine that "freedom was inherent in Christianity" or "that
Christianization opened the way to freedom" clearly preceded the economic enterprise of the New World, with its
concomitant exploitation of slaves.

Tension increased into a theological dispute between
the planters and their priests. If the planters were correct
in their belief that Christianity and freedom were inseparable ideas, one of two things would occur and either would
interfere with the central concern of economic development.

Thousands of slaves, cheaply bought for a lifetime of service, would have to be reverted to the earlier status of servitude, given contracts, and finally integrated into the life of the economy. This prospect took on nightmare proportions in the minds of the planters. The other possibility was equally repulsive. The conversion of slaves to Christianity and their baptism would require their being set free immediately as real human persons, potential brothers, entitled to be respected as sacred men and women. If the Anglican priests were right, Negroes could be both baptized Christians and slaves without being human beings. Planters understood the choice between being a baptized Christian and a real human being to be a contradiction in terms. Minimally, in their view, to be a Christian was to be a real person. The priests were concerned about the after-life, promoting a Christian burial as a fit substitute for free human existence.

This agitation over the theological definition of freedom continued for more than fifty years in Jamestown, which differed from the other colonies in coming to grips with the tension between faith and economics. The planters accepted the Christian understanding of freedom. They were unable to see how it could be compromised with their intention to dehumanize Negroes and therefore they assumed the honest position that slaves should not be confused with Christians or human beings. It was ironical that these laymen defended one tenet of the Christian faith. On the other hand, the clergy wished to make the Negro an exception. They were less concerned with the doctrine of freedom and more concerned with the doctrine of baptism. Neither side brought the full implication of the faith to bear upon the situation.

In the Virginia Assembly of 1667, it was affirmed that "Baptism doth not alter the condition of the person as to his bondage or freedom." [2] The point of view held by the priests had clearly won; but not for theological reasons.

The Roman Catholic priests who accompanied the Europeans to the West Indies were missionary-minded. They sought not only to establish the church on the islands but also to convert the Indians, no less the African slaves who were brought in to do the work at which the Indians balked. Roman Catholicism has always been a mission enterprise. In this way its missionaries differed from the seventeenth-century Anglicans who represented the Protestant, or at least non-Roman, wing of Christianity, which was barely a century old and preoccupied with discovering itself in the Western countries. In the process of converting the slaves, the priests came up against the same questions raised by the planters in Virginia. Roman Catholic priests appealed to European monarchies, such as Roman Catholic Spain which granted expansion charters and permitted the Church to evangelize on the basis of the European church-state relations; they gained a new interpretation with respect to baptism and freedom. European monarchs were committed, for the most part, to both economic and religious expansion. Assuming slaves to be heathens, Europeans justified slavery on the basis that it gave the Negro the privilege of having his soul saved. With this justification in hand, the Roman Catholic priests went to work on the slaves. They won the commendation of the planters because they succeeded in proving that the religious slave was more docile.

All the while that Roman Catholic priests were succeeding in areas like the West Indies, the planters in Virginia were facing difficulties with their slaves. The combination of rebellious slaves and the practical effects of the Roman Catholic priests aided the *rapprochement* between the Virginia planters and the Anglican priests:

Gradually the doctrine that freedom was inherent in Christianity began to wane in popularity and was supplanted by a point of view that was in itself a rationalization of the institution. This view was that slavery was good in that it brought heathens into contact with Christianity and led to the salvation of their souls.

Masters, far from discouraging the Christianization of slaves, should cooperate with the agents of the church and the result would be the creation of a more obedient servile class. The heathenism of the Africans thus became one of the important justifications for slavery.[3]

Thus, virtually from the beginning Negroes were introduced to the rewards of Christianity for the good of the planters in this world and for the good of the slaves in the world beyond. Negroes were exposed to Christianity quite apart from their participation in the Church and its full faith. They were treated as "exceptional" Christians from the earliest days and they came to understand themselves as exceptions. This theological laxity was the basis for depriving not only the helpless slaves of a firm grounding in the Christian tradition, but the vast majority of Negroes ever since. The idea of freedom as a theological and human fundamental was denied the Negro by the Church, and the Negro had to wait until forces for independence dominated the colonies to gain access to freedom. By then, religion was largely an otherworldly concern and freedom slipped in through the Negro leaders who were influenced in this concern by the doctrines of natural rights expounded by the Deists and Humanists.

Although the Anglican priests were enabled to carry out their clerical duties among the slaves by the consent of their white parishioners, who supported them with their taxes, they were largely ineffective. A limited number of priests, the lack of evangelical zeal, and insufficient funds all combined to restrict the outreach of the clergy. They were unable to reach many in the fields. Those few who were reached were simply baptized and given little instruction in morals, education, and doctrine. For these reasons, the real work among the slaves, many of whom were baptized Anglicans, was left to the evangelicals who were invited in by Anglican planters years later, to channel the energy of the salves.

The agitation over the question of freedom did not extend to the other Southern colonies where the Anglicans were established. The Maryland colony, dating from 1634, could point to statutory recognition of slavery as early as 1663. Prior to the settlement of Carolina, slavery was recognized in the "Fundamental Constitutions" written for the colony by John Locke—"every freeman of Carolina shall have absolute power and authority over his negro slaves, of what opinion or religion soever." Georgia was not permitted the luxury of slaves, founded as it was to rehabilitate English prisoners through hard labor, until the third and final petition for slaves was accepted under the sponsorship of the sometime Anglican divine, sometime Methodist itinerant preacher, George Whitefield, and his friend James Habersham.

The religion of the Negro which began in Jamestown and developed throughout Southern colonies during the first one hundred years was an emasculated one by every contemporary standard of Christianity in general and Protestantism in particular. The fact that these colonies were economic enterprises, religion being relatively incidental, is the conceded reason for this Anglican approach to the Negro.

In Massachusetts, economic and religious establishment were the twin goals of the Puritans and Separatists, who formed a Congregational theocracy on the strength of the Massachusetts Bay Company's commercial charter.[4] The Massachusetts colony was dominated by settlers who were not so much seeking freedom of all religion as freedom to develop a commonwealth based specifically on the religious principles advocated by English Puritans whose expression was curbed by the Church of England. In their own way, the Puritans were vigorous in their insistence upon religious conformity and sought to restrain or exclude dissidents in much the same way as they had been treated in England.[5] Along with having a rigid theocratic polity, Massachusetts attracted shrewd entrepreneurs, men who possessed few qualms with respect to slavery.

The Bay colonists began with a more vital religious tenor than their English brethren to the South, yet a debate over slavery and the Christian understanding of freedom was omitted. In 1641, twenty-six years before statutory recognition of slavery in Virginia, Massachusetts enacted the heralded "Body of Liberties" which included a statement prohibiting slavery "unless it be lawfull Captives taken in just warres, and such strangers as willingly sell themselves or are sold to us."[6] Such an open mandate to energetic traders to deposit slaves among the Puritans was justified as an economic measure, a means of supplying the manpower shortage. Fervently religious, this colony "not only fostered the slave trade like no other group in the New World but also countenanced the existence of slavery in their midst."[7] The Puritans were all but content to provide religious arguments as a justification for slavery: "Negroes were a cursed people, and enslavement was a proper method to bring them within the reach of God's grace."[8]

Although the Puritan masters retained a very limited number of slaves, they were experts at trading and sold thousands in the West Indies and to planters in the Southern colonies: "Down to the War for Independence New England Merchants regarded the slave trade as vital to their economic life and the very heart of the highly profitable triangular trade."[9] The theocracy of New England was no more opposed to the institution of slavery than was the established Church of England in the Southern colonies. Many of the same fears which discouraged the conversion of slaves in the other colonies were at work among the limited number of "saints" in New England:

Some feared that Christian slaves would take too much time out for Scriptural study and church attendance and, therefore, their economic value would be diminished. Others felt that upon conversion slaves would regard themselves as the equals of the whites and would refuse to obey orders. Another apprehension, generally held throughout the colonies, was that baptism conferred freedom on the slave. Still another objection, which was peculiar to New England, was that baptism would place the franchise in the hands of slaves, since church membership was the basis for exercising the franchise.[10]

The Puritans differed from the other colonists in providing more humane codes and conditions for the slaves, though their humanitarianism did not extend to opposing the lucrative slave trade. Some of the slaves were taught to read and write, the ability to read the Bible being a minimum Puritan requirement. By limiting the number of slaves, Puritans were able to do more with a fewer number.

Nevertheless, those few slaves who benefited from the ameliorative factors of Puritanism were never included in the Puritan theocracy, nor in the less rigid Half-Way Covenant of 1662 (an attempt to extend the "democracy" to those who previously were unable to qualify as "saints"). The Puritans were not enthusiastic in their teachings of religious rigidities to a limited number of slaves, but they were decidedly opposed to the slaves being "incorporated into the church, which then being connected with the state would grant them political as well as religious equality." [11]

Moreover, the Puritans did not provide their "Christian" slaves with a religious or theological understanding of freedom—as the Puritans understood freedom. Their slaves were left with the impression that to be a "Christian slave" was good enough for them, excluded as they were from the inner circle of their masters. Those Negroes, and their off-

spring, were permanently brainwashed. They were impressed by the humanitarianism of the Puritans, who led
the slaves under their control to believe that within the
Christian faith there were no grounds for freedom.

The Puritan theocracy differed from the Anglican Establishment in that not all residents of the Commonwealth
were considered members of the church. Puritans were under no compulsion to baptize those slaves who did not give
evidence of "true godliness" and "sound knowledge." The
perversion of religion for the purpose of controlling slaves
was unnecessary since the economy was supported by the
profit of the slave trade, rather than by the labor of the
slaves. There were less than 20,000 slaves scattered throughout New England in 1662, a measure of their sparsity in the
major slave-trading area.

By the end of the colonial period the vast majority of
slaves were unexposed to the Puritan religion. The few who
became Christians were instructed by masters who had
taken a personal liking to them. It is not clear that the slaves
were incapable of responding to the intricate theological
questions which concerned the Puritans, nor is it clear that
they were lacking in reason or native ability to deal with
complex issues—though the obvious lack of theological interest on the part of the Negro has been based on this assumption from the earliest days. What is evident is that a
limited number of Puritans gave of their leisure to a very
small number of Negroes.

The story of the seventeenth century in the colonies is
that of the dominance of religious establishment. It is clear
that Anglicans were relatively free of competing religious
perspectives, but the presence of religious controversy
within the state church was evident regarding baptism and
freedom with respect to the Negro. The inflexibility of the
Puritan theocracy grew out of the inner conflict of Puritanism

itself. Presbyterians were the largest body of dissenters migrating to Long Island and New York in 1640. English Baptists were forced to the frontiers of New England.

The plantation system of the Southern colonies and its
dependence upon cheap slave labor added to the accepted
priority of the economic over the religious establishment.
There was no question of this priority in the minds of either
the clergy or the laymen. Given this hierarchy of values, the
task of religion was to support the institution of slavery and
its adherents while providing some special ecclesiastical con-
solation for the slaves—short of aspiration toward complete
humanity and Christianity. The income which poured into
the Puritan economy from slave trading enabled members
of the Massachusetts colony to spend their intellectual and
spiritual energies in the refinement of theocratic principles,
and blinded them to their attitudes toward the slaves and
their white brethren of other persuasions. Favorite slaves
were freed or given preferential treatment, charitable action
made possible by the abundance supplied by the slaves. In
both North and South, there were the closest ties between
the church and state. In neither case were there protests
concerning conflicting interests with respect to the perception of the Negro as a breed apart. Thus, it is not surprising
that the identical concern with preserving the establishment
among religious men and entrepreneurs prevented any opposition to slavery. Given this seventeenth-century environment, it is generally assumed that religion was both the child
of its times and without roots for social reform.

A primary interest in economic well-being crushed out
neither the Quaker sensitivity to religious liberty nor the
concern for social reform. Quakers were an important group
among the dissenters from the Puritan theocracy. In 1682
they established an experiment in religious freedom at Philadelphia. This was a sound economic venture, guided by

the enterprising Quaker William Penn. Slaves were present there, in comparatively small numbers, as was true in New England. Prior to the charter obtained in 1681, the Dutch had already deposited Negro slaves in what was to be named Pennsylvania. The slow development of the Negro population was due in part to the presence of various European artisans who were attracted to this well-planned experiment which was free of fear and persecution. These artisans did not feel the need for slaves, since they were industrious persons who had migrated for the purpose of work.

Slaves were increased in the eastern section of Pennsylvania in response to the economic interest there. Great pressure was brought by the Royal African Company, as well, which saw in Pennsylvania a new and lucrative market. The religio-social ethic of the Quakers conflicted sharply with the economic interests of many others.

The significant witness of the Quakers was borne by a minority group in this religion of a minority. The great majority of Quakers held at least a few slaves or were in favor of the rewards of slavery. But this majority did not stifle the resistance of the minority.

In 1671, George Fox, the leader of the Quakers, visited Barbados in the West Indies, where he expressed concern for the human treatment of the slaves and the hope that they would be freed within the pattern of indentured servitude. Upon his return to England, George Fox wrote a testament to the Friends in Barbados against slavery, suggesting that they might well follow the Jewish law of liberating slaves as set forth in Deuteronomy 15. George Fox is a distinct witness to the truth that even in the earliest days of slavery Christians had Biblical authority for opposing slavery.[12] George Fox repeatedly admonished his brethren in New England to "teach and instruct Blacks" as well as to "preach the gospel to them."

The spirit of George Fox was taken seriously by the

Quaker women, who voiced their protest of cruelty and lack of education among slaves in 1678.[13] Quakers based their response to slavery on Biblical grounds. This was evident in the first American protest against slavery at Germantown, Pennsylvania in 1688.

Turning to the Golden Rule, a small number of Quakers of German descent presented a paper in a Monthly Meeting in which they stood against slavery:

Now, tho they are black, we can not conceive there is more liberty to have them slaves, as it is to have other white ones. There is a saying, that we shall doe to all men like as we will be done ourselves; making no difference of what generation, descent or colour they are. And those who steal or robb men, and those who buy or purchase them, are they not all alike? Here is liberty of conscience, wch is right and reasonable; here ought to be likewise liberty of body, except of evil-doers wch is in an other case. But to bring men hither, or to rob and sell them against their will, we stand against.[14]

Those who signed this paper respectfully requested clarification as to whether slavery was good or bad and whether Christians were at liberty to be involved in slavery. It was then considered at the Quarterly Meeting, which deemed it "a thing of too great a weight for this meeting to determine." It was allowed to die on the table of the Yearly Meeting.

What is significant in this rejected protest is its Biblical appeal to freedom for all men, here called "liberty of conscience" and "liberty of body." Some Quakers were slave masters like their fellow colonists, but unlike them they were free of the charge of appealing to the Christian doctrine of freedom as a means of supporting the institution of slavery. Those who defended lifelong bondage did so as an economic good. If the Quakers in the colonies were thinly spread, so was the minor voice within this communion in opposition to slavery. The spirited few who looked upon the Negro as a human being at least prevented their fellow Quakers and colonists of other persuasions from easily accepting slavery. There was no popular uprising among Quakers protesting slavery, but "in no other English colony were the forces for and against slavery so pronounced as in Penn's colony." [15]

Few Negroes came under the influence of the Quakers, partly because they were not the large slaveholders and partly because of the tension within the Society of Friends. The real contribution of the Quakers to the religion of the Negro was their early and vigorous insistence upon freedom and equality as the inseparable marks of Christian living. Only the Quakers took the Negro seriously enough to provide him with sustained instruction and thought enough of him to create a climate out of which anti-slavery groups grew. At least one Quaker, George Keith, began instructing slaves for the purpose of emancipation in 1693.[16]

The history of the seventeenth century was that of religious indifference to the Negro, with isolated exceptions. Limited time, interest, money, personnel, and energy were spent in his behalf. Religion was what the Negro was taught. He was totally dependent upon the white leaders for his religion and they were equally dependent upon the economy. On the whole, religious leaders thought of the Negro as a little lower than a human being and considerably less than a member of the Church. As a rule, Negroes who were interested in religion had to be satisfied with the sacrament of baptism and whatever training was necessary to meet this requirement. The failure of Protestantism in the seventeenth century perpetuates itself in each succeeding generation, and for many of the same reasons.

Protestant Missions and the Negro

The colonists were largely non-Roman Catholic. For
the most part, their religious affiliation was with the Church
of England and the various Protestant sects which grew out
of the Anglican communion. In Europe for more than one
hundred years following the birth of Protestantism in the
sixteenth century, the movement was engulfed by the dominant question of the relationship between the church and
the state. In a large measure, this tension was resolved in
England by the 1642-1648 English Civil War. The national
conflict settled, Protestants became engrossed in internal
problems which generated an Evangelical Revival that created a concern for missions.

A direct result of the Evangelical Revival in England
and the rise of Protestant missions was the organization, in
1701, of the Society for the Propagation of the Gospel in
Foreign Parts (S.P.G.). The S.P.G. was particularly concerned with aiding the growth of the Church of England
among those who had broken ties with it through travel to
the colonies. The Anglican Church in the colonies was solely
dependent upon the Church of England to supply priests
and was directly supervised as an extension of it. Prior to
the organization of the S.P.G., priests in the colonies were
limited both in numbers and in spirit. The S.P.G. sent the
bulk of its missionaries to the colonies, where the Church
was the weakest. Since colonists were usually communicants, the S.P.G. focused upon the Indians and the Negroes.

The first systematic endeavor by the Anglicans to bring
the Negro within the "pale of Christianity" met with the
opposition of the planters. The enthusiasm of these mis-

sionaries was at first directed to the instruction of the adult slaves. The missionaries were stymied by the unwillingness of the planters to grant these adults the time and opportunity to learn. The African heritage of the adults and the few hours on Sunday allotted for their instruction brought about a dilemma: whether first to ground the slaves in the basic principles of reading and writing and then introduce them to the doctrines of the Church, or begin with the African background and fuse therewith the Anglican doctrines, invited wide speculation. In 1704, Elias Neau established a catechetical school in New York for slaves who "were without God in the world and of whose souls there was no manner of care taken," and also offered a bill to Parliament

for the more effectual conversion of the Negroes and other servants in the plantations, to compel owners of slaves to cause their children to be baptized within three months after their birth and to permit them, when come to years of discretion, to be instructed in the Christian religion on our Lord's Day by missionaries under whose ministry they live.[17]

As early as 1727, the Bishop of London addressed a letter to the planters urging them to cooperate in the endeavor to provide slaves with religious instruction.[18] It was the hope of the missionaries that they might be able to influence the cooperation of the planters through the legislation of Parliament and, failing that, through appeal to ecclesiastical authority, for they frankly recognized that they were being thwarted by the planters. Even without this opposition, there were far more slaves than they could reach. It was hoped that planters would bear a considerable amount of this responsibility by providing instructors as well as time for instruction.

Within their limitations, these missionaries were effective. On some of the plantations and in some of the congregations the slaves responded eagerly to the efforts of the missionaries, often providing half the communicants. By 1743 the S.P.G. was represented in every colony along the Atlantic seaboard.

Unfortunately, these missionaries left no records regarding the religious behavior of the converts. The S.P.G. had to face the barriers of inadequate personnel and time. Because of exploitation on the part of many planters, religious instruction was as nearly nominal as possible. For example, two slaves in North Carolina in 1723 were baptized upon recitation of "the Creed, the Lord's Prayer, the Ten Commandments," as well as giving "sureties for their fuller information." [19] Despite such evidence of basic understanding, it is not possible to discover to what extent these converts returned to their "heathen" ways or combined new religious beliefs and practices with old ones. The missionaries were conscious of the difficulties surrounding the conversion of adult slaves. As a result, the S.P.G. concentrated upon Negro children, but since the family ties were tenuous at best and often non-existent, the normal pattern of nurture in which those children might instruct *their* children was unable to take hold.

The constant admonitions of the Anglican priests to the masters reminding them of their duty to see that the slaves were instructed in the principles of the Christian religion bespeaks the limited extension of the S.P.G. Jonathan Boucher, an Anglican priest, clarified the situation in 1763: "It certainly is not a necessary circumstance essential to the condition of the slave that he be not indoctrinated; yet this is the general and almost universal lot of the slaves." [20]

Anglicans were the first Protestant missionaries to evangelize the Negro. For more than a quarter of a century only the S.P.G. worked among the slaves, largely concentrated in the colonies along the Eastern seaboard. Anglicans required their communicants to undergo a period of instruction prior to being baptized and admitted to communion. Thus a relatively small and select group, more often than not closely associated in the household of the white planters, became adherents. The special treatment given the household slaves, in religous and other areas, developed in them a sense of distinction from the field hands and out of this association there continued those comparatively few Negroes of the Episcopalian persuasion in evidence down to the present. But the field hands, considerably more numerous, were generally neglected. The few missionaries among them were most ineffective.

The S.P.G. worked within the framework of the institution of slavery. To the Negro, they represented a purely spiritual approach, one of religious enthusiasm. Jonathan Boucher set forth the missionary spirit motivating the Anglicans:

You may unfetter them from the chains of ignorance, you may emancipate them from the bondage of sin, the worst slavery to which they could be subjected; and by thus setting at liberty those that are bruised though they still continue to be your slaves, they shall be delivered from the bondage of corruption into the glorious liberty of the children of God.[21]

The combination of duty and fervor impressed those slave masters of the Anglican communion who were susceptible to religious sanction and made them feel more "secure than ever in the righteousness of the institution."[22] In addition, Anglicans required of their Negro communicants the following oath, which was not only a reminder to them of their state but also a declaration of intention to the planters:

You declare in the presence of God and before his congregation that you do not ask for the Holy Baptism out of any design to free yourself from the duty and obedience you owe to your masters while you live; but merely for the good of your soul and to partake of the grace and blessings promised to the members of the Church of Christ.[23]

While the Anglicans were stripping the Gospel of its radical teachings and providing the slaves with a devitalized version of their tradition, the patriarchal system of granting privileges such as religious instruction to the favorite few was taking shape as the order of the plantation way of life. This paternalistic environment provided a climate in which slaves and masters could often worship together, closely associated as they were in the daily routine of the household and unthreatened by the small number of slaves granted the benefits of the intimate life.

Simultaneously, the commercial and industrialized colonies of New England, Pennsylvania, New York, and New Jersey developed a more businesslike approach to slaves. They were responsible for given tasks, but did not come into close association with the masters and their families. Even on a limited basis, slaves were less well known, since they were not depended upon in the North on a one-to-one basis. On the other hand, there were a recognizable number of free Negroes in these colonies. Except for the labors of the S.P.G. and the Quakers, Negroes were widely ignored by the other religious communions.

The religious centers of these colonies were dominated by Congregational, Presbyterian, and Baptist Protestants of the Calvinistic wing. In 1726, the Evangelical Revival in Europe erupted in the Great Awakening in the colonies. The spirit was that of Calvinism. Calvinism has everywhere and always lacked interest in the common man, preferring to oppose the sins of excessiveness and sensuality rather than those of inequality and injustice.

The enthusiasm of the Great Awakening resulted in theological controversy spreading throughout the East, South, and West of the American colonies. The vast ma-

jority of these congregations began to grow by congregational splits and mergers and by expansion into new frontiers. Presbyterians established the first American Presbytery in 1706 and grew so rapidly following the Great Awakening in 1726, that by 1775 they had the largest number of
congregations (588) in the Continental United States. The
dominant Baptist center dates from 1707 with the Philadelphia Association. It grew in both numbers and autonomy.
With six churches in Massachusetts in 1740, Baptists could
claim ninety-two in 1790, and a similar expansion occurred
in Rhode Island, Maine, and western New York. These
Calvinistic revivalists were largely preoccupied with nega-
tives—opposing licentiousness, juvenile delinquency, sab-
bath-breaking and other moralities with enthusiasm.

Evident in the history of the Great Awakening was the
Protestant interest in enlisting everyone willing to accept
the particular point of view of the evangelicals. The Negro,
like other uncommitted persons, was considered worthy of
evangelization. In the North, where the Great Awakening
started, it was the free Negro who was largely reached.
These religious enthusiasts were so filled with purifying the
religion of individuals that they ignored the question of
slavery, viewing the Negro and his dilemma as an individual
problem rather than a national issue. Negroes were converted
and some joined local congregations, although the population as a whole was virtually untouched.

Methodism was born in the English revival. John Wesley, its leading light, came to America in 1736 as an Anglican
missionary to the Indians for the Society of the Propagation
of the Gospel. The first Methodist society was organized in
1739. Methodism was late in coming to the colonies, beginning its work in 1766. Like John Wesley, the circuit riders
of Methodism never worked out a social philosophy, preferring to expound a doctrine of conversion which was preached
with equal fervor among Negroes and whites.

By virtue of the Great Awakening, most of the Protestant forces grew and spread out. The one exception was Congregationalism, which confined its activity in large measure to the New England area. A number of Negroes were reached, but the situation of the Negro was of little concern.

Quakers and the Free Negro

Among the Protestant sects which developed from the English church and state conflict and Civil War, the Quakers were unique in combining religious conversion with social reformation. They hoped and worked for a complete egalitarian society based on Christian ideals. This spirit was carried to the colonies. Because of this, and their radical ways, they were faced with persecution and forced out of New England. Much has been made of the notion that Quakers went further than any other American religious group in the development of a sense of dignity in the Negro because of their identification at the point of suffering. Rather, the Quakers equated an emotionally experiential religion with a sense of social concern. Quakers refused to allow their dedication to spiritual renewal to dissipate in fixation upon the world to come. They believed in and labored for the Kingdom of God on earth. It is not that they proclaimed a different gospel from that of other Protestants. Quakers were more concerned that the Gospel be revealed through their deeds than their words. Thus, they tested the meaning of the Gospel, specifically the Sermon on the Mount, in their individual lives and in the larger society in which they were involved. Primarily composed of the dispossessed and disinherited dregs of society, the early Quakers from England needed and promoted social reforms for

themselves and for others. New Testament piety and radicalism were Quaker contributions to the Negro and the colonies as a whole.

By the time the Great Awakening was well underway,
Quakers were economically sound and generally middle
class. But prior to the Revolutionary War they were in the
front ranks, not only of religious persons but of all colonists,
in the work among slaves. In 1743, John Woolman, of
Mount Holly, New Jersey, was beginning his effective work
in opposition to slavery which resulted in his gaining supporters in the middle colonies. By 1750, Quakers were providing numerous classes in basic skills for Negroes. While
the other Protestant communions were involved in theological controversies and denominational expansion, Quakers
had shifted from opposing the importation of slaves to the
opposition of the institution of slavery. This was as early as
1758. In 1775, Quakers organized the first manumission society, which provided the stimulus for other anti-slavery
movements, abolition, and the Underground Railroad.

There are several reasons why the Quakers did not attract large numbers of Negroes to their unique witness in
New Testament experiential piety and social radicalism.
Quakers were concentrated in the North where they worked
to provide the Negro with freedom and the means to make
his own way in the social and economic structures as they
had done. They believed that the Negro could move ahead,
unmindful of the impenetrable color barrier which differen-
tiated the Negro from the ordinary group of white persons.
In contrast to every other religious communion in America,
Quakers were the first, and remain the only, fellowship which
has consciously faced and dismissed racial consciousness—
but precisely because the other communions have failed to
do so, the Quaker record has been overlooked. The great
surge of Negroes to the North followed the Revolutionary
War. Quakers lost their dynamic during the War, largely

because they refused to participate in it. In the immediate aftermath of the Revolutionary War, they were at work with the Negro, but after they initiated the abolition movement, it was taken over by other groups. Quakers rapidly rose in the socio-economic sphere and lost their commitment to social radicalism, "although they remained widely influential as a creative minority devoted to social reform and humanitarian service." [24] Significantly, Quakers were not a part of the late eighteenth-century Protestant "counteroffensive to combat the forces of irreligion and to fashion a Protestant America." [25] The fervor of this offensive extended to the South as well as the North and West and pulled the Negro into this religious orientation.

The contribution which the Quakers made to the religion of the Negro was no less profound, if not so numerically spectacular. With the creation of the first manumission society, the Quakers provided the nucleus for the anti-slavery groups. These groups contributed significantly to the orientation and growth of the free Negro population. Colonists were sparked by the Quakers to see the inconsistency of their drive for independence from England and perpetuation of the Negro in bondage. The French philosophy of revolution, the Declaration of Independence, and the host of other provocative ideas in vogue provoked the emancipation of Negroes during this period.

The Quakers were in close touch with these free ideas and movements. At the same time, they were training the free Negro for employment and exposing him to the spirit of liberty, justice, and equality. The revolutionary philosophy continued for a few years following the War and the anti-slavery groups made capital of this spirit to free the Negro in the North.

The doctrine of natural rights was in the air. As the Quakers worked persistently with the free Negro in the North, the evangelicals were concentrating on the slaves in the South. Methodists and Baptists in particular were vehement against slavery during those first years following the Revolutionary War. They mixed the natural rights doctrine with the revival movement and the combination made a real impact upon the slaves. The 1780 Conference of Methodism opposed slavery and in 1789 the Baptist association of Virginia went on record denouncing the institution of slavery as directly opposed to the doctrine of natural rights. That doctrine and the revivalist spirit were born of enthusiasm and not rooted in the social implications of the Gospel. With the rise of the Cotton Kingdom and the demand for slaves following 1815, evangelicals were able to dismiss their radical beginnings and concentrate upon the regeneration of society through the regeneration of each individual.

Independent Negro Congregations

The spirit of abolition and the work of the Underground Railroad substantially increased the number of Negroes in the North. Many of these were Baptists and Methodists who took seriously the anti-slavery preachments of the white evangelicals. In the North they were joined with the free Negro who had been educated by groups such as the Quakers in the fundamentals of freedom and education. These better-educated Negroes became the natural leaders of the free Negroes.

Free Negroes were able to worship with their white brethren in the North as long as they were few in number. With the waves of Negroes migrating to the North and gravitating to the Baptist and Methodist churches of their persuasion, tension rapidly developed in the northern congregations. Northern whites were used to the exceptional

Negro, or to a cluster of a few Negroes, but a mass of Negroes caused them to react with the same prejudice as their brothers to the South. Northern white Protestants must be included from the first among those who "accepted the dogma of Negro inferiority and without compunction refused ecclesiastical equality to this race." [26] For it was among the free white and Negro Protestants in the North, the latter being emancipated during the American Revolution, that the independent Negro congregations based on race erupted.[27]

Richard Allen, who was born a slave in Philadelphia, was inspired by the movement for freedom. Along with his brother, he purchased his freedom in 1777 from a master who was receptive to the freedom movement, and in the same year he was converted by Methodist preachers. Three years later Allen was preaching. His talents as a preacher came to the attention of Bishop Asbury, who gave him assignments and allowed him to travel with white ministers.

In 1786, Allen began to preach frequently at the St. George Methodist Church in Philadelphia. When the Negroes increased in attendance the officials of St. George Church decided to segregate them by removing Negroes from the seats along the wall to the gallery. The die was cast when, on one occasion, Negroes mistakenly occupied that part of the gallery reserved for white Methodists. Allen, Absalom Jones and William White were dragged from their knees as they prayed by the white officials. They left the church and together with other Negro members formed the Free African Society.[28]

The Free African Society was not a religious organization, but a means for the expression of freedom and protest. One of the first concerns was the denouncement of slavery.[29] But it became the major vehicle for deciding where and how Negroes should worship. Allen believed that Negroes should form a separate congregation based on race, but re-

lated to the Methodist Church. Absalom Jones believed
that the Methodist Church did not welcome Negroes and so
he organized the St. Thomas African Protestant Episcopal
Church, and became the P.E.C.'s first Negro priest.

Allen founded the Bethel Church in Philadelphia, which
was dedicated in 1794. There was some agitation in Methodism over the separation of Negroes into separate congregations, and after an extended period of discussion, Bishop
Asbury ordained Allen a deacon in 1799. He was later ele-
vated to the status of an elder. By this time Allen and his
congregation were not satisfied with their relationship to
Methodism and decided upon a separate organization, based
on race, but patterned after the Methodist Church. As a
mark of this, Allen's congregation became known as the
Bethel African Methodist Episcopal Church.

In New York City, a secession of Negro Methodists
from the John Street Methodist Church was provoked by the
unwillingness of this congregation to accept Negroes in any
sizable number. Like their brethren in Philadelphia they
were unwilling to nurture Negro leadership and work out an
arrangement with a Negro assistant or co-pastor. Unwilling
to provide a Negro pastor or let the Negroes go altogether,
members of the John Street Church permitted Negroes to
have a building of their own. They later requested the privilege of a Negro pastor. When these arrangements did not
work out they withdrew from the white Methodist Church
and the white organization to form still another Negro Methodist body, the African Methodist Episcopal Zion Church.
Leaders in this movement were James Varick, George Col-
lins, and Christopher Rush. They were not as fortunate as
the newly created Philadelphia splinter group. No one in
either the Methodist or Episcopal Churches of New York
would ordain these leaders as elders, making it necessary
for them to do it themselves.[30]

The resistance to Negro leadership in the organizational

system of the Methodists in the North prevented the full incorporation of Negroes, but the system also allowed for an early separate organization of Negro churches. Lacking this system, Negro Baptists in the North were slow to assert their independence from white churches. In the South, where the white Baptists were less well organized than their brethren in the North, and were equally outside the Protestant movement and educational interests, the evangelicals were converting Negroes en masse. These evangelicals were farmers and laborers without concern for organization. In some of the cities, Negro Baptists became evangelists and started their own churches which sprung up during the Revolutionary War. George Liele founded a Baptist church in Savannah in 1779. Negro converts organized the Harrison Street Baptist Church in Petersburg, Virginia, in 1776. The African Baptist Church of Lexington, Kentucky was established in 1790.[31]

The events of the South during the decades prior to the Civil War prevented the Baptist churches from spreading as the Negro Methodist Churches in the North were free to do. Decentralized Baptist congregations usually associated with the white Baptist congregations and were thus unable to pull together for the improvement of the Negro in the area of religion.

Presbyterians, Episcopalians, and Congregationalists depended upon an educated ministry, and this emphasis limited their appeal to Negroes. In this way they were also able to curtail independent Negro organizations, though they developed separated Negro congregations. Presbyterians were more receptive to the Negroes than were Episcopalians, but like the Congregationalists they were concentrated in areas where Negroes were few and far between. Episcopalians were the large slaveholders along the Atlantic coast and their attitude toward the Negro is seen in their unwillingness to allow the single Negro Church, St. Thomas in Philadelphia, to participate in the deliberations of the Protestant Episcopal Convention:

In the year 1795 they declared it was only for the present. The same position, however, was taken in 1843 and it was adhered to throughout the period of slavery; for the Episcopal Church persistently refused to make slavery a matter of discipline.[32]

When Peter Williams, a Negro priest, became vocal on the question of abolition, the bishops silenced him "with a decree that he should preach merely the gospel without interfering with the political affairs of the times." [33]

The Presbyterian Church in the United States of America indicated its awareness of the slavery situation as early as 1774 in its General Assembly, but this question was deferred to the next meeting in 1780, and then no action was taken. The synod of 1787 stated that the "rights of human nature are too well understood to admit debate," and went on to commend the abolition of slavery to "all the churches and families under their care" as long as they were "consistent with the rights of civil society." Presbyterians first raised the question as to the moral evil of slavery in 1795, but the difference of opinion was such that those who wished to consider the problem were referred to the statement of 1787, since every "step which they deemed expedient or wise, to encourage emancipation, and to render the state of those who are in slavery as mild and tolerable as possible" had been taken by the General Assembly. The real concern of the Presbyterians was in the interest of harmony:

If Every difference of opinion were to keep men at a distance, they could subsist in no state of society, either civil or religious. The General Assembly would impress this upon the minds of their brethren, and urge them to follow peace, and the things that make for peace.[34]

Episcopalians were successful in keeping the few Negroes whom they attracted, for the most part household slaves, within the communion. Episcopalians were the first to engage Negroes in the area of religion, and some masters, like Bishop Polk, were exponents of the best in paternalism. Bishop Polk was also a spokesman of the most damaging error religion taught the Negro: the Good News "had little to do with the settlement of differences between the races in this world, since it was rather concerned with adjustment of affairs in the kingdom to come." [35]

Prior to the Revolutionary War, Congregationalists felt no urgency about opposing slavery. Conservative in politics and religion, Congregationalism remained provincial, middle-class, unable to sustain its missionary work even in the West where there was no "established and mercantile" society:

There it has found that type of educated middle class usually of New England origin, which feels at home in its atmosphere of highly respectable learning, doctrine, piety and ethics. Under the influence of this class alliance it has undergone changes through which most other churches of the bourgeoisie have passed. Its doctrine and its ethics have been accommodated to the culture, the needs and the interests of its clientele.[36]

The first response of Congregationalism to the Negro was through the independent, nonsectarian body known as the American Missionary Society, organized in 1846. By the time the Congregationalists, through the A.M.A., became interested in providing the Negroes in the South with education, the Negroes in the North had already been engaged in separate religious activities.

As a white institution, the church had declined as an effective institution among Negroes several decades before the Civil War. Negroes in the North had been indoctrinated with the ideas of freedom and equality and went about creating independent churches and organizations for this expression. Where these forces were thwarted, the result was a limited number of Negroes in white denominations, but even these were in separate congregations. Independent Negro congregations were a forced option, signal reminders that at the same time Christians in the North were vehement against slavery in the South, they showed an unwillingness to face and root out segregation at their door step.

Second Great Awakening: Baptists and Methodists

The second major revival in America began in 1800. With this religious movement Protestants were fashioning a Protestant America. The vitality which flowed found expression in various Protestant voluntary societies concerned with overseas missions, charities, and slavery, as well as personal conversion. The second Great Awakening was extremely moralistic in its approach to the problems it attempted to eradicate, lacking any real ethical dimension. Slavery had been abolished in the North and the movement to the frontiers of the West was underway. Baptists and Methodists grew by leaps and bounds in every section, especially the Southwest, which by 1815 was increasing the importation of slaves to support the Cotton Kingdom. In this area Baptist and Methodist evangelicals were ahead of all other Protestants in their religious impact, specifically upon the Negroes. Abolition, the Underground Railroad, and the appeal to freedom were of no interest to these Southern missionaries.

The momentum of the Great Awakening carried Baptists into the South and extended the work of Methodists. The evangelical mood was slow in reaching the Baptists but it continued longest with them. It was the intense fervor of an unrestrained emotionalism that continued among Baptists and Methodists long after the Protestant middle-class communions were concerned with national issues.

Proselytizing Methodists and Baptists gathered in the poor and ignorant white farmers en masse. The key to their success was the rise of circuit riders and farm-preachers who sprung up among the people. The major Protestant communions, particularly in their northern wings, demanded a trained ministry. With the movement to the frontiers there were an insufficient number of educated ministers to meet the situation. Baptists and Methodists were less concerned about the integration of the people into the life of the Christian faith than with the personal purification of individuals and the enlargement of piety.

Along the old frontier of the South where the Episcopalians were well established, the Baptists and Methodists promoted disestablishment. These enthusiasts were in keen competition. As the nineteenth century progressed, they drew into their respective circles more and more overseers who were left in control of the slaves by absentee plantation owners. The latter often instructed their overseers to allow their slaves to participate in the religous exercises. This contact with the overseers, and sometimes with the planters, provided the circuit riders and farmer-preachers with an open door to the slaves. Overseers and planters alike were receptive to the

. . . point of view articulated by Bishop McKendree when he said that "God's design in raising up the preachers called Methodists in America was to reform the continent by spreading Scriptural holiness over the land." A Christian society was not one of "wholesome laws" designed to conform to the overruling government of God but a nation blessed by the harmony of converted individuals.[37]

After 1820, the dependence upon slavery in the Cotton Kingdom was a fact accepted by these missionaries. The revival work among the slaves was not in opposition to the institution of slavery. Baptists quickly won the encouragement of the slave masters by proving that religious meetings made the slaves more slavish; they were unexcelled in their work among the slaves in the fields. This great mass of Negroes had not been reached by the Protestant coalition—Episcopalians, Congregationalists, and Presbyterians. Methodists were concerned with the redemptive love of God.[38] Somehow they were able to manipulate this love of God and the Wesleyan view that American slavery was "the vilest that ever saw the sun," [39] so that total acceptance of slavery and the endeavor to make the best possible slave became a hallmark among these southern Methodists. William Capers, later bishop, Superintendent of Negro Missions in South Carolina was a representative spirit:

So successful was the work of the Methodist Church under Mr. Capers, that soon Hon. Charles C. Pickney, one of the leading planters of South Carolina, and a very prominent political leader of his day, came to Mr. Capers and asked that a Methodist exhorter be appointed to his plantation, although Pickney was himself an Episcopalian. The matter was referred by Mr. Capers to the presiding Methodist Bishop and to the Annual Conference and as such a missionary was appointed. Before long other Episcopalians made such requests.[40]

The approach of these religious workers among the slaves emphasized revivalistic enthusiasm. These protracted meetings were repeated week after week, laying a permanent foundation for the religious expectation of the great bulk of Negroes. The meetings, based on emotion, were not different for the white dirt farmer, although the impact was decidedly different over the years. Slaves laboring in the fields were not instructed in the fundamentals of the Christian faith, for the farmer-preachers understood and embedded in the field hands the ideal of religion as frenzy. The religious experience of these Negroes was marked by the absence of instruction. Often their initial religious impressions were formed in "some camp meeting during a special effort in behalf of the lost." Slaves looked forward to these "big times" with a great deal of anticipation and these camp meetings were often as social and festive as they were religious.

Baptists made a real contribution to the dull and monotonous life of the Negro. By tying religion to festivity and encouraging Negroes to test their purity by the intensity of their feelings, they promised salvation. Undoubtedly, the white evangelicals enjoyed the performances of the Negroes. The emotions were whipped so high that they

. . . had a sort of hypnotizing effect upon the Negroes, causing them to be seized with certain emotional jerks and outward expressions of an inward movement of spirit which made them lose control of themselves.[41]

There was an excitement in these protracted meetings which the white evangelicals were not able to produce among the poor and ignorant whites.

In their more sober moments, white missionaries were able to drive home the central message they repeated to the slaves. Moral purity and humility were taught as if they were the only teachings of Jesus. Instead of the Christian faith, they emphasized the moral depth of Christianity. Christianity was equated with honesty, charity, obedience, industry, truthfulness, and kindness. Under the discipline of missionaries, slaves were kept busy in the evenings with these drills in the moralities of a substandard religion. Ethical issues were not raised. Moreover, salvation was misconstrued as depending upon the faithful following of morality codes. These religious teachings and services of selected scriptural memorization and recitation, and of prayers and lessons in etiquette drawn from the Bible, provided a most effective means of control. Negroes were provided with no means by which to judge the validity of these teachings. The constancy of this oral recital became the permanent understanding of religion for the masses of Negroes. At the same time these revivalists were indoctrinating Negroes, the movement for abolition was underway and Negroes in the North had begun to organize separate congregations based on race. The Negroes who slipped through the Underground Railroad carried this view of religion with them, swelling the churches of the North. At the same time these churches were being cut off from the historical and theological dimensions of the Protestant bodies they structurally imitated.

The vicious circle of the slave's finding freedom of expression in religion and seeking freedom of expression in society were not mutually supportive. Either way, freedom in any full measure was denied the Negro.

The paternalism of the evangelicals and the established communions were one in denying the Negro access to the Christian understanding of freedom and equality. While there is no evidence that the Protestant coalition would have done a thorough job of integrating the Negro into the mainstream of the Christian faith, there is evidence that the Baptist sect was as responsible as any other religious body for the defection of Negroes from the solid approach of the churches. Baptists, along with the Methodists, not only prevented the other communions from gaining a hold upon Negroes after 1820 and completely sabatoged their endeavors, they granted Negroes a literal license to turn religion into a social concern supported by intense feeling.

Baptists encouraged Negroes to become exhorters, or preachers, and few plantations were without them. Slaves who had been ripped from their native environs, family, and friends responded with fervor to the fiery messages preached by the black exhorters who had learned well from the white evangelists. Under the supervision of white missionaries and evangelists there developed a good many Negro Baptist exhorters who provided a simple bond of unity around a new way of life. But often, as well, these black exhorters were of such great conviction and emotional power that they were welcome among the whites of the community. The only criterion for a Negro Baptist preacher was his feeling of an inner call and evidence of his ability to preach. In this way, Baptists provided Negroes with an opportunity for leadership which was of some importance in a way not expected, as we shall see, by the whites:

God hath done great things for them, and their owners begin to discover that their slaves are of increasing value to them when they become religious. I am very very fond of teaching them; have preached to 300 of them at a time and not one white present but myself. They sing delightfuly, and those who are truly religious, in general far exceed the whites in love to each other and in most other duties. Many of them can read and are remarkably fond of hymns. We have several in our church who go to the plantations and preach to their own color on Lord's day evenings, and at other times when we have no service in this meeting house.[42]

Despite this paternalistic witness and the apparent fraternalism of the Negro, it became increasingly clear that the Negro exhorter was about more than mere emotional release:

When, however, these Negroes of unusual power preached with such force as to excite not only the blacks but the whites, steps were generally taken to silence these speakers heralding the coming of a new day. This opposition of the whites apparently grew more strenuous upon the attainment of independence.[43]

The Negroes enjoyed their religion, and they also used it for the achievement of an end which was more important to them than their masters surmised.

Independent Negro Organizations

While the white evangelicals were entertaining the slaves in the South and keeping them happy, their white counterparts in the North were excluding from their fellowships the free Negro and those who were escaping the bonds of slavery. In response to this segregating paternalism, the better educated Negroes in the North developed segregated organizations.

As has been pointed out, Negroes began with separate congregations. With the example of Richard Allen and the Bethel African Methodist Episcopal Church in Philadelphia, the movement for independent Negro congregations spread to Wilmington, Baltimore, Pittsburgh, Charleston and various communities in Pennsylvania and New Jersey. These churches were of sufficient strength to organize into an independent body. A conference was called in Philadelphia in 1816, and as a result Allen was elected bishop after the resignation of Daniel Coker. Patterning their discipline after the white Methodists, the African Methodist Episcopal Church grew into the leading body among Negro Methodists. There were 4,000 A.M.E. members in Philadelphia in 1820 and some 2,000 in Baltimore. Along with being a religious organization, the movement spread as an exponent of abolition. For this reason its spread in the South was stopped, because of the threats of insurrections in which Methodists were implicated. The African Methodist Episcopal Zion Church, which developed out of New York, developed into an independent organization and elected its first bishop in 1822. There were a small number of Negro congregations which remained in the fold of the white Methodist Episcopal Church in the North, when the split occurred over slavery in 1844. Following the Civil War, the Methodist Episcopal Church South excused its small body of Negro members to create a third Negro body. In 1870, the Colored Methodist Episcopal Church was organized in Jackson, Tennessee.

Negro Baptists were slower in developing a structure due to the local autonomy of each congregation. But the same socio-economic forces which separated white and black Methodists separated their Baptist counterparts. The First Baptist Church in Philadelphia included in its membership thirteen Negroes who were dissatisfied with their treatment in this congregation. In May of 1809 they petitioned the officials of the Church to permit them to worship separately and in June they were allowed to do so within the First Baptist Church. In this same year they formed the African Baptist Church, led by a Mr. Burrows.[44] Negro Baptists in Boston organized their congregation in 1809, at about the same time that the Abyssinian Baptist Church was being organized in New York City. In every case, Negro Baptists grew out of white congregations. The Baptist churches were among the first separate organizations set up by the free Negroes of the North and fugitives from the South.

When the Negroes were cut off from the white Baptists, they developed into associations. The rise of the Negro Baptists was rapid until it became clear that this would lead to total separation of Negro and white Baptist institutions and congregations unless a conscious effort was made at cooperation. One example of this was in the area of church school literature. White Baptists did not feel that Negroes were ready to enter into a cooperative arrangement. When

Negroes requested the opportunity for literary expression, white Baptists responded, in effect,

. . . that they look forward with the most pleasant anticipation to the day when the Negroes would be prepared to enjoy the good things for which they clamored, but that the time for the Negroes to dispense with the leadership of the whites had not come. Many years of education and social uplift were still necessary before the Negroes could successfully set out to do for themselves.[45]

If there was some truth in this position of the white Baptists, there was no help in it. Both groups were rapidly growing and the new sense of power in each overruled any compromise. Negroes were refused the opportunity to participate in the management of the Northern Baptist Home Mission Society. After some heated discussion the Society agreed to accept contributions from Negroes and then decided against it on protest from the southern churchmen:

The issue was then joined. The National Baptist Convention, a union of the Negro Baptists, was effected in 1886, and as the struggle grew more intense every effort was made so to extend it as to destroy the influence of white national bodies among Negroes.[46]

In 1865, Negro members of the white Primitive Baptist Churches of the South separated into the Colored Primitive Baptists in America.

The last movement for a racially separate religious affiliation was among the Presbyterians, after the Civil War. In 1869 and 1870, Negro ministers of the Cumberland Presbyterian Church moved to establish separate presbyteries and synods, which was encouraged by the General Assembly. In 1883, the Negro branch sought reunification, but it was denied.

This independent drive among Negroes in religion fell
short of Black Nationalism, which they vigorously opposed
along with the movement for the colonization of free
Negroes. The leaders of these independent drives were reflecting the freedom and pride newly emerging in the Negro.
They were not conscious of creating institutions based only
on race, a kind of Black Nationalism in the area of religion
of inestimable value during the centuries of transition. These
Negro movements produced the missionary Negroes from
the North, who, as black liberators and abolitionists, carried
the Good News of freedom to the brethren in bondage.

The Invisible Institution

Missionaries from the independent Negro congregations
in the North were as deeply influenced by the abolitionists
as they were by the religionists. Not only were the Negro
free men the first to carry the message of freedom to their
fellows still in bondage, but delivered though it was in the
form of religion, it reflected the philosophy of revolution
and the doctrine of natural rights. In fact, the religious congregations in the towns and the fellowships in the fields were
the home base for Negro liberators, who not only preached
freedom but provoked insurrections. They were as much
representatives of the fifty-odd anti-slavery societies created
by Negroes as they were representatives of religion. It is
certain that they were aware of religion as the key to
making contact with their brethren in slavery. While the
white man was using religion to keep the slaves content,
Negroes were using these meetings to sow discontent and
provide the means of revolt and escape. The effectiveness
of the ideas spread by the free Negro is clear in the insur-

rections led by slaves and free rebels and the response of the white planters.

In 1800, a slave known as Gabriel Prosser planned a revolt in Richmond, Virginia, which was betrayed by two slaves. He used the Bible to describe how they could assume the posture of the Israelites and discharge the bonds of slavery with the aid and comfort of God. Such Old Testament passages were strange to the ears of the slaves and the twist he gave to the usual message of obedience was so shocking that his listeners did not allow the plan to get underway. Little information is available concerning Gabriel Prosser, but his plan had apparently involved a large number of Negroes whom he refused to implicate after being captured.

Denmark Vesey led a celebrated uprising in Charleston, South Carolina, in 1822. A free Negro who worked as a carpenter in Charleston, Vesey gained the confidence of slaves and free Negroes. He was familiar with the successful conspiracy in Haiti in 1790 which he apparently used to motivate the slaves of Charleston to action upon every opportunity. A "faithful" household slave who was involved betrayed the uprising which also concerned members of the Negro Methodist Church. Thirty-five slaves were hanged and about thirty-seven were transferred outside the United States before the authorities completed their investigation and action.

Perhaps the most familiar insurrectionist was Nat Turner, who led a bloody revolt at Southhampton County, Virginia in 1831. This was the most far-reaching, if least well-planned, of the insurrections inspired by Negroes. Nat Turner was a Baptist exhorter and a mystic who discovered in the Bible the way out of bondage. Instead of making plans, he spent the months prior to the uprising in prayer and Bible-reading. Thus, with a small band, he began an assault upon whites by murdering those in the household of his master, then roamed the countryside killing whites.

Some fifty-five whites were killed before these slaves were suppressed by the militia and Turner was hanged with sixteen of his followers.

Prior to these events, religion among the slaves had been welcome; even the Negro evangelists had been given an opportunity to work among their fellows. There had grown up "the invisible institution" of the Negro church. The "invisible institution" was most effective where slaves were isolated from whites on the large plantations. The licensing of Negroes to preach, most often by the Baptists, was a recognition of how close these exhorters were to the people. But between 1830 and 1835 the fear of insurrection from these Negro-led meetings of inspiration became so widespread that most states outlawed Negro meetings not presided over by some white person or a "trusted" Negro:

In 1833, Alabama made it unlawful for slaves or free Negroes to preach unless before five respectable slaveholders and when authorized by some neighboring religious society. Georgia enacted a law in 1834 providing that neither free Negroes nor slaves might preach or exhort an assembly of more than seven unless licensed by justices on the certificates of three ordained ministers. Other Southern States soon followed the example of these, passing more drastic laws prohibiting the assembly of Negroes after the early hours of the night, and providing for the expulsion of all free Negroes from such commonwealths, so as to reduce the danger of mischief and the spread of information by this more enlightened class.[47]

As a result Negroes were coerced to attend the religious services of their masters. Thus the boast that many Negroes and whites got along famously in worship is placed in perspective. Usually the slaves were seated together in a special section or in the gallery. Among the earliest practices of the segregation of the Negro in America are these concerned with worship. An extreme case is that of the ingenious congregation which erected a partition several feet high to separate the slaves from their masters. By this time the "invisible institution" was well underground.

It is difficult to recapture the compulsory and segregated situation in worship, or its effects on the slave, but the following report of a scene in South Carolina was made by an eyewitness:

I think there is quite as large a portion of the negroes in the churches generally, as the whites, particularly of the Baptist and Methodist denominations—not so many in the Presbyterian. About one-fourth of the members in the churches are negroes. In the years 1832, '3 and '4 great numbers of negroes joined the churches during a period of revival. Many, I am sorry to say, have since been excommunicated. As the general zeal in religion declined, they blackslid. Our churches are furnished with galleries, or portions are set apart for the accommodation of the negroes. They pay good attention, and preserve order. There are a few licensed preachers among them of the Baptist and Methodist order. It has been thought they do some good. They hold meetings only by permission, and not frequently.[48]

Another report reveals more fully the paternalistic encouragement which the slave early received and the background which led to the Negro minister's becoming the white man's contact for control in the period following Reconstruction:

There are 4,212 negroes in the District of the county in which I reside and labour. Upon a rough estimate 1,000 of them are members of the different churches: say 350 to the congregational church: 550 to the Baptist—and 100 to the Presbyterian and Methodist. There is one Presbyterian minister who devotes the whole of his time—and one Baptist minister who devotes the half of his time to the religious instruction of these people. There is one coloured minister connected with and under the supervision and control of the Congregational Church, who preaches to the coloured congregation of that church between morning and afternoon services in the white Church, when the white missionary is not present: he performs marriages—attends funerals, etc., but administers no ordinances, this is always done by our white ministers. He also visits as he is able, and receives permission, the different plantations, and holds prayer-meetings with the people and attends to their spiritual affairs. There are coloured watchmen, regularly appointed in both the congregational and Baptist churches. Their duties are expressed by their name. They conduct plantation prayers in the evening where they reside, in connection with prominent members of the Church, of their own colour, and on other plantations when invited and permitted. They exhort the people: give instruction to inquirers— assist members in their Christian walk—warn and reprove, and report cases of delinquency. They are appointed by and are amenable to the white churches. We have no coloured churches independent of the whites. Such organizations we do not deem expedient.[49]

Negro Spirituals

Negro spirituals represent the spirit of the "invisible institution," a spirit born of aspiration but not of faith. Spirituals lie outside the Christian faith precisely because they were expressions of fervor, even religious fervor, related to situations of struggle which ended in 1890.

The complexities which made religious and social intercourse between Negro and white communions impossible increased following the periods of the Civil War and Reconstruction. It has been argued that, given the independent movement of the Negro in religion, there is no reason why he could not have developed an independent theology, the most likely source being the spirituals. But while, in a deep sense, spirituals were songs of great belief, perhaps of hope, they were neither songs of faith, nor songs of a growing body of critical theology. The dignity, beauty, insight, and classic quality of the spirituals as the creative contribution of the Negro to the world is a matter of record. They are most significant when placed against the background of insurrections, protracted camp meetings, religious festivities, moral exhortations, and the urge for freedom planted by the free Negro. Indeed, the Biblical literalism and abundance of moralities taught the slave made a profound impact and led to a spontaneity of surprising power.

As an expression of religion, rather than of faith, some Negro spirituals were songs of protest, in acceptable and thinly veiled form, against the conditions of this life. As such, they were songs of defiance, revolt, and escape. On this level, the rhythm and messages of these spirited songs aided slaves to be religiously or psychologically supported in their feats of courage—to be tenacious, resolute, and militant. In the present era of massive protests, Negroes have returned to spirituals, not as songs of faith but as sources of spirited support. This is natural since in times of distress and trouble it is a human tendency to fall back upon the past. Freedom rides, sit-ins, and jailhouses rather than formal worship are the context in which spirituals are helpful—a context close to that of the slave heritage. Negro spirituals are used as mood music for retreats, are the source of jazz, and are occasionally used in the setting of an anthem. The religious relevance of spirituals as songs of protest or feeling, rather than as creedal affirmations, identifies these works as expressions of religion and not of faith.

Where they are not used for inspiration, Negro spirituals are generally valued as works of art. The rhythm is African; the text of the majority of spirituals is an adaptation of the King James Version of the Bible. The earliest spirituals followed the leading lines and response of African songs cast in a religious setting.[50] Just as religious meetings were used by Negroes for purposes other than worship, so the spirituals projected beyond the entertainment interests of the white people who loved to hear "those darkies singing." Not all spirituals were concerned about the things of the "spirit," though they were concerned with all things spirited.

In addition to the African rhythms as a mode of expression, there are four fundamental elements without which Negro spirituals are not fully appreciated. These four elements are the cataloging of historical events, the various forms of protest, the individual and personal reflections, and the worshipful expressions. These elements are significant for the understanding of why many Negroes who found their life in religious communions independent of the mainstream of Protestantism were unable to hammer out an independent body of beliefs from the teachings codified in the Negro spirituals.

A historical perspective gives the best setting for the interpretation of spirituals. African music was the thread connecting the history of these people. With their gift of song, Africans were torn from their native ties and set down in the colonies. The first extended collection of songs by slaves was promoted as an authentic document of the Negro people.[51]

Negro spirituals are the creation of the slave field hands, the masses, who were also the "invisible institution." After the insurrections of the 1820's, which led the white masters to abandon the widely held view that "true religion makes good masters and good slaves," Negro worship was proscribed and monitored. At the same time that whites used worship to indoctrinate the Negro with moralities, to keep him busy, to keep tabs on him, and to snuff out uprisings, the Negro was using religion as a "front" for surreptitious activities. In the cool of the evening, Negro spirituals served the purposes of the white man as well as his slaves. Hearing

the religious words against haunting African rhythms, overseers and masters knew that slaves were both "faithful" and
contented fools. Aware of the white man's credulity at the
point of religion, slaves lulled them to sleep while their
brethren were beating their way to freedom; sometimes to
the freedom of the next world, more often to the freedom of
this world.

It is widely known that camp meetings and revivals,
prior to the insurrections, provided occasions for Negroes to
gather en masse to hear the "word," at times of God, but
usually of man. This setting provided unusual opportunities
to risk escape, but those who failed to participate were in
an even more dangerous predicament:

> Sinner, please don't let this harvest pass;
> Sinner, please don't let this harvest pass, harvest pass;
> Sinner, please don't let this harvest pass,
> And die and lose your soul at last.[52]

Spirituals were used to call secret meetings at midnight
and at the break of dawn:

> Let us praise Gawd together on our knees.
> Let us praise Gawd together on our knees.
> Let us praise Gawd together on our knees.
> When Ah falls on mah knees
> Wid mah face to de risin' sun;
> Oh, Lawd, hab mercy on me.

The African colonization movement, to relocate Negroes outside the United States, was widely supported by
many white Protestants and denounced by such outstanding
Negro spokesmen as Frederick Douglass, Sojourner Truth,
Harriet Tubman, and Richard Allen. However, the idea got
through to enough slaves to develop a sense of expectation
about the camp ground across the waters:

> Deep River, my home is over Jordan, Deep River,
> Lord, I want to cross over into camp ground;
> Lord, I want to cross over into camp ground;
> Lord, I want to cross over into camp ground.

Bishop Francis Asbury of the Methodist Episcopal Church North was instrumental in the late eighteenth-century declarations by Methodists against slavery, later revoked. In what he called the "Egypt" of South Carolina, Bishop Asbury lost his health in behalf of the Negroes for whom he was Moses:

> Go down, Moses
> Way down in Egypt Land,
> Tell ole Pharoh
> Let my people go.

The tumultous days following the Nat Turner insurrection were extremely difficult ones for the slaves. This was the period when Negroes were no longer permitted to be inspired by black exhorters without the most scrutinizing supervision:

> Oh what a mournin',
> Oh what a mournin'
> Oh what a mournin'
> When de stars begin to fall.

Reconstruction days brought about tremendous changes in the life of the Freedmen, full of uncertainties:

> Nobody knows de trouble I've had,
> Nobody knows but Jesus,
> Nobody knows de trouble I've had.
> Glory hallelu! [53]

From this historical point of view, Negro spirituals are records of meaningful events in the lives of the slaves. These events were not seen as the mighty acts of God; they were the record of situations which were the result of human affliction and response—not the judgment of God upon an unfaithful people. Thus, as "secular" history, these events represented a past which the Freedmen were trying to out-live. While it is true that many of these spirituals could be used in worship, they were not so used following the 1890's. In the late nineteenth century and throughout the twentieth Negro spirituals were without meaning and relevance, nor did they inspire faith for the independent Negro Protestants who were the direct descendants and heirs of the field hands who produced them.

If the historical element in the spirituals did not provide a basis for a growing and dynamic faith, the protest element was of even less moment for the participants in the strictly Negro congregations following the turn of the twentieth century.

Negroes were conscious of being excluded from the churches of their white teachers in the North and in the South:

> When I get to Heaven goin' to sing and shout,
> Nobody there for to turn me out.

In order to meet the Underground Railroad and escape the cruelty of the overseers, Negroes found it advantageous to

> Steal away, steal away,
> Steal away to Jesus,
> Steal away, steal away home,
> I hain't got long to stay here.

Canaan for Negroes seeking refuge was the North,

> O Canaan, sweet Canaan,
> I am bound for the land of Canaan,

the promised land:

> I am bound for the promised land;
> I am bound for the promised land;
> O who will come and go with me?
> I am bound for the promised land.[54]

It is difficult to express, much less develop, a faith out of protests which are essentially negations rather than affirmations, one reason why Negroes have never been able to set forth theological tenets based on their quasi-religious experience. The protest of spirituals was meant to provide escape from desperate circumstances. The god whom the missionaries revealed was not interested in freedom and equality, as was the God of the Negro preachers. Rather than to God, slaves looked for relief of their burdens to their fellow Negro leaders, who were influenced by such shining examples in the darkness as John Woolman and the abolitionists.

On a close reading of the spirituals, one is impressed with their deeply private and often individualistic utterances, the common thread running through all of them. Indeed, a spiritual has been defined as the expression of a single Negro concerning his experience "that had universal application at whatever time that song was popular." [55]

Spirituals are of real vitality only for the individual and group experiencing the trial by fire out of which they were forged. As songs of faith, spirituals have no universal appeal —they are powerless to evoke an affirmation of faith in the faithful. Their power to evoke deep feeling depends upon the ability of the artist to draw the listener within his frame of reference or that of the singers to simulate the situation of oppression. Their vigor comes primarily from the African rhythm and only minimally from the beautiful English of the King James Version of the Bible.

Perhaps the singular factor preventing spirituals from developing as a body of faith was their religious context. The usual claim is that Negroes "took complete refuge in Christianity" and that the Negro spirituals are the searing evidences of this "religious fervor." If Christianity is defined as "the religion of compensations in the life to come from the ills suffered in the present existence," [56] or as the religion which implies the "hope that in the next world there would be a reversal of conditions," then the Negro really was besieged with religion in the name of a modified Christianity. For, to my mind, the doctrine of rewards and punishments is not basic to the Christian faith; at most it is incidental. The Christian faith does not, and did not, rise and fall with compensations, though this be the persuader used by sincerely religious people who are also Christians.

We have seen that the Negro did not seek the religion of Christians. He was beset by and nearly coerced into the religion of white Protestant missionaries, who, incidentally, did not represent the best in their tradition as it was expressed in their time. Despised, deprived, dehumanized, and deceived, the slave responded to what was interpreted as Christianity as to a diversion, a channel for the release of bis repressed desires.

The missionaries, however, were convinced that Christianity is a "religion of compensations in the life to come," and they knew what they were about in withholding from the slaves the great demands of the Christian faith, demands which the white ambassadors of Christ and of the slave masters were able to ignore. The missionaries and the evangelists interpreted the Gospel to fit the situation as they chose to perceive it. This "comedy of errors" was so repetitive and impressive that it led Negroes to the false conclusion that the religion of feeling and compensations is the Christian faith. The revivalists seized upon the defenseless Negro in his impressionable state of ignorance, permanently damaging the opportunity for the slaves and their offspring to participate in either the fruits of the Christian religion or the Christian faith. The dominant moralities of the period were disguised in terms of "faith, hope, and love."

The spirituals, as we have seen, were not forged out of the Christian faith but were shaped by the fiery brands of white Christians who were not able to choose between their faithfulness to God and Mammon. Of course some Negro spirituals did carry forth the intention supplied by the words and thoughts caught from the revivalist enthusiasts, some-time-representatives of God, sometime-representatives of slave masters and overseers.

When the songs of worship are studied, at least eight different kinds of materials are discoverable, among which are the psalms and hymns of such renowned writers as Isaac Watts, Charles Wesley and Richard Allen.[57] Despite this revival influence, there is considerable evidence that antebellum spirituals rarely contained Christian themes.[58] Old Testament ideas, characters, symbols, and stories pertinent to the Christian faith are isolated and misrepresented nearly as frequently as they occur. We must remember that the oral tradition was the basic method used by the missionaries to the field hands, who seldom were able to read or write, and this tradition accurately reflects the content, beliefs, and aspirations of the people involved. Thus, what issues from the spirituals is primarily the tale of how slaves revolted, responded to the colonization movements, became pacific, and finally placed their hopes in the world beyond as a final resort.[59]

Negroes took the vocabulary, Bible, lessons, instructions, and messages of the white teachers and expressed them in the form of spirituals. Jesus was seen as the protector from violence. The death of the "Lamb" assured slaves they would not have to die:[60]

> O de Lamb done been down here an' died,
> De Lamb done been down here an' died,
> O de Lamb done been down here an' died,
> Sinner won't die no mo'.

A great many spirituals reflect the missionaries' emphasis upon morality:

> You'd better min',
> You'd better min'
> For you got to give account in Judgment,
> You'd better min'.

Still others reflect the evangelists' preoccupation with purity:

> You must be pure and holy,
> You must be pure and holy,
> You must be pure and holy,
> To see God feed his lambs.

The fixation on death in some spirituals is indicative of the revivalists' emphasis upon being prepared for this momentous event:

> O Lawd, when I die,
> I want to go to heav'n
> My Lord, when I die.

Slaves were aware that religion was used to make them pacific. One of their reactions was to use a theme for purposes other than those intended by the whites. The chariot was a "sledlike" form of transportation for tobacco, providing a theme for reincarnation in Africa:[61]

Swing low chariot! Pray let me in!
For I don't want to stay behind.
Swing low chariot! Pray just let me in!
For I don't want to stay here no longer.

The Christian faith per se was poorly communicated, if
at all. The few spirituals which refer to the birth of Jesus
are extremely late, occurring sometime between Emancipation and Reconstruction. There are few more than the following:

> Go tell it on de Mountain
>
> Three Wise Men to Jerusalem came
>
> Lit'l Boy, how ole are you?
>
> Dar's a Star in de East
>
> Mary had a Baby
>
> Rise up Shepherd an' foller

The Biblical Marys are never distinguished. Jesus is usually
given the title of power, "King Jesus," and He is indistinguishable from God. The spirituals concerning the Crucifixion and the Resurrection—core of the Christian faith—
tend to be verbatim statements of description, rather than
affirmations of the faithful, often interwoven with themes
of withdrawal:

> Calvary
>
> Crucifixion
>
> De Angel roll de Stone away
>
> Were You there when they Crucified my Lord?
>
> Look-A how dey done my Lord

Many spirituals deal with the imagery in the Old Testament by simply setting the words to music. By far the great

bulk of the spirituals deal with the Old Testament, especially its suggestions of escape from this life. No other theme gives such clear evidence that the missionaries taught primarily a religion about another time and place. Seldom does the theme of freedom enter the spirituals, but when a spiritual speaks of freedom it is outside the context of the Christian faith:

> Oh Freedom! Oh Freedom!
> Oh Freedom I love Thee!
> And before I'll be a slave,
> I'll be buried in my grave,
> And go home to my Lord and be free.

The predominance of the otherworld theme is fundamental to the following spirituals:

> Ride on, Moses
> All God's Chilluns got Wings
> Dere's no hiding place down here
> Lis'en to de Lam's
> Stan' still Jordan
> By an' by
> Roll Jordan, roll
> Git on Board, Little Chillen
> Keep A-Inching Along
> Give Me Jesus
> You God A Right
> Sometimes I Feel Like A Motherless Child
> In Dat Great Gittin' Up Mornin'
> Religion Is A Fortune I Really Do Believe
> Walk in Jerusalem Jus' Like John
> I Want God's Heab'n To Be Mine

To See God's Bleedin' Lam'
I Thank God I'm Free At Las'

The popular view that Negro spirituals are of Christian
origin is based upon the preponderance of otherworldly
themes, Biblical words, and the instruction and messages of
the missionaries. These were the tools the Negroes had at
hand. But this view assumes the credulity of the slave. It
overlooks the awareness of Negroes that religion was me-
thodically used to hold them in check, and their capacity to
use it for other purposes than worship. Thus, the distinction
between spirituals being forged from materials presented by
Christians and forged from the Christian faith itself is essential to understanding the mind of the Negro.

Yet, the claim of Christian origin for these songs is more
of an indictment than a source of pride for Protestants. The
very content of these religious expressions dispels every
doubt about the quality of proselytism among the slaves.
When Negro spokesmen counterattacked with the Good
News of freedom, slaves fled from the churches, and when
Negro leaders went to their own with the call to pride
following the Civil War, Negroes left the white communions
in droves.

But the argument that through the spirituals, the only
general body of religious knowledge possessed by Negroes,
there might have developed within the independent religious
movement a full understanding of the Protestant faith, tradition, and theology is sound so far as it goes. Negro independent religious groups, based only on race, never intended
to be other than Protestant, although they underestimated
the complexity of this commitment. But the idea that they
could develop an independent Protestantism falls by its own
weight—both because Protestantism is not racial in its intent,
if it may be in practice, and because Negro spirituals were

historical documents, protest expressions, as well as poetic interpretations of a peculiar time and place. After all, the Negro was desirous of leaving that past behind because in the call to freedom he believed that his day would come— hopefully, it is coming. He had no way of knowing that his past would remain deftly with him in his future.

Finally, the religious or worship-centered spirituals were essentially individualistic, the key to Negro religion and a sign that Negro religious organizations have yet to learn to participate in and contribute to the overarching community of faith. The so-called religious spirituals, then, were the creations of religious aesthetes and not theological inter- preters:

> Somebody'. Knocking At Yo' Do'
> I Couldn't Hear Nobody Pray
> It's Me, O Lord
> De Blin' Man Stood On De Road An' Cried
> I'm Troubled in Mind
> Who'll Be A Witness For My Lord
> Ev'ry Time I Feel De Spirit

In each of these spirituals there is a sense of drama, an ap- peal to emotion and a highly personal demand, fundamentals of the existential decision embodied in the community of faith. But these spirituals were decidedly about the future in an unknown world. Such a one-sided emphasis, so often combined with transitory moralities without any sense of corporate morality or the wholeness of faith, was not con- ducive to a full understanding of faith:

> O, Gambler, Git Up Off O' Yo' Knees
> My Lord's A-Writin' All De Time.

Negro spirituals are a criticism of the missionaries, revivalists, evangelists, and the whole Protestant coalition who
were enthusiastic about casting out the devil in the Negro
but who became for the Negro, in the deepest theological
or Biblical sense, the very devil himself. Negro spirituals
are also helpful in understanding why, when the Negro
responded to exclusion by the very same Protestant forces
which would "save" him through the development of a
pseudo-Protestantism based on race, there was no basis for
nurture in the Christian faith. In the twentieth century,
when Protestantism began seriously to recover the historic
Christian faith, the religion of the Negro was frustrated in
the quest for the freedom and equality which their slave
ancestors thought they had achieved in their escape to
freedom.

Civil War to World War II

The social disorganization preceding and following the
Civil War disrupted the church life and religious education
of the independent Negro Baptist and Methodist movements. A considerable amount of their energy was spent in
freeing and bringing relief to their southern brethren.
Negro Baptist and Methodist congregations and institutions,
legally prohibited from expanding in the South, were at
work through their charismatic leaders among the free Negroes in the cities and towns of the South, as well as among
the slaves on the plantations. Here the "invisible institution"
was taking root under the aegis of the Negro missionaries of
freedom, whose heroism and integrity made a greater impact
upon the Negro than the labors of the white missionaries for
the status quo.

Between the Civil War and World War I independent
Negro Baptist and Methodist communions mushroomed. The
"invisible institution" merged with the Negro independents
to form visible Negro congregations. Negro preachers and
recruiters swarmed among their brethren who had been held
in check so long within the "invisible institution." By simply
reminding the Freedmen of the cajolery and indignation they
had suffered for centuries at the hands of white religious
leaders, Negro independents received an overwhelming response. Not only did the "invisible institution" become the
backbone of the visible Negro religion, but free Negroes,
North and South, departed in large numbers from the white
Protestant and Roman Catholic congregations. The immediate growth of the Negro religious organizations was a
phase of the emancipation of the Negro from white supervision.[62] Negro envoys for independent Negro religious organizations were aided by the fever for freedom which they
helped to impart and when it broke they were able to
capitalize upon sentiment, pride, and the opportunity to be
in on the ground floor of a seemingly sure-fire organization—
as well as identification on the level of race. Without these
elements, the sizable number of Negroes in the South who
were expelled from the white congregations might have
joined all-Negro congregations of white denominations—
the actual response of a minority of Negroes. Once the independent movement was set in motion it was virtually unchallenged in the proselytism of Negroes. Through the
added measure of contributing to the material, as well as
spiritual, relief of the Freedmen during Reconstruction,
Negro independents solidified their hold on the masses.

The free Negroes in the North who enjoyed the rewards
of employment as common laborers or domestics and, less
frequently, the benefits of a skilled occupation were widely
dispersed throughout the white community. Often they had
a feeling of superiority *vis-à-vis* the Freedmen, one sign of

which was participation in white congregations. This was possible so long as they remained more of a curiosity than a threat. In isolated areas and inconspicuous numbers free Negroes affiliated with Episcopalian, Presbyterian, Congregational, Baptist, Methodist, and Roman Catholic churches. With the expansion of the old Negro middle class, composed of the professional Negroes who were free prior to the Civil War, its members continued to distinguish themselves from the masses through association with white denominations, but more often than not they were forced to form their own racially identifiable dependent congregations.

In the South there arose the other tradition of the free Negroes, distinguished by their obvious blood ties to the old planters and referred to as "mulattoes." These free Negroes worked as household servants in the homes of the planters or as skilled artisans. The largest number of Negroes in skilled occupations prior to the Civil War were the *gens de couleur* in New Orleans.[63] Household workers and artisans were both in a position to become familiar with and accrue the mores and manners of the aristocrats, whose sons and daughters they were. Indeed, they were nurtured in the bourgeois mold and, being free prior to the Civil War, developed an upper class among Negroes, the descendants of whom dominated the professional and old white-collar classes. This traditional Negro upper class distinguished itself from the folk culture through its religious affiliation— becoming Episcopalians, Presbyterians, Congregationalists, and Roman Catholics instead of Baptists and Methodists.[64]

Although this traditional upper or bourgeois class emphasized the typical aristocratic virtues of gentility, morality and hospitality they were unable to escape the segregation which followed the Civil War. Their previous status and security threatened, they were forced to establish dependent class congregations which would mark them off from the

"religious emotionalism of the black masses" who were independents.

These congregations of the bourgeois Negro were also
based upon racial foundations, differing from the Negro
masses in their reluctance and dismay at being set apart, as
well as in respectability born of their positions of "status."
Middle-class Negroes were more solid in their family relations and attitude toward sex. As blood relatives of prominent persons in the community they could protect their
women and build a meaningful family life in a way denied
to the masses whose women continued to be the prey of the
white male. This stability of family was reflected as keenly
in the religious context as anywhere. Thus, this middle-class
Negro, often the vestige of the patriarchal system, was as
impoverished with respect to the Christian faith as the
masses. Household slaves passed on to the free Negro middle class the less emotional, but no less emasculated, tradition of religion based on the moralities most often taught by
the mistress of the plantation. Because of this close association they were even more fully indoctrinated. The one
advantage these dependent Negroes had over the masses in
religion was their experience in the white patterns of life,
enabling them to develop a life of worship which could not
be easily distinguished from that of their would-be white
peers.

With the rapid growth of independent Negro organizations and their undisputed success among the masses, white
Protestants ceased to proselytize and/or evangelize the Negro masses. From the post-Civil War period down to the
present, white Protestants have almost completely ignored
the Negro as a prospect for conversion and membership in
their congregations. This was not simply a result of the
success of the independents or of the desire of white Protestantism for exclusion. In a sense, Reconstruction days gen-

erated a feeling that it was not only natural but right that
Negroes should go their own separate way in religion. This
feeling was abetted by Negro independents who led whites
"to assume that the Negroes felt freer in their worship and
had easier access to positions of leadership," [65] although the
dependent Negro congregations were reminders that this
assumption did not express the universal feeling of all Negroes. Nonetheless, white Protestants were optimistic about
the outcome of Negro organizations. Given the optimum
they would have preferred to nurture Negroes in separate
racial congregations with white supervision, but since whites
could not accept Negroes in large masses and Negroes would
not accept segregation by whites, there was no optimum.
On the wings of freedom Negroes segregated themselves,
considering this the more noble evil of the two.

In this situation white Protestants ceased to evangelize
the masses, but they did not abandon the Negro. They
turned to the promotion and staffing of educational institutions in the hope of providing the Negro with sound morals
and learning as a means of helping him to make the fullest
possible use of his newly won freedom and sense of independence. The Negro colleges are the outcome of the
missionary work of Baptists, Methodists, Presbyterians, Episcopalians, and the American Missionary Association (Congregational), and they aided the Negro at the time of his
deepest need in a crucial period. While the hope was to lift
the entire race by educating the few, who would go out to
teach the masses, actually these institutions created an elite
so impressed with the morality taught in these colleges that
they were unable to communicate with the masses.[66]

Negro independents, along with Negro dependents and
white leaders of Protestantism in the North were overly confident of the good will of white southerners and northern-
ers. They were one in the belief that the Negro would be

integrated into the society as he increased in ability and that this could be accomplished best by the separation of the races. The error has persisted which affirms that paternalism can be successfully countered by fraternalism, that white supremacy can be nullified by black cohesion, that a racial minority can be a microcosm indistinguishable from the macrocosm of the American culture, and that a few gifted Negroes can alone lift the whole body of their outcast brethren to the height of acceptance on merit while at the same time they are cut off from inner workings of the socio-religio-economic complex. The effect of this pervasive error, provoked by whites and perpetuated by blacks, has nowhere been more compounded than in religion.

In fact, by the end of Reconstruction, religion had come full cycle. Prior to the Emancipation Proclamation whites used religion to keep the Negro in his place of servitude, while the Negro was using religion to gain equality with justice. But with the end of Reconstruction there returned the doctrine of white supremacy along with the rise of independent Negro religious structures, and the Negro religion developed as the most effective means whereby white superiority was once again assured. As an agency in accommodating the Negro to his subordinate role in society, the Negro congregation was without a peer.[67]

Prior to the twentieth century, the history of the Negro in religion is that of his response and reaction to Protestantism. Roman Catholics had little stake in colonial America. The endeavor of Protestantism to make this nation Protestant rather than Roman Catholic is a long and sordid one, reflected in many ways including conflicts centered upon the Negro.[68]

Considerable evidence is available to support the contention that Catholics were not free to work with Negroes, prior to 1829, in areas other than Maryland, Louisiana, and, later, Kentucky. This places in perspective the surge of interest in the Negro in the twentieth century:

Not before the beginning of this century was there anything like a concerted effort to win the Negro to the Catholic Church, and at least another decade elapsed before the effort gave unmistakable signs of success.[69]

The absence of a radical approach to social problems and the tendency to reflect the mind of the state in civil matters is characteristic of the Roman Catholic Church. Thus, it appears improbable that Catholics would have supported the Negro's thrust for freedom in a way different from that of Protestants, had they been in control. Where Catholics were engaged with Negroes the endeavor was to ameliorate, educate, and indoctrinate, in much the same manner as Protestants.

Prior to 1829 the limited number of Catholics, priests, and opportunities led to individuals working unilaterally among Negroes. Since Roman Catholicism has always considered itself a mission Church, it is understandable that the most was made of the few contacts available. A great many Catholics, many of whom were Negroes, fled to Maryland and Louisiana following the San Domingo revolution in the 1790's. Even here Negroes were primarily neglected prior to the formation of the American Roman Catholic hierarchy in 1808. The insufficient number of priests, for Roman Catholics did not early depend upon laymen, for the mission to the Negro was a major topic at the Second Plenary Council of Baltimore in 1866. Here the decision to set up separate schools and churches for Negroes was formalized, though the first Catholic Church for Negroes was St. Francis Xavier of Baltimore, 1863.[70]

Of the four million Freedmen, at best five per cent were

Catholics. The decrease in the number of Negro Catholics during the post-Civil War days was brought about by Negro independents, movements of Negroes North, lack of priests, lack of discipline of the Roman Catholic Church, and the zeal of Protestant missionaries. In 1871, the Josephite Fathers from Mars Hill, England became the first organized society to win Negroes, joined by the Sisters of the Blessed Sacrament in 1889. From 1871 to 1892, the Josephite Fathers carried the major responsibility for work with Negroes on behalf of the entire Church.

The Negro has been a low priority among Catholics prior to the post-World War II period. Yet, the Roman Catholic Church was the first religious communion to appoint a Negro bishop in a predominantly white area.

In 1875, Father James A. Healy, born in slavery to a Negro woman and a white planter, was sent to Boston for his education. There he had to fight the twin evils of being a Negro and a Catholic. But his celebrated work among the poor was so effective that even his white parishioners were able to see him as a personable priest, rather than as an outcast Negro. On one occasion when a child confessed that he no longer referred to the priest as being as black as the devil, Father Healy replied that it was all right to refer to him as black as night, or as black as coal, as long as he did not state that he was black as the devil. In addition to his hard work and compassion, Father Healy was the most outstanding Catholic orator of his time. He was called to Rome and appointed Bishop of the Diocese of Maine and later made an Assistant to the Papal Throne.[71] But as Albert Foley's *God's Men of Color* indicates, the limited number of Negro priests has been the major handicap of Catholics *vis-à-vis* the Negro.[72]

Whether in independent Negro organizations or in congregations dependent upon white denominations, the story of religion and the Negro from 1900 is that of segregated con-

gregations, reflecting to various degrees the polity and orders
of worship of the particular mainstream denominations after
which they are patterned.

Having discharged their duty to the Negro through the
development of special "commissions for Work Among Colored People," or the creation of special organs for the Negro
to lead his own people with some connection to the mainstream, white Protestant denominations promptly ignored
him. In the twentieth century white Protestantism has concentrated its personnel, time, energy, intellect, and finances
on isues that it has deemed more significant than the "American Dilemma": pacifism, politics, liberal versus conservative
controversies, prohibition, socialism, Marxism, labor and
management aspects of economic justice, civil liberties, to-
talitarianism, overseas missions, fascism, war and peace, reorganization of ecclesiastical structures, and ecumenical
issues.[73]

In addition to the social gospel which neatly compartmentalized the Negro under the assumption that the battle
had been won, white Protestantism engaged in a theological
renewal which has continued since the late 1920's. In this
period Protestantism began to take seriously its Christian
commitment as a way of viewing its mission in the world in
interdependence with, but not dependence upon, the disciplines of philosophy, psychology, sociology, history, and economics. Theology was reinstituted as a contributor to the
clarification of human problems and their solutions. It is
enough to suggest the complexities of this renewal: liberalism as personified by Harry Emerson Fosdick; fundamental-
ism exemplified in the trial of John Scopes at Dayton, Tennessee; the enormous influence of continental theology
highlighted by the writings and works of Karl Barth and
Emil Brunner; the surge of neo-orthodoxy with its liberalism
in politics and reformed theology, identified with Reinhold
Niebuhr; and the ecumenical movement which has awak-

ened in all the mainstream communions a sense of the tension between faith and culture, as well as the demand for the unity of all Christians—expressed in the increasing mergers of denominations.

While white Protestantism was deeply involved in the rediscovery of faith and its meaning for culture, Negro fellowships were saddled with the singular issue of being all things for the Negro. Partly because of this overriding demand to provide a medium for the spiritual and material relief of the Negro, partly because it was never a part of historic Protestantism, the theological activities of white Protestantism appeared to be the white man's concern, just as the Negro's struggle was seen as his problem.

Given the malaise of segregation and discrimination, it is understandable that Negro religion centered its life on a single issue: race. Religious education, theological growth, and social issues were overshadowed by race consciousness, providing little time or energy for the development of independent religious thought. In these areas where there was concern, Negroes depended upon the views of their white brethren.

The meeting house became considerably more than a place of worship; it evolved into a community center, a club, a political arena for budding politicians, a recreational hall for social activities, the major outlet for emotional repressions, the town hall, and the school room. The minister was its publicist. His encouragement from the white community was by way of financial aid to support his program; he was also placed on social agencies and consulted by white philanthropists.

Negro religion was the one organization which the Negro controlled and which was strong enough to carry the load of a social institution. Moreover, ministers were the best trained leaders in the Negro community. Because the minister was almost unique and was often able to administer to the needs of Negroes as they conceived them, he was able to extend the nonreligious functions of the congregation and in so doing nearly turned it into a nonreligious community. The meeting house became the agency for influencing social behavior through face-to-face relations and was the world of escape from the hard experiences shared by all. In this way the minister exercised power over the subcommunities and families by regulating behavior through the penalty of expulsion from the church, often controlling by means of public censure the young radicals who dared act contrary to community opinion. The Negro religion was the center of the Negro community and the minister was its undisputed leader. One measure of the esteem in which the church and the minister were held by Negroes was the growth of the institution.

Baptists exceeded all other Negro religious societies in growth, with about 3,000,000 members in approximately 22,-000 congregations in 1916. The African Methodist Episcopal Church was next in line with 548,355 persons on the rolls of 6,633 churches. The African Methodist Episcopal Zion Church with 250,000 in 2,716 congregations paralleled the Colored Methodist Episcopal Church with a like number in 2,621 churches. In 1916, too, 300,000 Negroes were registered in Negro churches of the Methodist Episcopal Church North, compared with about 23,329 members in 265 Congregational and Christian churches. The Protestant Episcopal Church totaled nearly the same number. Negro members in white Roman Catholic, Presbyterian, and the Northern Baptist communions numbered about 50,000 in each. There were approximately 4,602,805 Negroes in smaller bodies in 1916.[74]

The church as the outstanding institution in the Negro community and the minister as its acknowledged leader formed the nucleus for its dynamic and strength throughout the first quarter of this century:

The preacher is the most unique personality developed by the Negro on American soil. A leader, a politician, an orator, a "boss," an intriguer, an idealist—all these he is, and ever, too, the center of a group of men, now twenty, now a thousand in number. The combination of a certain adroitness with deep-seated earnestness, of tact and consummate ability, gave him preeminence, and helps him maintain it.[75]

During this period the vast majority of Negro congregations were in the rural South—23,744 or 62 per cent, as late as 1936—where the people were restricted in social activities and economic well being. The rural Negro was more dependent upon the church than the Negro in the urban South where there were located 9,486 Negro churches or 25 per cent.[76] In 1936 less than ten per cent of the Negro churches were in the North and more than 75 per cent of these were in the cities. In both the South and the North the Baptists were the most populous body, followed by the Methodists.

Two factors disturbed the monolithic control of the minister and the church. With the outbreak of World War I and the return of immigrants to their native land to take up arms, northern industrialists journeyed South recruiting Negro labor. The flow of Negroes North to employment disturbed the developed pattern in the South and overflowed the Negro churches in the North. The Negro ministers and churches were not prepared to care for either the spiritual or material needs of this influx. The need of these in-migrants created the opportunity for "storefront" congregations and sects which multiplied by the thousands and continue to vary between two extremes—capitalizing upon the poverty and ignorance of many Negroes and providing them with spiritual, moral, and nutritional relief.

The other factor was the small band of Negroes who made up the old black middle class, primarily professionals, whose clientele was Negro. These Negroes expanded into a new and larger middle class following the 1930's, when opportunities other than professional ones opened in the North

and accelerated after World War II. The new black bourgeoisie are the white-collar workers.[77] This new black middle class is obviously not dependent upon the Negro church
to supply all its needs in the old pattern of a community
center. The old middle class was motivated by respectability, morals, and manners which gave them special privileges
among the whites. The new middle class is motivated by
high living and well-earned status. The ranks of the black
bourgeoisie were swelled by more than the descendants of
the old middle class; they included capable Baptists and
Methodists able to rise on the basis of ability. These former
Baptists and Methodists joined the churches which attracted
persons of their status. This new black bourgeoisie was
ready to join white congregations, but had to settle for Negro middle-class churches of the white denominations, since
white Protestants departed from the cities of the North with
the first increase in the Negro population.

With the development of a more heterogeneous community Negro professional people and businessmen, politicians, social workers, and civic leaders emerged and forced
the minister and the church to compete for a previously un-
contested role of leadership, even in the sphere of race advancement. With the increase in opportunities, college-
trained men discovered other areas for recognition and
concentration in which they could make use of new ideas
in a way hampered by the emotional conservatism of Negro
religion. The religion of the Negro was perceived as intellectually bankrupt, dependent upon showmanship rather
than craftsmanship.

The Negro minister as a race leader and the Negro religion as a racial institution met the needs of the Negro at
the turn of the century. As shown by the statistics for 1916,
the Negro responded. But as the forces of segregation con-
gealed, the Negro minister became a negative power, holding his people in check. Once a rebel with a cause, the Ne-

gro minister developed into a reactionary—partly because he had no philosophical or theological roots. By 1936, Negro churches were decreasing in membership, or were just maintaining the 1916 membership:[78]

Negro Baptist	3,801,962
Lutheran Mission	8,813
African Methodist Episcopal	507,248
African Methodist Episcopal Zion	411,461
Colored Methodist Episcopal	335,666
Colored Cumberland Presbyterian	10,668

While it is difficult to determine the accuracy of religious statistics, those available for the recognized Negro bodies indicate that by 1962 growth depended in large measure on organizational schism. Statistics are not available for the number of Negroes who have joined white Protestant or Roman Catholic congregations, nor for those who are involved in the "storefronts" and other sects:[79]

National Baptist Convention of America	2,668,799
National Baptist Convention, U.S.A.	5,000,000
Lutheran Missions	8,531
African Methodist Episcopal	1,166,301
African Methodist Episcopal Zion	770,000
African Union First Colored Methodist	5,000
Central Jurisdiction of the Methodist Church	367,000
Christian Methodist Episcopal	392,167
Reformed Methodist Union Episcopal Zion	11,000
Reformed Zion Union Apostolic	12,000
Union American Methodist Episcopal	27,000

Nonreligious functions of Negro fellowships are being fulfilled by community organizations. Race consciousness is the single remaining factor contributing to the cohesion of Negro congregations, but the issues of segregation and discrimination are being worked out more effectively by other community forces supported by the churches. Whatever stability there is in Negro religious fellowships, it is due to the non-acceptance of Negroes in the mainstream congregations. The new philosophy of massive nonviolence has added to the image of the minister as worthy of the earliest exhorters. There is still absent any theological depth to provide meaning beyond the era of protest.

Yet, while the attrition of Negroes from Negro fellowships is not encouraged by white Protestants who have retreated into restricted neighborhoods and suburbs, the work of Roman Catholics has been intense among Negroes in the urban centers. Independent Negro fellowships have not only been unable to meet the needs of the migrants from the rural South, they have also failed to develop a ministry meaningful to the Negro middle class.

Having outlived its usefulness as a community center and never having been permitted to attune its life to the dynamics of the Protestant tradition of the Christian faith, independent Negro religion is a most extraordinary phenomenon. As we have seen, Negro religion is an attempt to develop fraternalism in response to the paternalism of white Protestantism. Although it intended to imitate Protestantism, it developed solely into a racial fellowship with no other reason for existence. This pervasive spuriousness has so confused its interpreters that nearly all have concluded that "the Negro church is an ordinary American church with certain traits exaggerated because of caste." [80] But the contrary is true. Negro religion was never steeped in the theological, Biblical, cultural, and historical reality of Protestantism. Negro religion would wither away were it not for the forces of segregation and discrimination which demand its existence as an option for Negro outcasts.

Chapter 4

CHALLENGE TO NEGRO AND WHITE CHRISTIANS

The record of the dominant religious forces in America is clear—"No Negroes Allowed," or to put it in the affirmative, "For Whites Only." The real story of the American Negro is his exclusion from the currents of mainstream Protestantism and Roman Catholicism. He has been forced to find his way outside of the life and work of the historical traditions. In reaction, the Negro has developed separate operational machinery, differing both in content and intent from his white contemporaries. For the most part, white Christians have viewed the Negro as a sign of trouble, sometimes widespread trouble, but never as evidence of a great religious issue—a real crisis. White churchmen and scholars have been satisfied with the designation of independent Negro religious organizations as "heroic," obscuring the tragedy of the whites' refusal to allow the Negro to take part in the faith common to Christians. The Negro has been satisfied with the "separate but equal" arrangement in religion, selling his soul for a mess of pottage.

As suggested earlier, Americans today recognize five major religions: Protestantism, Judaism, Roman Catholicism, secularism and the religion of the Negro. The religion of the Negro differs from all others in being defensive, reactionary, and lacking in universal or historical appeal. It alone is stagnant, without the possibility of developing beyond its own problems of inheritance or expanding to attract those who are not born into it. The reality of religious separation by race is not understood, nor can it be changed, by scholars who are as much outside the Christian community of faith as the Negro:

The educator blames ignorance and proposes education; the sociologist cites the impregnating pressures of mores, folkways, and traditions and suggests arbitrary changes in the societal systems; the historian reminds us of those insensate forces which, like the invention of the cotton gin, coerce man, willy-nilly, into prescribed patterns of thought and feeling and action, and he recommends patience; the Marxist sees racial prejudice solely as a rationale for exploitation and is confident that the equalizing of material goods among all people will prevent class and race conflict; the psychologist speaks in terms of the frustration-aggression hypothesis.[1]

White Protestant Forces for Compartmentalization

Compartmentalization is the traditional pattern of Negro-white religious life in America and full participation with Negroes in the life of the church has never been the intention of the white religious forces in the United States: "The case is plain; until the middle of the second decade of this century the major denominations of the church did not officially rebuke themselves for their division of the body of Christ along racial lines."[2]

It is one thing to point out that churchmen are indistinguishable from their neighbors in their discrimination and segregation of the Negro in all areas of community interest. It is quite another to make the judgment that within their own sacred sphere of endeavor churchmen refuse the Negro admittance to the community of faith, a denial more humili-

ating than the physical discrimination and segregation on
Sunday mornings, which is but the logical conclusion of
what these churchmen have been doing all week long. But
this disarrangement is not to be compared with the irrepara-
ble damage done by literally blocking every access to the
resources of the Christian faith, a faith which churchmen
declare is vital for the renewal of life. The church which
moves out of the area where Negroes reside or the church-
man who stands in the door and screens the worshippers as
to whether they are black or white are widespread instances
of stupidity that can be tolerated by so recognizing them.
However, when the Christian enterprise selfishly reserves
the tradition and its dynamics, channeling the spirit of Christ
and his Church to white people only, that is the greatest
crime against man and defiance of God ever perpetrated in
the name of love, justice, and mercy. This is the peculiar
and primary sin of white Christians in America and it cannot
be laid at the door of socio-economic pressures. White
churchmen alone are responsible for the creation of an exclusively white Christian community of faith.

Negro congregations have a Christianity divorced from
the mainstream of the Christian faith. What is at stake here
is more than the socio-economic factors which divide Negroes from Negroes and Negroes from whites of the same
social background. There is a theological division between
Negroes and whites of the same denomination and class, be
they Congregational or Presbyterian or Episcopalian or Lutheran. The caste system in these denominations forecloses
the historical, cultural, social, and psychological ties with
the Christian, essentially European, heritage. In white congregations and seminaries today's theological renewal is not
American-born. Every important theological interpretation
and insight begins in Europe and spills over into England
before it trickles to America. In part this is due to the seriousness with which Europeans involve themselves in the

Christian heritage, in part to their scholarship. But whatever the reasons, these theological inheritances are kept alive through conversation with theologians in Europe as well as by the presence of Europeans in America who foster the constant ferment of the contemporary Christian tradition. White Americans identify easily with their European heritage, while Negroes have no easy access to this cultural lifeline.

Thus, not only past alienation from the earliest roots of Protestantism in America has affected the perspectives of Negroes and led to the anemia of their arrested religion, but also the continuing refusal of whites to give blacks full participation in the community of faith. There is no such thing as white Christianity, but there is white control of the historical resources. It is possible to be a Christian without native roots in the dynamics of the Christian heritage, but it is not possible to contribute to or live within the community of faith without a sensitivity to its growth and change. In effect, white Christians operate on the "separate but equal" principle in religion. The futility of this principle is reinforced by the lack of communication between the white congregation and the Negro congregation of the same denomination (which is little more than a superfluous imitation of its namesake around the corner) in city after city, town after town, all across America.

White Christians insist upon compartmented religion because they are unaware that racial exclusion always has and always will deny Negroes the opportunity to be an integral part of these three Christian communities: faith, Church, and Protestantism. Without these communities the Negro has no way of increasing his understanding of and commitment to the "body of Christ." White communicants have yet to see that their exclusion of the Negro from the Christian community is not the same as segregation in seating arrangements. The withholding of full responsibilties and rights within the Christian life has left the Negro with only cheap substitutes. Theologically speaking, white Christians have been concerned with the establishment and disestablishment of the churches, American independence, religious revivals, denominational growth, frontier movements, urban life, overseas missions, social gospel, alcohol, church and state relations, unity of Christendom, war and peace, economic problems—all the great issues of society over which or within which they have some influence. But within their own life Christians (laymen and theologians) have refused the responsibility of nurturing the Negro. Of course Christians have been willing to offer the Negro salvation in the next world as long as he plays the game and allows whites to work out the meaning of salvation in this world. Yet the offer of salvation is not the proper province of the churches; salvation was the mission of Jesus Christ. The mission of the churches is not to duplicate that which has been done once and for all, but to bring persons into this awareness through participation in communities of meaning and purpose. If salvation, rather than witness, was the work of the churches they would have nothing to do. Sealed off in tight compartments, the white Christian is free to damn his Negro neighbor to a life without ultimate direction, goals, purpose, relevance, or meaning.

It is well known that the African slave was almost always considered to be an inferior being, though he was sometimes viewed as being human. From the beginning, Christians failed to contribute a Christian view of freedom to the Negro, with the result that he was never introduced to this dimension either as a way to seek his freedom from slavery or find his dignity in equality throughout the twentieth century. There was no way out of slavery or second-class citizenship through the Christian faith, conspicuously stripped of its inherent social protests, an unknown history to the Ne-

gro. It is no surprise to find that the protests of Denmark
Vesey, Nat Turner, Adam Clayton Powell, Jr., and Martin
Luther King, Jr., were rooted outside the teachings of American Protestantism. Denied access to the theological doctrines of Protestantism, the Negro sought equality upon
moral grounds and Christian principles divorced from the
Christian faith.

Within the Christian community, as without, the Negro
is an exception running parallel to the mainstream of the
Christian tradition. This pattern is not substantially different either in the South or in the North. And the segregation
of the Negro from the Christian community is not fundamentally economic, or even cultural. The crux of the matter
is that eleven o'clock on Sunday morning is the most intimate and social hour in the week—a private hour of white
faith on public display.

It is difficult enough for white Christians to be in genuine fellowship and communion with each other within and
across theological, social, and denominational barriers—but
to add the factor of race is tantamount to opening Pandora's
box. Decompartmentalization of religion would mean recognizing all Negroes and providing them with keys not only
to local church doors but to the kingdom of ecclesiastical
equality, leaving whites without the benefit to their egos of
their small investment in "Negro missions."

There is no guilt among white Christians in separating
Negroes into national or racial congregations. White Christians really believe compartmentalization is the right way,
primarily because it is the only way they know. White
Christians do not believe they should relate with the Negro
in communion and community, except on special occasions.
Genuine relations on the local level would mean reciprocal
demands and Negroes might just enter the congregations in
large numbers on an unexpected Sunday, rather than in twos
and threes on special occasions. This the white community

does not want, and does not believe in. It is the fear of this possibility which sends them fleeing to the suburbs with gentlemen's agreements.

There is a preference, and with no guilt attached, on the part of white Christians for their own kind. Whites point to Negroes who gather in groups as if Negroes were not carrying out the pattern set up for them to follow. What the white Christian wants is private control of a public faith. Without separation, it would be impossible for the white community of faith to distinguish between personal preferences and the demands of the Christian faith.

Compartmented religion allows the white Christian an escape from reality. By this means he does not need to face the fact that religion as a voluntary society of personal preferences is a recent and largely American innovation which excludes the Negro. Neither the Christian Church, faith, nor the history of Protestantism stem from societies of personal preference. Protestantism began as a coalition of constituents who affirmed certain religious doctrines and codes, but race was not a factor in the beginning. Certainly religious societies were not based upon the codes of private clubs which reject "highly visible" persons. The idea that local churches exist for private containment is in direct conflict with the Christian claim that the local community of Christians is a mission center. Whatever restrictive codes other communities wish to embody, the Christian community has no theological grounds for exclusion on the basis of personality; to do so is to deny the person of Jesus Christ. This is not news to white Christians. They know precisely what they are doing. It is their intention that churches continue as private social clubs for "whites."

There are some white Christians who are able to live with the exclusion of the Negro from the community of faith by addressing him thus: "We will include you in our Christian communities when your entire race has pulled itself up to our level and proved to us that you are worthy of our fellowship." Usually this speech is from the soul of a middle-class seminary professor or church administrator who, like the constituents he represents, assumes that it is not possible for Negroes to join with whites on the various intimate levels of the caste and class ladders. He may be right, but the assumption that the Negro can do for himself what the white man does not do with him is the joker in the pack, about which the white Christian has no misgivings. He knows there is only one Christian community, not two, and the forces which control this community will either include or exclude the Negro at will. The Negro cannot pull himself up by his bootstraps into the community of faith from which he has been excluded for nearly 350 years—the white Christian knows this.

White Christians are fully aware that until the Negro is included within the community of faith on the various levels of the socio-economic ladder he cannot begin to be faithful. By keeping the Negro out of the community of faith, whites have succeeded in keeping him out of their congregations. The intent of white Christians is clear, for even the concessions are limited by

(1) situations in New England and the upper Midwest where the Negro population is small and of a relatively high cultural order and where the presence of one or two Negro families has meant the difference between an exclusive and an inclusive church;

(2) situations in large cities or academic centers where there is available a sufficient population of intellectual, social and religious liberals to sustain an interracial church;

(3) integration from the top, beginning with official church pronouncements continuing with the appointment of Negroes to official boards and staff positions but not reaching down to the local church;

(4) integration on the fringes, beginning with such church-related organizations as the American Bible Society, the World

and National Councils of Churches, the Y.M. and Y.W.C.A., and locally, on the edges of the church in such groups as the Boy Scouts of America, the Girl Scouts, the United Church Women, the Inter-Church Athletic Leagues, etc., yet never entering the core of the real church;

(5) integration in communities in transition where the Negro population is growing and the white population is rapidly diminishing and where the interracial church will by all practical definition soon become a Negro church attended by a few remaining whites;

(6) a few churches which were deliberately organized to attract and serve a racially mixed constituency. In a word, there is little evidence that the local white churches are as yet taking seriously the resolutions and pronouncements of their respective official bodies.[3]

Roman Catholic Forces for Compartmentalization

Roman Catholicism has come into its own in America at a relatively recent date. It is difficult to ascertain its influence upon the Negro, for there are comparatively few Negroes within this communion. What is clear is that there is an unprecedented movement of Negroes toward Catholicism. Catholics are willing to seek members among the majority of Negroes who have turned from the Church or who have never been concerned with its life, and the Roman Catholic Church is not unreceptive to the Negro who no longer finds his needs met in Negro communions and is unwelcome in mainstream Protestantism.

It is true that the Roman Catholic hierarchy in America exercises considerable control over its people, but not in ignorance of the mood and temper of the people. The South still thinks in terms of compartmentalization, even in Roman Catholicism. What a Roman Catholic Archbishop will do in New Orleans in 1963 will not be what he will do in northern Louisiana or in Mississippi. But the tide toward an inclusive communion is the unmistakable trend of this Church, unlike the Protestant, a trend which is impressive beyond the fact that its organizational structure provides for this action. Protestantism is not particularly concerned about these inroads into the world of the Negro which the Protestant communions once had complete access to in every area of America. Protestantism would be relieved of a real reformation if Negroes were attracted in large numbers to the Roman Catholic Church and ceased to seek inclusion within Protestant ranks.

In those areas where Roman Catholics deny Negroes the opportunity to participate in the community of faith, there is compartmentalization which does not take on the same degree of exclusion as within Protestantism. Roman Catholics, where they have been in power, were as responsible as Protestants for the rise of the independent Negro communions. A great many Negroes were once lost to this Church with the rise of the independent Negro societies. Those Negroes who remained within the Roman Catholic fold were segregated into congregations for Negroes only, largely without access to the decision-making processes and as excluded from the Christian community as their Protestant brethren. The paternalism which the Catholics demonstrated and their acquiescence to the gods of segregation yielded few educated Negroes, and even fewer candidates for the priesthood. While the Roman Catholics frequently have their parishes defined on an ethnic or racial basis in urban areas, though the trend is decidedly away from such grouping, their structure in America is such that Negro priests are only now being placed over Negro missions. A clear signal of the progress of Roman Catholicism among

Negroes will be the promotion of Negroes to positions of prestige beyond the local church and over white and colored Catholics.

Roman Catholics have been very slow, in comparison with Protestants, in taking an official position with regard to the total acceptance of the Negro—but it has been very sure. With the heavy concentration of Negroes and Roman Catholics in the urban centers of America and the withdrawal of Protestantism it is to be expected that the growth rate of each will increase. Whether or not the emerging importance of laymen will affect the Roman Catholic encounter with the Negro remains in the speculative state.

The forces for compartmentalization have been challenged in the past by the Catholic interracial councils, Catholic social welfare groups, Catholic youth groups, clergy conferences on Negro welfare and the Catholic Committee of the South. Through long-term, peaceful adjustment between Negro and white communicants by means of education these groups have paved the way for the official action of the ecclesiastical leaders. The interracial councils appeal chiefly to the middle-class, better-educated Negro and white Catholics. The social welfare groups single out the spiritually elite. The youth groups work with Catholic youth, the clergy conferences with clerics and the Catholic Committee of the South with educated Southerners.[4]

There are about 615,000 Negro Catholics, excluding those in non-national churches. Whereas the bulk of Roman Catholic Negroes are in these national churches it is difficult to evaluate the real work of the Church among Negroes. It is certain that Roman Catholics have far less responsibility for the mission to the committed Negro Christian than do Protestants if one is to take into account relative memberships. What the response of Catholics to the large number of Negroes will be is yet to be determined, though like Protestants they have studiously avoided advocating assimilation.

The Roman Catholic educational system and patterns of
worship, even in segregated Southern churches, have impressed Negroes with a sense of belonging to the universal
Church so profoundly that there is a deep sense of identification with the Church among Negro Catholics; they do not
think themselves as Negro Catholics but as Catholics. This
is in contrast to Negro Protestants, who have no sense of
identification with the Church or Protestantism or faith, but
consider themselves Negro Baptists, Methodists, Congregationalists, Presbyterians, or Episcopalians.

The problems facing Protestants and Roman Catholics
are not equal. Until recently, only Protestantism reflected
in its life the warp and woof of America. There is a sense in
which Protestantism cannot solve its racial conflict without
solving it for the entire nation, although Roman Catholicism
could conceivably become totally integrated, yet leave un-
affected the status quo. This is particularly revealed in the
Roman Catholic approach to compartmentalization through
education and the stress upon supernatural ideals, means,
and ends. That is, Roman Catholicism is less a social body
than is Protestantism, but as Roman Catholics increase their
numbers among Negroes they may increase compartmentalization.

Compartmentalization in Roman Catholicism takes the
form of an unreal approach to the issue of race in America.
Serving as a refuge for Negroes in their flight from congregations of their past, the Catholic Church has a tendency to
concentrate on peripheral concerns or those in which it has
been preceded by the state. A great deal of work has yet to
be done among Catholic fraternal organizations. Negro
priests and sisterhoods were begun in response to a strangely-
felt need of working among Negroes, but the number of Negroes within Catholic schools in positions of leadership does
not differ from that in Protestant institutions. Part of this
dearth of leadership is due to Roman Catholic missionaries,

who are not only supported by local constituents but who also possess an extreme paternalism which limits opportunities for Negroes.

Essentially, the Negro Catholic is tired of Protestant segregation, but he is not impressed by the intellectual questions in Roman Catholicism. The Negro turning to Catholicism seeks a common life of worship which involves mystery, drama, and ritual. In addition, there is an emotional appeal based upon unquestioning acceptance rather than a rational appeal based upon understanding. The limited lay understanding among Negro Catholics reflects their Protestant background; the lack of a mission sense is indicated in their intention to join Roman Catholicism not as a commitment to the Christian Church, faith, and mission— but as a commitment to racial unity, even of the lowest common denominator. It is not a vision of the true Church which excites Negroes, but the possibility of an authentic acceptance. Having gained whatever dignity they have from legislation and laws, Negroes see in Roman Catholicism a parallel force.

In the North, Roman Catholic compartmentalization takes the form of white priests, teachers, and administrators in authority over Negro persons. Catholics have not taken seriously the full inclusion of Negroes on every level, and have tended to be concerned about social problems which have captured the imagination of the Negro. In the long run, Negroes will not be satisfied with an approach which tends to do things for instead of with them. A deliberate and sustained effort to accept Negroes in strategic places will be necessary if they are to be recruited for the mission of the Church. Without substantial endeavor at the point of equal participation, Roman Catholics may be able to make capital of the Negro's drive for desegregation and against discrimination, but its Negro members will be largely dead weight.

Negro Forces for Compartmentalization

Theoretically, the religious center is the symbol of solidarity for the Negro. It is clear that American Negro folk
religion, with its thrust for justice and equality, has per-
vaded all Negro congregations, regardless of socio-economic
level or denominational affiliation. To varying degrees,
North and South, congregations of Negroes put theory into
practice. Negroes argue that their churches remain racial
for reasons other than the fact that whites are conditioned
to worship elsewhere. The basis for the Negro fellowship is
its service not only as a pivotal point for escape and refuge
from white oppression but as a springboard for action. Thus,
the argument continues, if Negroes were to open their ranks
to the white community (assuming they would respond) or
infiltrate the white communions (assuming they would be
welcomed) such a movement would serve to undermine the
resources necessary to withstand the white world.

There is no disputing the fact that in the North the segregation-discrimination picture is not appreciably different
from the South. The laws of the North are rigid informal arrangements—educational, residential, social, and economic.

Insofar as congregations function to break down these
barriers or give relief to Negroes in these times of tension,
their consciously perpetuated separation is valid (from the
perspective of the folk religion). Negro congregations do
not generally serve this function. Negro independent institutions, like Negro middle-class congregations, have not
contributed to social action. Racial themes are introduced
in sermons and Negroes join together for fellowship, but
these are only incidental to the particular religious enter-

prise. Indeed, precisely because Negro congregations have simply provided a means for relieving anxieties, it was necessary for the nonviolent direct action movement to take over, using the meeting house as a center of operation while the congregations continue uninterrupted in their activities.

Since the Negro congregation has perverted the traditional folk religion (as a congregation, it is not involved in social justice) and merely imitates white congregational procedures (uninvolved in the mainstream of the Christian community of faith), its only indispensable function is that of a social center. On this level, the tacit affirmation of compartmental religion by Negroes may be essential for the community, but the assumption that it is essential for the Christian community breaks down by its own weight.

Whereas the fragmented Negro religious institutions actually serve as compartmentalized fellowships for social cohesiveness (existing only as potential for radical action), it is not helpful to conclude that they are thereby motivated by the faith of the Christian community. Social institutions, inspired by religion or other concerns, do not need the Christian faith for purposefulness. This would be the case even if Negro fellowships existed for the historical purpose of achieving racial justice. For, as we have seen, the earliest Negro missionaries of freedom and their contemporaries both discovered resources outside the Christian faith and Church (if not outside of Christian principles), certainly outside of Protestantism. White Christians continue to seek comfort (it is to the strategic advantage of the Negro that they do so) in the vain idea that the Negro's militancy for human dignity is an outgrowth of their teachings. White Protestants affirm that Negroes are expressing their faith (which they have been too timid to express); some go so far as to state that the Negro is their "child prodigy"; still others claim they have given birth to a virtual monster. Nothing could be further from reality. Negro and white Christians are not opposite ends of the same faith, but rather are expressions of two different ultimate concerns. Alas, it is strange that white Christians really believe the Negro has discovered a source of action and power in the religion taught them by their cousins, cousins who have hardly been religious revolutionaries in matters of social concern and have hardly been aware of this dimension of faith. Perhaps it is plausible to maintain that this is a Christian nation and that therefore nothing occurs within its life that is without debt to Christianity, or that Christian principles have been linked with non-Christian resources, thereby providing a basis even for the social action among Negroes. But to link this interpretation with the Christian Church, faith, and Protestantism in the context of the Negro-spawned revolution is to misunderstand the fundamental drive in the Negro.

While the Negro draws upon the white man's vagueness (everything good is Christian) to perpetuate religious compartmentalization, he is being more clever than wise. The forces of the Negro for compartmentalization are for social relief; they are indifferent to equal rights and discrimination, and oblivious to the faith of the Church. A social group, whatever its religious dynamic, can engender a life without faith, dignity without meaning, opportunity without purpose, and status without responsibility. In the compartmented social religion of the Negro even the claim of cohesiveness for racial justice is a façade.

Negro middle-class congregations segregated within white denominations are compartmentalized—severed from the Christian community—by social decree and not by choice:

The ambivalence of the Negro middle class is manifest in their churches, which underwent marked changes with the emergence of the bourgeoisie. An organizational style appeared, the emotionality of the folk religion rejected, services became formal and dignified; congregational life was elaborated in various activities and recreational groups; moreover, the committees, children's groups, men's and women's activities, and recreational interests of the organization church appeared full blown within the churches of the Negro middle class.[5]

Unable to participate in the historic community of faith, "the middle-class Negro wants a religious style which insulates him against his Negro identity and yet acknowledges formally his bond with the people upon whom he depends financially and to some extent emotionally." [6] Whether Negroes commune in dependent or independent churches there is the inescapable racial bond which unites them above class distinctions and separates them from parallel white congregations at the point of communion in the Christian faith. A noted sociologist explains the development in this fashion:

The Negro Protestant group is an especially interesting situation, sharing as it does much of the social heritage of white Protestantism, but existing in a totally different environment. For roughly the first two thirds of its existence, Negro Protestantism was a religion of slaves in an agrarian setting. Currently it is becoming the religion of a depressed urban proletariat. In short, it has been obliged to exist in environments which provided minimal opportunities for development. In many ways Negro Protestantism resembles a tree growing on a mountain close to the timber line, and hence having characteristics which do not reveal its potentialities.[7]

While this interpretation is helpful, it is inaccurate. Similarly Gunnar Myrdal is helpful in pointing out that Negroes "have made no innovations in theology or in the general character of the church service";[8] but inaccurate in stating that the Negro's "theology and church service are the same as in white Protestant churches." [9] Both are errors of sociologists desiring to be fair to the Negro, but unwittingly providing him with props which aid him to feel pity and pride in separation. Through the "eyes of faith" there is no such thing as "Negro Protestantism," although middle-class congregations are sure imitators of Protestantism and therefore the best evidence of the fiction of "Negro Protestantism." If theology is the map which guides the community of faith in its journey and Negroes have never been participants in that community, there is more sentiment than reality in the belief that the Negro has a theology, much less the affirmation that his theology is "the same as in white Protestant churches." If less desirable and therefore less defensible, compartmentalization is no less real for the Negro fellowship.

The difference between compartmentalization as a reality among the Negro middle class and compartmentalization as a right among the independents is a significant one. Independents are desirous of perpetuating the status quo because they are committed to the organization above and beyond its qualitative worth. The defense of Negro communions is never made on the high ground of theology; it is made on the low ground of tradition. Independents argue that since they were forced to create their own congregations and organizations as a matter of dignity they should be fostered in the present out of respect for the past, even if this means continuing outside the Christian community in an era when they might demand and achieve the very fellowship in faith they were once denied. It is not the body of Christ but the body politic which takes precedence in the minds of Negro independent communions.

Negroes insist upon their right to independent religious communities, pointing out that in this way they are no different from the Norwegian or Swedish Lutheran, German Baptist, and the Dutch Reformed congregations. The parallel between these national bodies and racial congregations is not what it seems. National churches of European descent developed out of national divisions and with varying theological emphases, but within the Christian tradition and particularly Protestantism, to which they contributed diversity in unity. Of course Lutherans, Presbyterians (reformed), Arminians (Methodists and Evangelical United Brethren), Anglicans, and the Free Tradition (Baptists) are not of one mind in such areas as communion, baptism, the doctrine of the church and the relationship between church and state. But they are one in their endeavor to contribute their perspective to the common body of Christ which transcends their peculiarities. National loyalties may not aid, but they do not prohibit life within the community of faith. Protestants may tend toward diversity but they are bound by unity in the spirit of Christ. It is true that the worldwide ecumenical movement (which has heightened the unity of Christians while exposing the sharp differences and common loyalties among Protestants and between Protestants and Roman Catholics) reflects the social division of mainstream American Protestantism from the evangelical lower class. It is also true that the denominational mergers of Protestants indicate a willingness to heal old wounds and ruptures of previous theological battles. Unity in the area of socio-racial divisions is microscopic compared with the binding of previously separated brethren.

Here the argument of racial separation for the declaration of the Negro's independence in the one area of religion is inapplicable. Believers in the ecumenical movement are bound by a sense of history and a sense of the Church, the precise elements of unification which the Negro knows and cares least about. The religion of the Negro does not participate in and therefore cannot draw upon the tradition of the Church. The religion of the Negro has a different history, one of social release and protest, affirmation of race and not of faith. There is nothing comparable to the ecumenical movement as a point of identification for Christians the world around; and as a point of separation between

white and Negro Christians in America. Negroes are conspicuous by their absence in the ecumenical movement simply because whites and Negroes do not share the same history. Were it the case that Negroes involved themselves in
the ecumenical movement as an independent or dependent
Protestant body they would have nothing to contribute but
race—and one of the marks of the ecumenical movement is
the historical contribution of each denomination to the other,
with a sense of dignity and pride. The Negro could only bring
the spectre of the despicable, however enmeshed the image
might be with the missionary influence for good in the world
beyond.

It is common knowledge that the Negro is not involved
in the ecumenical movement nor in its major concern with
mission. This is a peculiar problem of the Negro in America,
for Africans are involved in mission within the triple communities of faith, Church and Protestantism. The advantage
of the Africans is obvious; they are the potential directors of
their society and know themselves to be identified with and
responsible for its life—even its life of faith.

Price of Compartmentalization

As the present situation confronts us, whites and Negroes are unwilling to decompartmentalize religion (it is
important to be reminded here that, for different reasons
which we shall presently see, neither is unable to do so).
Like salt and pepper, black and white religion belong together, although they are capable of a less successful life
apart. The religion of the Negro (social action for racial
justice with equality) does not need white religion (the historic Christian community of faith) to carry out its mission

of working toward full participation in the community. When this is accomplished, or on the way to that accomplishment, the Negro may well become part of that block of Americans who feel no need for the unknown or rejected white community of faith. White religion (as it is practiced in America) does not need black religion for its inauthentic mission of exclusion. Neither of these missions is an illusion —both are delusions. White religion does not understand (or understands too well) that one of its true missions in America is to include black religion within the context of the Christian faith and Church. Black religion does not understand its need for ultimate roots and meaning and, therefore, its true mission as revelation to white religion of its unfinished reformation. Both religions are preoccupied with missions which deny the truth of faith and the ground of unity within the Church. There are, however, no theological reasons for compartmentalization. Unless there is a realization of the seriousness of effective compartmentalization, the immediate future for which we are responsible will proceed with its Negro-white compartments sealed off from each other and against the Holy Spirit of God.

The central theological questions of faith, particularly the teachings of the Church on social issues, have not entered the religious realm of the Negro. Theologians in particular and Protestantism in general have never taken seriously the revolutionary element in the social teachings of the Church and, therefore, no theology of revolution has been formulated. The teachings of the Church to which the Negro has been exposed emphasizes gradualism. Thus, the Negro has gained his insight with respect to social action outside the Christian community. The moral nerve of the Negro is sure, but it is limited to the single sphere of racial justice.

Being a victim of both society and the Church, the Negro has been able to think of very little without the perspec-

tive of race. This is understandable. The failure of democracy is obvious. But the failure of the Church to include the
struggle of the Negro deprived him of a sense of the universal, as surely as American democracy has deprived him of
his basic rights. The singular theme of the Christian faith
is universality, a concern for the whole of life. Although the
theme of universality has suffered at the hands of American
churchmen, it is still one which the Negro fails to find relevant. His religion, the thrust of the Negro revolution, has
only to do with justice and equality for the Negro in the
American society. Lacking the universal thrust of the
Church, the Negro is not involved in the universally-perceived social, political, economic, and military questions so
germane to the Biblical faith and the contemporary world.

Yet the very revolution which the Negro leads for existential reasons cannot be confined to his plight. It is apparent that the success of the revolution requires the affimation of the American promise by all citizens. This new
commitment to the ideals of democracy is one by-product
of the revolution; another could be the radical realignment
of Christian congregations, their teachings and practices.
Putting democratic and Christian theories into practice demands a recognition that the Negroes constitute a pressure
group which seek social justice for its own members without knowledge of or concern for the development of a broad
sense of social justice for all people, but that this pressure
is so inclusive as to leave no area of life untouched. It is
possible that the movement toward equality in politico-
economic areas may leave Negroes a permanent pressure
group insofar as they are excluded from white social groups
and Christian communities, and are without a sense of the
universal and a feeling of responsibility for the whole of society.

Of course the Negro cannot realistically be expected to
take other groups and persons into account since they have

not taken him into account, but this reality exposes the viciousness of exclusion from the Christian community. The Church has withheld from the Negro a universal concern for others, and by forcing the revolution to take place outside the context of its life, has shunned an opportunity for vitality.

Responsibility of White Christians

The concept of integration is presently understood as the opportunity and freedom of the Negro minority to enjoy the fruits and shoulder the responsibilities of the American society without merging with the dominant group. In this sense, integration is a realistic first step supported by specific laws, a sense of respect, the tradition of justice, and executive orders. This concept is predicated on the assumption that the Negro minority can maintain its own identity and aspiration with human dignity and separation.

This realistic and temporary movement is widely accepted as a proper blend of the ideal with the practical. It is based upon the concession that the Negro may be able to work interdependently with real progress in all areas, exclusive of primary relationships in the social and intimate spheres of life. Both Negro and white Americans, at least in the growing middle class, see interdependence in all nonsocial concerns as the acceptable pattern for the present and future. In many respects this tacit agreement is but a step beyond the past, symbolized by Booker T. Washington at the Atlantic Exposition of 1895 in his speech called "Let Down Your Bucket Where You Are": "In all things purely social, we can be as separate as the fingers, yet one as the hand in all things essential to mutual progress."

The strength in this position lies in realism. Interdependence or politico-economic integration appeals to a common interest of both white and Negro Americans. Insofar as the Negro can gain his place in the political and economic interests, he can be indifferent to the social sphere. But while the Negro continues to advance in vital areas, there is some real question as to whether he is a full participant in the culture. With all due acknowledgment of the Negro's achievement there is no parallel advance in the area of status, the final measure of his acceptance in the culture. However exceptional or however many exceptions, the Negro qua Negro is not comparable with his white counterpart. It is difficult to consider this singular fact without seriously questioning whether the defensive social separation on the part of the Negro and its offensive affirmation on the part of the white American is really in the best interest of the American society.

Admittedly, it is not helpful to dream about some imaginary ideal which is without effect in the present and immediate future. Neither is it helpful to hold rigidly to the concept of integration which is without power to motivate the changes necessary if there is to be full participation of the Negro in the culture. This is of particular importance for the Christian faith and tradition.

Within the context of the Christian faith and tradition assimilation may be a more idealistic concept, but it is no less realistic than integration. In a sense, integration is a dead concept which defers to the status quo, while assimilation is a dynamic one which need not be viewed as an impossibility. Integration is the logical outcome of Washington's articulation of a meaningful symbol. But full participation in the culture requires a symbol more dynamic than integration, with its conservative arrangement expressed through compartmentalization. Integration is a constant which cooperates with the larger society while becoming an independent whole distinct from that activity in which it is engaged. That is, integration does not necessarily lead to pluralism—it leads to separation without concern for the full life of all. The Negro minority tends to become an independent component in the purely social sphere, while becoming interdependent "in all things essential to mutual progress."

The Negro as an independent component is a Negro separated from all things essential in the American spirit. It is one thing to gain the economic rewards of the culture. It is quite another to participate in the spirit of the culture which is only partially revealed in its economics. Whatever identity the Negro has apart from this infused spirit is irrelevant and, finally, superfluous. In effect, integration provides the Negro only with the power to react to that which is and prevents his becoming determinative in the dynamics of the culture. Pluralism differs from integration in that it is a way of being determinative. The deadness of integration is seen in the fact that while we live in a pluralistic society composed of various minorities, the concept of integration is reserved for the Negro.

Although integration as a concept has had and will continue to have real support, it is a defensive, rather than offensive, measure of the past which will be detrimental if allowed to continue. If there is to be "mutual progress," a more dynamic concept describing the direction of the Negro in the culture is indispensable. This is particularly true in the area of Protestantism and the Christian faith, where the idea of integration means for the white Christian the acceptance of an occasional Negro or group of Negroes in small numbers—but is entirely rejected by the Negro religious bodies as a whole, which consider integration as a white issue they are unwilling to entertain because of its lack of universality. Moreover, the realism which persuades the white Christian to go slow, "picking and choosing" in integration, evokes in the Negro that realism which defends the status quo as an acceptable arrangement, however indefensible when compared to the Negro's dogmatic opposition to a fenced-off life in every other but the intimate area.

The concept of integration blinds both Negroes and whites to the realism that a life apart does not lead to a life together. The Negro is as yet unaware that his acquiescence to the white man's support of integration as something less than merger with the dominant group forces him outside the Christian faith and tradition and into a variety of Christianity which can only be described as black religion. The Negro is so impressed with the fact that the Negro congregation "antedated by many decades the monogamic Negro home" that he all but forgets that, regardless of its results, its roots are without pride or sustaining power. The Negro has forgotten that his religious organization was and still is necessitated by exclusion. The Negro has yet to realize, and his fellow white American to be convinced of, the truth that segregated and "equal" religious communities separate the Negro from more than social intimacies—they separate him from the very faith he proclaims, and belong to the past as solidly as do separate and equal educational facilities. It is utterly inconceivable that the Negro can be expected to contribute to the renewal of the Church from which he is excluded. It is ironic that the Negro has contributed least through the very mode of religion to which he first turned and which he still holds up as the most stable product of his own creation. It is ironic because the only force holding Negro religion intact is the bond of color which the Negro seeks to reinforce to the disadvantage of his own spiritual development and that of the Church. There is no regenerative power in that which exists because of dynamics external to its life.

If only in the realm of the Church, the Negro needs as much as his white neighbors a different concept from that of integration to provide the tension needed to correct errors of exclusion which are inevitable in the ideal of the Negro as an integrant. While integration is of the past, present, and future its strength lies in the absence of alternatives. It is realistic to assume that were another concept to enter the thinking of both Negroes and whites (backed by the awareness of the exclusion of the Negro from the Christian faith through the cornering of fellowship by mainstream Christians for "whites only"), the Negro would have a reason consistently to seek acceptance in the Church, as in every other realm, and his excluders would become far more vulnerable and less indifferent in their vicious reservation of the Christian faith for non-Negroes.

Assimilation is not a new concept, but its depth and relevance for the Negro as a dominant mood has been rendered ineffective through its confusion with miscegenation. While the risk of miscegenation is involved in authentic assimilation it is not inevitable—assimilation and miscegenation are not interchangeable terms. Assimilation as homogeneity is the kind of interdependence Negroes and whites seek in the economic realm and have generally agreed upon as the emergent pattern of activity. In other areas of life, such as education and politics, integration is still the dominant basis of action. Large blocks of Negroes are forced to confine their activities to separate zones and are provided the opportunity to reinforce a racial mentality. The trend in education and politics is away from integration and toward the end of assimilation; few persons would defend integration as the objective in education and politics, although these areas of the American life are hindered in their advance toward assimilation by housing restrictions.

Assimilation is a mediating concept—more realistic than integration and less provocative than miscegenation. If Negroes and whites are to the "one as the hand in all things essential to mutual progress," a heightened sense of assimila-

tion beyond integration is the conscious process toward this
objective. It is visionary to place confidence in integration,
for the realization of the Negro as integrant will hardly lead
to the desired end of assimilation. As an integrant the Negro
perpetuates compartmentalization, and in the specific area
of faith this means a continuance of a heritage without roots
in the Christian tradition, cut off from the Protestant perspective.

Were the concept of assimilation to enter the thinking
of the Negro it would no more include all Euro-Africans
than does integration. Yet, a conscious sense of assimilation
among even the most selective of this body could emerge
into a movement with a sense of urgency and, combined
with white emergents, produce through immediate action
presently unpredictable consequences. It is certain that
without some such conscious concept in the fact of exclusion
from the Christian community, satisfaction with the present
condition will dominate the future, disguised as necessity
born of virtue. The dynamics in the idea of assimilation
consist of realistically creating opportunities for Negro
Christians to enter the mainstream of the Christian tradition and become indigenous and homogeneous persons in
the dominant system. Regardless of his defense of separate
religious organizations, they are the Negro's response to
exclusion from faithfulness to the Lord Jesus Christ. Yet,
there are possibilities for the Negro and white Christian
who are conscious of the truth that the Negro is neither a
part of the American society nor of the Christian faith in
its Protestant and Roman Catholic expressions.

Whether Negro or white, those who hold to separate
religious expressions without actively seeking to assimilate
the Negro are gradually but surely extinguishing the light
and cursing the blackness, in lieu of engaging in vital action.
It may be too much to hope for assimilation, but it is a hope

born of the certainty that these persons need not find their acceptance only in the life beyond. Presently, there

. . . still broods silently the deep religious feeling of the real Negro heart, the stirring, unguided might of powerful human souls who have lost the guiding star of the past and are seeking in the great night a new religious ideal. Some day the awakening will come, when the pent-up vigor of ten million souls shall sweep irresistibly toward the Goal, out of the Valley of the Shadow of Death, where all that makes life worth living—liberty, Justice, and Right—is marked "For White People only." [10]

The major responsibility in assimilation lies with the dominant white group, which has the power to include or exclude the Negro, however highly assimilable he may become. Negroes will not become conscious of the need to assimilate nor participate in this process, short of a concerted Protestant movement intent upon fulfilling this long-neglected mission (as we shall see, the advance of this movement will need to be outside of the established Negro organizations).

When white Protestantism becomes convicted of its role in denying the Negro a life within the Christian community and becomes conscious of the rationalization that separate Negro religious institutions are simply lagging behind and need only encouragement with education to be truly equal and separate, the moment of decision will not be far off. It is possible that awareness of this unbridgeable chasm between Christian community and racial separation may be the factor which leads to the mobilization of time, energy, and finances necessary to commence the most significant responsibility facing Protestantism.

Realization that "separate but equal" religious organizations do not amount to equal participation in and commitment to the Christian faith is a proclamation as true in the area of religion as it is in education. There are no legal powers which can broadcast this truth and force compliance with its demand. The initiative resides with white Protestants who are committed to the mission of renewal and related with the vast majority of Negroes who are similar in religous identification. In lieu of a Supreme Court decision, the awakened consciousness of Protestantism must suffice to get on with the responsibility. All of the organizational genius of Protestantism (together with sociological, psychological, and theological corroboration) is necessary for a Protestant-wide movement at the grass roots level to confront local congregations with the mission of which each must be a part and in which no delegation is possible.

Protestantism has the potential to work out the techniques, which will vary from situation to situation. This book is a call "to do it" rather than an explanation of "how to do it." The truth is that Negroes care no more about Protestantism than its adherents care about Negroes, and the Christian faith is quite possibly seen by the former as an obscurant. Indeed, the Negro as a Christian has obviously learned to live with certain limitations and will hardly enter the doors which have so long been closed to him. Where there is dissatisfaction, he has a choice between turning to Roman Catholicism or to some religious cult, or of having no religion. Moreover, the future religious life of the Negro appears more definitely to be drifting toward Roman Catholicism, with its hold on the urban area where the Negro increasingly finds himself isolated.

The only force which can bring depth to the religion of the Negro is a Protestantism alert to its present failure and its future possibility. But only a Protestantism that is willing to risk its life for the sake of a limited minority can bring meaning and purpose to the religion of the Negro who is potentially Protestant. Nothing short of a full scale, across the board movement will be effective. If such a realistic mission were undertaken, a renewal in Protestantism might well result.

A mission toward the assimilation of the Negro into the Christian tradition and faith would need to face head on, if there is to be any general movement, the issue of sexual fear. A conscious exploration in every local congregation of the belief that the Negro is not worthy of intimate association, that "white" implies "superiority" and "Negro" "inferiority," is of the highest priority. Precisely on this level will the choice be made between including the Negro in the Christian community, with his possibilities for renewal, or not. Working through the fear of sex and its defensive mechanism expressed in the inferiority-superiority complex, we may understand that assimilation may well involve critical situations bordering on miscegenation, yet realize that these human exceptions may be creatively endured for the sake of a fuller assimilation without miscegenation. A Protestant movement lifting to the conscious level the fundamental fear whites have of Negroes, with extended opportunities to think through the issues, would provide the preparatory context for decision. The number of years of intensive work required for this preparatory climate may be considerable, but without education in depth the possibility for conscious rejection of both well- and ill-founded fears and hatreds cannot emerge.

At some point, denominational organizations and their entire constituency will need to decide whether or not the Negro is to be brought within the "household of faith." Since any consideration of this question in Protestantism will be based on individual and corporate decisions, no coercion is available, short of recognizing whether they or the Lord Jesus Christ is the determiner of the Christian community. The steps which have been taken along this way have been few and far between. Here and there heroic individuals and communities have taken unprecedented steps toward inclusion of Negroes, usually under peculiar circumstances. These fragmented and isolated instances have fallen short of wrestling with the fears and hatreds which rage beneath, partly out of expediency or the possibility of fracturing these fellowships into splinter groups. The difficulty with this "catch as catch can" approach is not simply that persons who have not worked through and rejected their fears and hatreds are able to move over to the next community and find a local community of faith with less pressure. The real problem with pecking away at integration is that the uncertainties of acceptance are so acute the Negro can never be sure where he will be welcome. The conscious objective is to make the Negro certain that whereever he moves he is welcome in the community of faith. The immense complexities in achieving this openness are undeniable, but this does not mean a beginning cannot be made whereby the Negro knows he is accepted in the fellowship of his choosing as surely as he knows he is accepted in any federal institution across the nation.

The task of Protestantism, instead of wishful thinking or pointing with pride to exceptional situations, is thorough preparation through which the decision to include or exclude the Negro can be consciously faced. It would be in the best interest of the Christian faith to have a careful examination of this decision without the acceptance of any Negroes rather than to rest upon the acceptance of Negroes in isolated instances. The issue is not whether there should be Negroes in white congregations, but whether or not Negro Christians will be included with white Christians in "the household of faith."

The test of any Christian fellowship is the choice it gives to those who seek involvement in its life—the dignity and freedom it provides its adherents. It is questionable whether Protestantism has seriously provided its constituents (let alone the Negro) with a live option. Hithertofore, superfluous time and energy have centered upon strategies which are important only after thorough preparation includes Protestantism in general instead of experimental stations in particular. It is commendable to point out that in one locale there are two Negro families, in another twenty, and forty elsewhere. Such figures are largely meaningless, for the problem is not the acceptance of exceptional persons in exceptional circumstances but the inclusion of a previously excluded people in every local situation.

It is difficult to imagine more than a beginning in awareness in the next generation. If the movement toward assimilation beyond integration (short of the brink of miscegenation) is to be a permanent guerrilla warfare rather than spontaneous border incidents, each community will need to begin preparation for its moment of decision. Communities may well work through a pattern of authentic acceptance and find few or no occasions to declare their openness. The objective must not be that of integration, where there is some pressure to include immediately a Negro or two as symbols of desegregation and non-discrimination. The objective is readiness to include Negroes into the Christian community wherever they are located, whether or not they take advantage of this opportunity, and whether or not they are merely accepted if they seek out the community or are actively invited and encouraged to find fellowship in a particular communion. There is little naturalness about integration as a manipulative approach in a sphere where one becomes a member of the community by choice and acceptance rather than by power and legal pressure. Were a given community to work through to a positive acceptance of Negroes on the basis of integration, supported by the enthusiasm of the pastor or laymen, who were then forced to wait a number of years or decades for its realization, a sense of being cheated or inspired without fulfillment might easily result in wide frustration. The objective of assimilation requires eternal vigilance in each community without visible proof but with perpetual openness. A persuasive commitment to the inclusion of Negroes within the Christian tradition will need to well up out of the same kind of loyalty evoked when *The Star-spangled Banner* is played. At public functions, the singing of the national anthem is assumed. In the worshipping community, the inclusion of the Negro will need to be as natural.

The creation of this kind of climate in the local congregation through the organizational procedures of the denomination is a major responsibility. The basis for this widespread affirmation is the faith that within the Christian community there is always and everywhere the possibility of renewal, while in black religion the basis for renewal has been truncated. The possibility for renewal within the Negro, as within the white Christian, remains constant but without the community of faith individual maturation remains a frustrated potential. Denominational organizational machinery can be helpful in pinpointing *what* the congregations are called upon to do (provide the context for the assimilation of the Negro though conscious rejection of sex fears and their expression in the inferior-superior complex) and *why* (the Negro has been excluded from the Christian community and faith). The *how* and *when* is the decision of the local congregation.

White Protestantism, through its organizational structures, is in a key position to take the initiative *vis-à-vis* assimilation. The leadership on the upper echelon has considerable power at the point of procedures and dissemination of information. White Protestant denominational bodies have a positive contribution to make where Negroes are concerned, while Negro organizations have no positive contribution to make. The difference between these two organizations is that between a booming enterprise and a holding company. Neither white nor Negro religious organizations have been willing to face this issue. The difference is not a matter of capabilities, but of ultimate purpose and resources. One organization intends to further the mission of the Church; the other to maintain racially religious societies. If the bond of race were suddenly withdrawn from Negro religious organizations, they would have no reason for existence. If the identical situation occurred in white organizations, their basis for existence would be enhanced, not jeopardized.

It is certain that Negro religious organizations are not about to commit suicide. It is equally certain that white Protestantism is not about to become expendable for the well-being of the Negro. Without a Supreme Court decision as a lever, there is no pressure for Negro religious organizations to adhere to single standards of quality. In the sphere of religion the Negro organizations qua Negro organizations seek integration (they are thoroughly opposed to assimilation), by which they mean that white organizations should open the doors to Negroes and that Negro doors need not be open to white aspirants. Further, integration means the denial of merger with the dominant group and the carrying out of Negro identity. Negro organizations are bereft of objective idealism and seek only to maintain the advantages accrued over long years of separation.

White Protestantism, organizationally, has accepted this outlook of Negro organizations and has perpetuated it through financial aid for building houses of worship. It has assumed that all Negro organizations need is more educated and alert ministers—in utter disdain for the fact that a separated religious life, like a separated educational one, is definitely and unalterably inferior. White Protestantism has in reality been unable to overcome its belief in the inferiority of the Negro qua Negro, because the actual inferior Negro religious organizations have been shored up for the understandable but mistaken purposes of charity.

Where mainstream religious organizations have awakened to the evil of separated Negro communions, the approach has been that Negro religious life is the same as white religious life and that the exclusion of Negroes is theologically indefensible. It is a long step from this theological sensitivity to the reality that the question is not a matter of mere integration of equals but of assimilation of Negroes into the Christian community.

The Negro confuses the defense of Negro religious institutions with loyalty. One may have loyalty to that which has purpose and meaning, but defensively perpetuates that which is endearing rather than enduring. White Protestantism has assumed that the Negro's defense of his religious institutions is based upon loyalty. Neither group recognizes that Negro religious organizations as racial institutions are no more worth saving than Negro educational institutions, although both will continue to exist on the periphery of the mainstream.

In effect, the most charitable contribution to the Negro as an American is to provide an alternative to preserving Negro religious institutions, in the awareness that this opportunity will not be readily acted upon by the majority of Negroes in any foreseeable future. A good beginning would be in the area of consciously overcoming the fear of miscegenation on the local level, where the decision to include the Negro or exclude him will ultimately be made.

Having initiated the process wherein local congregations distinguish between integration, assimilation and miscegenation, the next step would be for mainstream Protestant organizations to be permissive but not supportive of Negro religious organizations. Up to this era, white organizations interested in some rapport with Negro organizations and congregations have assumed that the inclusion of Negroes must be through the channels of organizations. Negro religious organizations and congregations are too entrenched and too suspicious to consider mergers seriously. Since Negro religious organizations are outside the bounds of the Christian faith and tradition, through the forces of socio-economic separation which they seek to maintain, no worthy end is served through direct attack upon them or conscious support of them. Negro religious organizations must be by-passed in the best interest of the Negro and the Church. Three hundred years of separation cannot be undone, nor need it be continued.

Assimilation into the mainstream is the endeavor of the Negro in every field except that of social relations and the religious life. The responsibility of white Protestantism is to create conditions wherein the Negro will realize assimilation is in his best interest and that of the Church. To do this, Negro and white Christians will need to affirm the truth that without pain there is no social growth and that the pain of new life and growth is preferable to the pain of meaninglessness. Were congregations open to assimilation of the Negro Christian into the Christian community, it would not be a question of how many Negroes would take this opportunity, but of the quality and kind of Negro. An analogy may be helpful at this point.

It is widely agreed that desegregation of educational institutions is in the best interest of the American people and specifically the Negro American, however much this has been resisted by some people. It is also well known that with the opening of mainstream American colleges to Negroes, there has been no appreciable decrease in the quantity of Negroes who attend predominantly Negro institutions, but there has been a decided decrease in the quality of Negroes who attend the predominant Negro institutions of higher learning. The more ambitious, able, and alert Negroes have matriculated in mainstream colleges, leaving the Negro institutions to work for the most part with the ghetto Negro.

There is little danger of creating elite religious com-

munities. Were the Protestant congregations to accept assimilation, there is every evidence that inclusion of the
Negro would follow the pattern in education, but such a
decision can hardly be effective if the opportunity is provided in *ad hoc* fashion. The demand for assimilation in the
Christian faith cannot wait for the Negro religious institutions to collapse or concede—the mainstream of any movement necessarily involves detraction.

The fact that a high percentage of the most able Negroes are matriculating into mainstream colleges and others
are increasingly finding acceptance as white-collar workers
provides white Protestantism with an alternative to organizational inclusion of Negro religious institutions. There
are a limited number of these Negroes. Their predominance
is in the far-distant future, which means that the possibility
of an emergent commitment to assimilation within Protestantism can be rooted in the unconscious spirit of its adherents without anxiety over integration. Negroes whose daily
routine in the mainstream partially frees them from the
anxiety about being a Negro are open to alternatives beyond
materialistic acquisitions. In this group there are latent
questions of meaning, purpose, and fulfillment which are
ripe for direction in the Christian community, inevitably
thwarted or ignored in Negro religious communions. It is
within the college communities and the mainstream economic endeavors that Protestantism has the opportunity to
include Negroes within the Christian faith. It is this mission
which should provide the motivation for assimilation within
mainstream Christian communities.

If the approach to the Negro continues along organizational lines, the frustration will continue at an impasse. Organizationally viewed, the difficulty for the Negro qua Negro
and for the white qua white lies in the choice of action which
denies two cherished values. So long as Negroes are requested in their institutions to choose between the vacuities

of segregated institutional life and integration they will tend verbally to support the latter. But if a specific proposal is actually made to merge, they will continue to balk. So long as white Protestants are requested in their organizational life to choose between including Negroes within their life and excluding them from the local community, they will make pronouncements verbally upholding the former. But if specific proposals are made to integrate the Negro into Christian communities at the expense of exclusive fellowships, the latter will continue to be the dominant choice. Within the Christian context as without, men choose that course of action which is the denial of the least important value.

This principle of social hedonism is generally appealed to in support of the status quo. It is assumed that, since the established white and Negro religious organizations support two opposing Christian norms, Negro religious organizations demand the inclusion of Negroes at every level and all at once, or else continuation of the separate and segregated patterns. White institutions, on the other hand, either affirm token integration and are satisfied with limited numbers or leave the question of the Negro to those persons and congregations having a peculiar interest in the Negro—the least demanding norm tends to win the majority and therefore the least committed of both groups. In effect, there is no way for inclusion of the Negro in the mainstream.

There is a stalemate when those established and institutionalized religious bodies are in conflict as to the inclusion and exclusion of Negroes. A third alternative, beyond the integration or merger of religious organizations, provides a critical setting for radical decision. The real choice before white Protestantism is whether it will consciously exclude the Negro from the Christian faith and tradition, a far more serious matter than whether or not it will choose to integrate. It is a question of assimilating or denying the Negro entrance into the spirit of Protestantism. Whether or not white Protestantism seeks to assimilate the Negro, Negro institutions have no choice but to exist as racial bodies outside the Christian tradition. Only the dramatic and radical commitment on the part of white Protestantism to the Christian faith, above exclusive communities and in the spirit of assimilation, can overcome religious hedonism.

Protestantism has the choice of continuing to support the patterns of the past or of beginning to participate in the wave of the future. The organizational structure can initiate the decision with respect to the assimilation of the Negro on the local level. This decision can be focused upon the marginal Negro, whose vision of the purpose and meaning of the Church opens the way to his seeking a fellowship that has the possibility of renewal, though it is thoroughly human.[11] These marginal Negroes are increasingly found in mainstream colleges where each year there is an increase in the number of Negro students. Beyond the provision for fellowship in local communities, the work of the Protestant organizations is to focus its mission at the college level.

What makes the college-trained Negro so vital is the knowledge that it is he who is increasingly turning away from the religious background of his parents because these congregations are often directed by fundamentals other than a relevant existence and the search for meaning. At least his white peers, often in the same predicament, stand under the corrective judgment of theology—a far more significant means of renewal and direction than is often acknowledged. Normally Protestant, the Negro now tends toward Roman Catholicism or no religion because he does not find guidelines in the faith of his fathers, nor acceptance in the mainstream of Protestantism. What white Protestants need is this awareness. What the Negro needs is the experience of acceptance. Perhaps for the first time in his life, the college community provides an opportunity for the Negro student to be involved in an authentic relationship with mainstream Protestantism.

It is extremely likely that the potential represented by Negro students will not really result in responsible members of campus religious communities, or of larger religious communities, until they are seriously considered and their problems respected. The increase in Negro students generally has not resulted in any comparable increase in participation in religious communities.

Why this predicament? First, there has not been a consistent authentic welcome extended. This "mission within a mission" has seldom received high priority. Though extraordinary effort is occasionally exerted to engage Negro students, it is often met with apathy or hostility. So, it is resolved to try again next year. Such approaches lack continuity and perseverance, and the lack of openness is pervasive, infectious and immediately perceived. The history of Negro and white relations—particularly in Protestantism —leaves the Negro with a sense of suspicion toward whites even where there is a deliberate, genuine attempt to overcome this psychological barrier. The Negro yet requires special cultivation to overcome his historical despair.

Second, the Negro has been cautious about involving himself in groups which desire to "pepper their salt" as a symbol of their liberality. This spurious approach is understandably rejected by the majority of Negroes, who do not wish to be subtly exploited. However, the Negro is often not willing to face reality and see that the price of belonging means the inevitable recognition of some less-than-noble-motives. Since he cannot jump out of his skin he might as well enjoy its advantages while tolerating its disadvantages. But this caveat is worth consideration by those whose interest in the Negro is for purposes other than an authentic human relationship.

Third, it has been suggested that the Negro minority

prefers its monistic fellowship of color even while pursuing education in a pluralistic environment. But this observation is usually accompanied by little experience of what occurs when white Americans find themselves in a minority. Of course this description can be empirically verified on campus after campus where "birds of a feather flock together." Negroes do seek each other out and limit their fraternization to this in-group. One would expect this, though not applaud it, in commuting situations where Negroes leave the campus to move again in a restricted sphere. But the chasm between white and Negro students who live in dorms cannot be attributed to fear of miscegenation. Here the custom of avoidance rears its head, and discloses an illiberal preference for certainty to the frustrating rhythm of uncertainty.

Fourth, the elimination of Negro and white Protestants participating in the life of the church means the loss of identification with the same theological roots and religious awareness. By this omission, Negro religious bodies become the instruments for security, salvation, moral guidance, and social protest. Consequently, Negroes are not generally prepared to communicate with their peers of the same denomination.

Finally, and this is the crux of the matter, where Negroes have managed to hurdle these obstacles it has not been followed by an earnest endeavor to hire Negroes in positions of leadership, namely, those on the faculty and staff. Especially is this true of religious leadership on the campus. This missing link distorts the image of the Negro in the eye of his peers; moreover, it wreaks havoc with the Negro student, who is thereby robbed of the basic support he needs to extend himself in what is at best a precarious predicament. Negroes will be in token preparation as long as their white peers are robbed of the experience of working with a qualified Negro in the daily routine and as long as the Negro is without symbolic representation in the life of the community.

In addition to preparing the larger community for the forthcoming Negro, a prior step of preparing the Negro for assimilation bears real consideration by the decision-making instruments of Protestantism. The college community is, by and large, open to the Negro, but his partial acceptance of this opportunity is because of images of the white man in places of leadership. Particularly in church-related colleges, denominational organizations are presented with an opportunity to develop the potential faith of the normally Protestant-oriented Negro student through providing him with the support of an image which will draw him out and into the mainstream. However distant and future the possibility of including Negroes in positions of leadership on mainstream campuses, the present is not too early to think of its implications.

Beyond assimilation on the local level and local campuses, organizational Protestantism can take the initiative in providing conditions whereby potential Negro leadership can be groomed for symbolic posts. Negroes have not been supported at the level of aspiration, so that they naturally aspire to be seminary professors, denominational executives, and pastors of mainstream congregations. In the past, it has been widely felt that the Negro should minister to the Negro and that the training of Negroes in seminaries was for a segregated ministry. Insofar as Protestantism takes seriously assimilation of the Negro into the Christian faith this previous distortion no longer is relevant. In the local churches, on the campuses, and in the seminaries, promising Negro students will need to be given special consideration and an opportunity to be "in" with persons who make the decisions, not unlike the special consideration given to white students who are to proceed to appointed positions.

Of all the signs of promises in today's world, none is more heartening than the growing rebellion of youth against the un-Christian practices of their elders. It is a peaceful rebellion and surely an ironic one, for the rebellion consists in the determination of youth to do what their elders have taught them. More and more, all over the nation, there is arising from the youth of the Christian churches and fellowships the demand that the church either practice Christianity or stop preaching it. They are restless and, being restless, they are on the move. Happily, Christian leaders in touch with Christian youth are aware of this and realize that organized Christian bodies face one of the supreme crises of their lives and that, unless they change, young people will be lost to them. Happily, too, young people want them to change so that they can stay with them and in them, and they balk only when the churches, colleges, Y.M.'s, and other such groups balk at letting them be Christian.[12]

Negro religious institutions were the result of socio-economic forces. They have served their function as an alternative home for the Negro prior to the development of the monogamous Negro family or his acceptance in the economic sphere. As a social and racial institution for the development of Negro leadership, and a meeting house for the free exchange of ideas, the "Negro's Church" has made its contribution and now only exists as a defensive operation. Negroes have reached the stage in history where they can, however small in numbers, find their development in the community of faith outside a sheerly racial institution. Negro religious institutions are without sources for renewal, reformation, and relevance. He who is both a Negro and a Christian will increasingly find his fulfillment in the mainstream, though not without tension and formidable obstacles. The weakening of Negro congregations in the next generation will not spell their obliteration but their passing worth and the end of a creative era. Hopefully, the way will be cleared for the new Negro to live out his life in the Church denied his forebears.

The past, present, and future provide no way for the Negro to forget that he is a Negro. But the route of assimilation provides the direction in which this identification tag may be creatively used in those spheres where it is more important to be than to be a Negro. Unqualified participation in the Christian community is the only way to awareness of the Christian tradition, which in turn is the only way to participation in the Christian faith. The Negro as an entire race, or more precisely those members of various Christian and racial organizations, may never be included in the Christian community. There is an increasing remainder to be assimilated—unconscious of their purpose to be indigenous and responsible Christians within the historic Christian Church. If the mainstream can begin to work toward the end of including that remainder within the length and breadth, height and depth of the Christian community, there will be joy rather than sorrow at the withering Negro religion.

Responsibility of Negro Christians

If the responsibility of the white communions is to take the lead in declaring the full acceptance of the Negro as a person who should be encountered with respect and welcome as a son or daughter, the responsibility of the Negro is to insist upon this. The time has long since past when the Negro should defer this basic right and be defensive in the sense of denying that marriage with another regardless of race is his full due. Rather than a plea for miscegenation, the Negro needs only to plea for the right to accept or reject, the right of all persons. It is not miscegenation that the Negro must seek, but full participation in a church which is based upon social intimacies that exclude him. Until this central issue is recognized, acknowledged, and accepted by the Negro, he will not be. Whether or not miscegenation takes place is totally irrelevant. That he is no longer denied full participation in the community of faith is the central unfinished business of the Negro. Heretofore, Negroes have been frustrated in the area of religion because their basic assumption has been that they could achieve community in faith independent of the dominant society. In this frustration Negro organizations have become defenders of the status quo and victims of personalities and their ambitions.

The real task is for Negroes to enter the community of faith in the knowledge that, in the words of St. Paul,

God has placed everything under the power of Christ and has set Him up as Head of everything for the Church. For the Church is His Body, and in that Body lives fully the One Who fills the whole wide universe.[13]

But there are no signs of this discovery,

. . . for they live blindfold in a world of illusion, and are cut off from the life of God through ignorance and insensitiveness. They have stifled their consciences and then surrendered themselves to sensuality, practising any form of impurity which lust can suggest.[14]

Compartmentalization will be the future until their white brethren welcome all Negroes, even if according to class, into their communities, as "no longer outsiders or aliens, but fellow-citizens with every other Christian," [15] a message which the Negro will be suspicious of until his white brother acts so as to live the message which has never been delivered in face-to-face relationships within the intimate chambers of Protestantism: "You, my brother, are not a servant any longer; you are a son." [16] Only within the community of faith will white and black brother know that the central message of the Christian Church is decidedly not,

. . . slaves, obey your human masters sincerely with a proper sense of respect and responsibility, as service rendered to Christ Himself not with the idea of currying favour with men, but as servants of Christ conscientiously doing what you believe to be the will of God for you. You may be sure that God will reward a man for good work, irrespectively of whether the man be slave or free.[17]

It is this very continuance of the superiority and inferiority overtones of an era gone by which expresses itself in sexual fear of the Negro and in hatred by him of the white man. The message of the Christian faith is a love without fear or hate, and this can only finally be realized through intimate community in depth:

Love contains no fear—indeed fully-developed love expels every particle of fear, for fear always contains some of the torture of feeling guilty. This means that the man who lives in fear has not yet had his love perfected.

Yes, we love Him because He first loved us. If a man says "I love God" and hates his brother he is a liar. For if he does not love the brother before his eyes how can he love the One beyond his sight? And in any case it is His explicit command that the one who loves God must love his brother too.[18]

The Negro has sufficient evidence that his European blood and culture relative "hates his brother" and that his Christian community reveals him to be "a liar." Excluded from the Christian faith, the Negro will never be convinced of the "explicit command that one who loves God must love his brother too" until the white guardians of the Christian community take this admonition so seriously as to live by it: "Finish, then, with lying and tell your neighbor the truth. For we are not separate units but intimately related to each other in Christ." [19]

But "separate units" there are, and this means that Negro and white Christians are neither "intimately related to each other in Christ" nor a unity in the one spirit of Christ. This lack of intimacy in the Christian tradition grows out of the lack of intimacy in the movement of Protestantism. The lack of intimacy within the spirit of Protestantism has resulted in the underdevelopment of the Negro in areas other than those of faith, for Protestantism is more than a movement within the Church—it is also the dynamic perspective which has profoundly influenced the American society.

In every other sphere of life he actively seeks full integration, but in religion the Negro within independent and segregated communions is not really interested in decompartmentalization. This lack of openness does not only mean the Negro recognizes that such a movement would destroy a solid area of security—it also means that the Negro does not identify the Church as an inclusive community, toward which he must work by going out of business as a racial compartment and a spirit which he cannot know apart from renewal within the sources of the tradition. As a society for religious organization the Negro congregation has a very definite future; as a community of faith it has neither past nor future. The religious fellowship, even in middle-class Negro society, represents the last refuge from the social exclusions of culture even as the Negro religious society was the first refuge from the politico-economic exclusion of the previous centuries. The difference between these two reasons for seeking out religious societies is that, having begun to receive politico-economic rewards with limited social benefits, Negroes have no desperate need for the religious society.

The future of segregated Negro and dependent congregations is growth, through education and good organization, into large congregations which will attract communicants from every corner of the urban community—but without depth and objectives. Where there is no point, however minute, of sensitivity and allegiance to the tradition above race and clan, there is no possibility for renewal. To spend time, energy, and money in the vain hope of reconstituting these bodies for purposes other than those which they now attend would not only be of meager value—it would actually be a fatal concern with the symptoms rather than the disease.

Compartmentalization is a past-present-future malaise of such severity that the only real mercy is to allow these symptoms in Negro congregations to die a natural or quick death. What the Negro needs is choice, not restriction. What he wants in religion, as in all of life, is the opportunity to develop in the context of the mainstream—this is the wave of the future beyond immediate generations. He will certainly resist this distant future at the same time that he will know it to be his ultimate intent. Any attempt to shore up religious apartheid is sure to be hardly more than an illusion that the clock can be turned back a hundred years. The immediate future means superficial exchanges on the upper echelons of the denominational hierarchies. Those who perpetuate "the Negro's church" in the present will be many, not a few, Negroes—but they will not have the respect of their peers now or in the future. The spurious Christian notion that, through education, members of the Negro religious community can be held in readiness for the day when they will be accepted into mainstream faith and community lends support to apartheid compartmentalization in religion. Such compartmentalization needs no support, since it functions very well irrespective of interest in the mainstream Christian community. The idea results in the wrong thing for the right reason. Neither Negroes nor their white counterparts will admit that it is no less realistic (though far more relevant) to be engaged in the process of disestablishment through spending energy in the failing efforts that will finally prevail than to succeed in religious compartmentalization that will finally fail.

The immediate future, like the present, will have an increasingly segregated and dependent Negro religious society based on conformity, homogeneity, economic integration, and active affability—largely without variance from white exclusive and private religious clubs. The difference is that the Negro imitation is but a reaction to the other without its possibility of renewal, since the culture has cut the Negro off from communication at the source of renewal. Negro religious societies will continue to differ from their white images in their intent to search for security and wholeness in reaction to the rejection of their contemporaries. These realities, which will continue to constitute a religious groping without the possibility of faith, mean the prevention of seriousness of purpose beyond functional activities devoid of meaning and responsibility. There is no available evidence that factors will emerge to curb the warped potential of these congregations in the search for economic gain rather than freedom from the pressures of technological conformity and mass-mindedness. The possibility of seeking meaning, purpose, relevance, fullness, and authentic identity cannot but continue to be an impossibility for a body forced to seek its equilibrium in the conscious kingdom of race.

Only the marginal man, the outsider, whose experience by accident or design engages him in a vision of the Church as meaning and purpose (however its particular form falters in the peculiar locale), will be able to join the Christian community. While the case of the white Christian varies little—he, too, often seeks authenticity beyond the bounds of the Christian fellowship—the white Christian knows that the sick church to which he is committed is not beyond the possibility of renewal, because its Lord is not race but Jesus Christ. The white church may exist to exclude Negroes, but this it does in denial of the Church and its faith, while the Negro congregation has nothing but cultural guides to commend this separation, encouraged as it is by racial pride and socio-economic necessity. The white church exists because of faith in a tradition; the Negro congregation exists because of social conditions which take precedence over faith and tradition—the denial in the former may be turned to affirmation, but the affirmation of the latter must finally be denied.

Increases in numbers as well as compartmentalization among middle-class dependent and segregated assemblies is the wave of the future insofar as Negroes find their way in white-collar jobs. This religious style which distinguishes middle-class from lower-class Negroes is little more than a mode of non-awareness of the Church as a responsible influence in public affairs. The Negro middle class is concerned with privacy of religion. Successful Negroes have arrived without the aid of religion, which hardens their understanding of religion as a private affair. They are a step ahead of the less successful by virtue of managerial hierarchies, civil service, and other bureaucratic escalators. Advancement in these areas may free Negroes to work through various organizations for the health of the community, but not within the Christian community for its health. The religious societies are sought by private individuals and families for the "rounding out of life." Private and public life have nothing to do with each other, except that the private area of religion gives encouragement to, but is not involved in, the public sphere. Religion is a collection of individual devotions. Sermons and messages are expected to reflect the current situation in race tension, but to the middle-class Negro there is no conception of a faithful existence through socio-politico-economic structures leavened by a people who faithfully respond in the daily activities. At the other extreme there is no concern for the approach which claims that spiritual purity is the way to change society and that a mission to others is therefore based upon the religious identity of the individual. In this way middle-class Negro congregations do not differ from their white branches except at one decisive point. Negro congregations have no theological tradition or basis for correction—the theological idea of the Church is not a framework they have ignored, for Negro congregations are cultural societies without reasons for existence other than cultural ones. The privacy of Negro congregations excludes any spiritually ameliorative purpose, and, apart from reaction to their cultural activities, their members find no real purpose.

From the point of view of the Christian faith, Negro bodies are in a very precarious situation. There is no theological judgment urging them to work for an open and inclusive Christian community. It is on tactical grounds that Negro congregations are as rigid against the inclusion of white participants as white communicants are opposed to the inclusion of Negroes except where either body finds it tolerable to accept token numbers. Without a theological undergirding, there is no basis for the doctrine of inclusion (more implicit than explicit in the Christian tradition), nor for discovery of the meaning of life and work and other latent depths in the white middle-class congregations. However feeble, the stirrings for inclusion are centered in white and not Negro congregations—partly because there is a theological dimension which serves as a lever outside the culture.

Self-expression, entertainment, recreation, aid in meeting crises, otherworldly orientation, and the hope of salvation are no more crucial to the middle-class Negro congregation than is the search for meaning and relevance. The real function of these economically integrated religious societies is to witness to the fact that ambition and good fortune are worthy values which are then offered in evidence among persons of a select but segregated community. These congregations contribute to the American apartheid system by their reinforcement of a style of life in a segregated religious society.

Style without depth is insufficient to hold those who feel no loyalty to a racial institution which offers nothing unique. The loss of youth to these congregations is not incompatible with an old religious sentiment in the new garb of organizational activities with precious little relevance for the real issues of life. Instead of perpetuating respectability within the confines of religion, the youth find their outlets in authentic fellowships with rather definite objectives. Thus, the importance of religion declines with the rise of Negroes to the middle class:

There are indications that the next twenty or thirty years will see a wakening of the Negro Protestant churches, but since most members of the other major groups are unwilling to establish primary-type relations with Negroes, it seems unlikely that the development will weaken the internal solidarity of the group.[20]

It is the loss of the vitality of youth and their imagination to the Negro congregations which indicates the quality of these religious communities. The loss of youth is not peculiar to Negro congregations, but the tendency for Negro youth to abandon religion is even greater than in white churches.[21] Increasing education and sophistication, along with the separation from white peers in this singular area of life are contributing elements. Moreover, religion viewed as a reservoir to be individually tapped and allowed to surge forth when needed, or when ritualistic rhythms of life de-

mand, means that the religion of the Negro does not speak
to its youth.[22] Indeed, Negro religion is of importance chiefly
to the older generations who need activities to vary their
monotonous routines—with the number of elder citizens
the continued existence of compartmentalized religion is
assured.

The Negro middle-class and dependent congregations
are the most secure and least revolutionary religious group.
In this religion, which avoids faith and seeks privacy, there
are no cross-currents *vis-à-vis* the mainstream. The growing
middle class in religion is not anti-white, just realistically
Negro. There is no deep resentment nor movement for
change. If the Christian faith is understood, it is seen as
the white man's peculiarity, and the repudiation of the
Christian community as a theological way of life is not an
act of aggression. It is a misunderstanding of religion as the
private sphere for control and security. Negroes have historically viewed religion differently from their white peers.
Disestablishment of Negro congregations and their decompartmentalization concerns middle-class religionists least of
all. Excluding religion, the middle class is the most excited
about integration and the least open to entertainment of
assimilation of all Negro classes, since its members see segregation as the path for all Negroes in the intimate spheres of
life.

Indifference to assimilation and affirmation of integration means that the middle-class independent and segregated
Negro religious societies are oblivious to the fact that the
Negro minority as a minority cannot participate in the fullness of society without merger with the spirit of the majority,
wherein its racial identity is lost. Integration means maintenance of the Negro identity, which takes precedence over
the Christian faith and community in favor of compartmentalization. The very fact that the middle-class Negro now

settles for integration supported by laws, justice, and respect for human dignity widely accepted in the culture means that this attitude will be carried out in religion. And while the Negro will gain opportunities to advance in economic endeavors, this success will reinforce the illusion that religious integration may be equally successful—when, in reality, without replacing racial identity with the identity of faith in community, there can be neither openness to the Christian tradition, nor renewal.

The responsibility of all Negro congregations which exist essentially because of racial ties is to go out of business. The total revolution in which the Negro is involved has only begun. It will be hampered by educational and economic deprivation, housing restrictions, and social exclusion, yet in all these areas the Negro has access to legal and moral resources. But if he is to be included in the Christian community, he will have to work at it virtually alone.

Thus far the revolution has taken place outside the context of the religious community. It is incumbent upon the Negro now to close his houses of worship and enter the white congregations of his choice en masse. This may be impossible in large areas of the South today; it may be impractical in many urban areas where white Protestants are in flight from the Negro. But it can begin in all the small towns and medium cities of the North and West where Negro congregations are obviously inadequate and lack vital leadership. Such a movement may need to begin with Negro youth, who have the least to lose and the most to gain. It is assumed that the separation of the races in the congregations is not the will of the denominations but the intention of the local congregations. Negroes will need to impress upon these congregations their seriousness by their presence at worship, application for membership, and committee involvement. Wherever he travels the Negro must make a point of worshipping with his white brethren. In resort towns and suburban communities the Negro will need to go out of his way to participate in worship.

In this way, both the historical and contemporary functions of religion in Negro meeting houses may be preserved. Historically, the meeting house was the congregation for freedom and justice and equality. Presently, it is the place of community and social identity. Negroes would be free to use these centers openly for social action and community fellowship.

Without some voluntary sacrifice of the unessential areas of its past for the essential life of the future, the Negro congregation will simply wither away, a liability rather than an asset to the spirit and the community.

A religious life which is not rooted in the structure of society is ultimately transitory and ineffective. Moreover, the religious perspective which is rooted in the history of a people provides a creative dimension even when it is rejected. Negroes have yet to learn that the Christian faith is the warp and woof of the Western world, and to be excluded from this sphere is to be preempted of full participation in its ethos. Participation in the Christian community is the *sine qua non* of contributing to that society. Without admission to the Christian community, Negroes may be able to change the external structures of democracy, or help them to be realized, but this does not lead to a sense of responsibility and the imperative of contributing to the social milieu. The religion of the Negro has proved that religion is indispensable, whether relevant or irrelevant.

However, militant direct action for participation in the Christian community does not mean that the Negro has to accept the non-Christian tenor of Christian communities. In fact, not only is it true that unauthentic Christian communities can only be changed from within, but it is also true that the Negro provides the greatest opportunity for narrowing the gap between principle and practice. By his very racial difference, he can be a permanent revolutionary within the Church, providing the creative tension necessary to sharpen the teeth of justice in the community of love. Insofar as he is isolated from the white community, the Negro is under no pressure to foster a truly dynamic fellowship, but the very process of demanding acceptance within that community forces both Negroes and whites to come to grips with the mission and message of the Christian Church.

By voluntarily giving up their segregated worship life, Negroes would be taking the offensive. This burial of the old forms in order that new ones might be reborn would contribute to the purpose of the Church and America. Were Negroes to be assimilated into the Christian community, they would gain much and add new life.

But if Negroes do not take the offensive and demand assimilation in the Christian community their gains in material goods will hardly be matched by spiritual growth. Separate and segregated worship centers may well continue as the symbol of impoverishment of a segment of the society in all things essential. The choice between being a part of the whole or attempting to be a whole apart is the decision of the Negro. It is within his power to begin the long process of assimilation into the Christian community and therefore the American society, from strength, declaring not that he wishes to have what the white community has nor his intention to be like white people; rather, his declaration must be that alone and separated, white and black America are antagonists of the American dream and the Christian community.

A NOTE ON *THE NEGRO'S CHURCH*

The image of "Negro Christianity" or, more precisely, of the "Negro church" has led some scholars erroneously to seek its verification, only to conclude that the concept is untenable.* To a considerable extent, this misunderstanding is traceable to the most influential book concerning the religious life of the Negro that has appeared so far: *The Negro's Church.*** Every writer on the subject has been forced to take it into account and give it the most serious consideration. Unfortunately, this book has been misleading to a good many scholars, including Gunnar Myrdal.

The authors specifically entitled the book *The Negro's Church.* It was intended as a sociological study of the function of the church in the life of the Negro, based upon extensive research in 609 urban and 185 rural churches, North and South. The title accurately reflects the findings of the authors which led them to conclude there is a religion identifiable by race but not a "church." It is clear in this book that for the first two decades of this century the Negro was totally dependent upon the racial bond of fellowship in the church to support him at every crucial area of his life. In large measure this has been the case throughout succeeding decades. These findings are verifiable and valid.

* The most glaring example of this is Chapter 40 of *An American Dilemma* by Gunnar Myrdal (New York: Harper & Row, Publishers, 1944), which the author goes so far as to title "The Negro Church," only to reject the title later.

** By Benjamin E. Mays and Joseph W. Nicholson (New York: Institute of Social and Religious Research, 1933). Although this book is thirty years old, there is nothing comparable to it on the market. The results of the field research point out what would be expected from the victims of caste in the society.

But while Mays and Nicholson paid deference to their experiential and library research in the title, the book really deals with an empirical study of 794 congregations. Their library research led to the conclusion that they could only be concerned about "the Negro's church," its function as a unique social institution developed by Negroes to carry out their needs. However, the authors also wished to emphasize the data gathered in their field research which revealed the poverty of the institutional life of the Negro. As a result, Mays and Nicholson repeatedly refer to "the Negro church" without differentiating this concept from *The Negro's Church*.

In the final chapter of the study, entitled "The Genius of the Negro Church," the authors give the results of their findings, here quoted at length because they are still relevant:

The analysis reveals that the status of the Negro church is in part the result of the failure of American Christianity in the realm of race-relations; that the church's program, except in rare instances, is static, non-progressive, and fails to challenge the loyalty of many of the most critically-minded Negroes; that the vast majority of its pastors are poorly trained theologically; that more than half of the sermons analyzed are abstract, other-worldly, and imbued with a magical conception of religion; that in the church school less than one-tenth of the teachers are college graduates; that there are too many Negro churches; that the percentage of Negro churches in debt is high; that for the most part the Negro church is little concerned with juvenile delinquency and other social problems in its environment; that less than half of the reported membership can be relied upon to finance the church regularly and consistently; and that the rural church suffers most because of the instability and poverty of the rural Negroes.

During the decades since this study was made, there has been a general upgrading of ministerial standards, religious

education, financial responsibility, and institutional outreach to meet the needs of the community.*

Despite these qualitative changes, Negro religious organizations and congregations have not outstripped the rising standards of white churches, and they continue in the
present, as they will in the future, to be comparatively inadequate, insufficient, and substandard. Negro institutions
are not inherently inferior. Regardless of how feverishly
their members labor to improve them, and however substantial this internal improvement, the underlying socio-religio-
economic factors out of which they were created will not
thereby be appreciably changed. Unfortunately, many Negro leaders and institutions are so caught up in the defense
of their religious heritage that they do not see this basic
problem and spend energy in the preservation of Negro religious congregations, an energy which might better be
spent in the eradication or alleviation of the causes. But in
truth these maintenance operations are based on the perception that the stigma attached to the Negro will not soon be
removed; therefore, the Negro must make the most of an
impossible situation. Negro religious organizations and their
leadership resist the truth and its consequences: "separate
but equal" religion is not equal religion, for exactly the same
reasons that "separate but equal" education is not equal education. Of all the Negro institutions, the churches are foremost in their attempt to negate reality and the least open to
Woodrow Wilson's dictum: "It is better to fail in a cause
that will ultimately succeed than to succeed in a cause that
will ultimately fail."

It is apparent that no contribution can be made through
the study of Negro congregational life (e.g., updating the
statistical study of churches organized and dominated by

* The best available evidence, although it does not deal with details
of the above study, is in *The Religion of Negro Protestants* by Ruby F.
Johnston (New York: Philosophical Library, 1956).

Negroes). The issue is no longer whether or not Negroes are capable. It is clear that they are relegated to an unenviable position as long as their church life exists for the purposes of a deprived people. Moreover, whatever standard might be developed to measure the ineffectiveness of the Negro religious communities, there would be no significant change from a comparable study of white religious communities. There are too many exceptions and intangibles for a scientific comparison of Negro and white congregations, although the Negro organizational structures might well show decided deficiencies—but even these could be accounted for, given the pattern of segregation in America. Negroes are as Christian or non-Christian as are whites, varying in their emphases upon specific criteria, perhaps, but this is not the question.

The Negro's Church has had a remarkable effect upon those scholars and lay people especially interested in the religious life of the Negro. Its implication, which reflects the mind of many Negroes and whites, that "the Negro church" exists* has been particularly influential.

Mays and Nicholson appear to begin with the hypothesis of "the Negro church," which they proceeded to study sociologically. Perhaps because so little evidence was available to support this hypothesis, the title of the book became *The Negro's Church*, and its subject a cross-section of Negro congregations in need of higher standards. Granted the validity of this analysis of Negro congregations, neither the evidence nor the conclusions corroborated the hypothesis that Negroes

---

* This misnomer was introduced in *The History of the Negro Church* by Carter G. Woodson (Washington, D.C.: Associated Publishers, Inc., 1921). Mays and Nicholson corrected the discrepancy in their title, but the non-clerical researchers were not perceptive of this change. See *From Slavery to Freedom* by John Hope Franklin (New York: Alfred A. Knopf, Inc., 1947), and Chapter 14, entitled "The Negro Church," in *The Negro in the United States* by E. Franklin Frazier (New York: The Macmillan Company, 1947).

have created an independent church—an identifiable, unique, form of Christianity. Rather, Negroes manifest in their ecclesiastical life a form of disinherited Protestantism, cut off from Protestant roots and allowed to wither away—in glory or in ignominy, but inevitably.

However, the great weight of the final chapter is not concerned with the sociological analysis, which offers little hope for the future church life of 12,000,000 people. It is concerned with the authors' experience with the Negro church, which they consider to be a significant American institution:

The authors believe that there is in the genius or the "soul" of the Negro church something that gives it life and vitality, that makes it stand out significantly above its buildings, creeds, rituals and doctrines, something that makes it a unique institution. For this reason, the writers, in this chapter, lean more heavily than in previous chapters upon the observations and personal experiences gained during the two-year, intensive study of the Negro church; and these are supplemented here and there by the experiences of the race.

The conclusions of their formal research and study of history reported throughout the book and in capsule form in the final chapter reveal a real "genius" or "soul" in this "unique institution."

In my opinion, there is no "genius" of "the Negro church," but there is a real "soul" or "genius" of the American Negro folk religion. The findings reveal that the Negro has created, out of the scraps of Protestantism provided by white missionaries, an ingenious "technique" for survival and a creative means of calling forth pride in achievement to disprove the white assumption of Negro inferiority. He has been hampered in his efforts by the segregating forces of the white power structure which circumscribes, but at the same time acquiesces before, the undeniably impressive

Negro advance. The "genius" or "soul" of the Negro folk religion is its incidental or token bow to Protestantism, about which it knows and cares so little. Because of their isolation, independent congregations have preserved in arrested form the religious behavior of the evangelicals on the American frontier between 1800 and 1890. Since they had no other criterion for religious expression, the frontier pattern became traditional. Evangelism is to the folk religion what "Christian doctrine" is to the nonviolent movement—a red herring.

Negro folk religion is deeply involved in one area of Christianity, the ethic of love-justice-equality, about which they have learned from people other than white Protestants. The Negro folk religion is fundamentally and unequivocally dedicated to freedom, expression, independence, and the rise of Negroes to equal status in the society. The "genius" of the Negro folk religion is not the "church" but the use of this structure as an instrument for the fulfillment of its participation as a race in every area of life. This is what Mays and Nicholson suggest in the phrase "the Negro's church."

NOTES

Chapter 1

1. Martin Luther King, Jr., *Stride Toward Freedom* (New York: Harper & Row, Publishers, 1958), p. 84. This work forms the basis for a considerable part of this chapter.
2. *Ibid.*, p. 62.
3. Louis E. Lomax, *The Negro Revolt* (New York: Harper & Row, Publishers, 1962), p. 125.

Chapter 2

1. See Gerhard Lenski, *The Religious Factor* (Garden City, N.Y.: Doubleday & Company, Inc., 1961), *passim*. Lenski does not include secularism as a religion, but emphasizes the importance of the other four.
2. St. Clair Drake and Horace R. Cayton, *Black Metropolis: A Study of Negro Life in a Northern City* (New York: Harcourt, Brace & World, Inc., 1945. Reprinted by Harper & Row, Publishers, 1962).
3. *Ibid.*, p. 422.
4. Benjamin E. Mays and Joseph W. Nicholson, *The Negro's Church* (New York: Institute of Social and Religious Research, 1933), p. 278.
5. Hylan Lewis, *Blackways of Kent* (Chapel Hill: The University of North Carolina Press, 1955), pp. 64 ff.
6. See Mays and Nicholson, *Negro's Church, passim,* for dated but helpful statistics.
7. *Ibid.*, p. 198.
8. See Paul Harrison, *Authority and Power in the Free Church Tradition: A Social Case Study of the American Baptist Convention* (Princeton: Princeton University Press, 1959), *passim*.
9. *Ibid.*, p. 165.
10. *Ibid.*, p. 227.
11. *Ibid.*, p. 162.
12. Adam Clayton Powell, Jr., *Marching Blacks: An Interpretive History of the Rise of the Black Common Man* (New York: Dial Press, 1945), p. 95.
13. *Ibid.*, p. 18.
14. *Ibid.*, p. 94.
15. *Ibid.*, p. 198.
16. *Ibid.*, p. 200.
17. Quoted in Drake and Cayton, *Black Metropolis*, p. 631.
18. Lomax, *Negro Revolt*, pp. 46-47.
19. C. Eric Lincoln, *The Black Muslims in America* (Boston: Beacon Press, 1961), p. 235.

20. Earl E. Thorpe, *The Mind of the Negro* (Baton Rouge, La.: Ortlieb Press, 1961), p. 116.
21. Howard Thurman, *The Creative Encounter* (New York: Harper & Row, Publishers, 1954), p. 140.
22. *Ibid.*, p. 139.
23. Howard Thurman, *Jesus and the Disinherited* (New York: Abingdon-Cokesbury Press, 1949), pp. 30-31.
24. *Ibid.*, p. 31.
25. *Ibid.*, pp. 33-34.
26. *Ibid.*, p. 33.
27. Howard Thurman, *Deep River: Reflections on the Religious Insight of Certain of the Negro Spirituals* (New York: Harper & Row, Publishers, 1955), p. 22.
28. Howard Thurman, *Footprints of a Dream* (New York: Harper & Row, Publishers, 1959), p. 24.
29. *Ibid.*, p. 38.
30. *Ibid.*, p. 51.
31. *Ibid.*, p. 52.
32. *Ibid.*, p. 54.
33. Thurman, *Creative Encounter*, p. 152.
34. Howard Thurman, *The Growing Edge* (New York: Harper & Row. Publishers, 1956), p. 176.
35. Howard Thurman, *Deep is the Hunger* (New York: Harper & Row. Publishers, 1951), p. 176.
36. Howard Thurman, *Meditations of the Heart* (New York: Harper & Row, Publishers, 1953), p. 15.
37. E. Franklin Frazier, *The Negro in the United States* (New York: The Macmillan Company, 1947), pp. 350-357.
38. *The New Day*, July 27, 1963.
39. Frazier, *Negro in the United States*, p. 357.
40. J. Milton Younger, *Religion, Society and the Individual* (New York: The Macmillan Company, 1957), p. 189.
41. Lincoln, *Black Muslims*, p. 21.
42. *Ibid.*
43. Lomax, *Negro Revolt*, p. 177.
44. Gunnar Myrdal, *An American Dilemma* (New York: Harper & Row, Publishers, 1944), p. 866.
45. Ruby F. Johnston, *The Development of Negro Religion* (New York: The Philosophical Library, 1954), *passim*.
46. Ruby F. Johnston, *The Religion of Negro Protestants* (New York: The Philosophical Library, 1956), p. 20.
47. *Ibid.*, p. 20.
48. *Ibid.*, p. 27.
49. *Ibid.*, passim.
50. *Ibid.*, p. 25.
51. *Ibid.*
52. Mays and Nicholson, *Negro's Church*, p. 290.
53. H. Richard Niebuhr, *The Purpose of the Church and its Ministry* (New York: Harper & Row, Publishers, 1956), p. 80.

54. E. Franklin Frazier, *Black Bourgeoisie* (Glencoe, Ill.: The Free Press, 1957), p. 32.
55. *Ibid., passim.*
56. Interview with a Lutheran seminarian in New Orleans, La., October, 1962.
57. Interview with a Negro clergyman in Boston, Mass., September, 1960.
58. Myrdal, *American Dilemma*, p. 866.
59. Gibson Winter, *The Suburban Captivity of the Churches* (Garden City, N.Y.: Doubleday & Company, Inc., 1961), p. 116.
60. *Ibid.*
61. Thurman, *Jesus and the Disinherited*, p. 112.
62. Thurman, *Footprints of a Dream*, p. 82.
63. Mays and Nicholson, *Negro's Church*, p. 171.
64. *Ibid., passim.*
65. *The New English Bible*, Acts 8:31.

Chapter 3

1. John Hope Franklin, *From Slavery to Freedom: A History of American Negroes* (New York: Alfred A. Knopf, Inc., 1947), p. 71.
2. *Ibid.*, p. 85.
3. *Ibid.*, pp. 85-86.
4. Kenneth Scott Latourette, *A History of Christianity* (New York: Harper & Row, Publishers, 1953), p. 953.
5. Williston Walker, *A History of the Christian Church* (2d. ed., rev.; New York: Charles Scribner's Sons, 1959), p. 433.
6. Franklin, *From Slavery to Freedom*, p. 100.
7. *Ibid.*, p. 103.
8. *Ibid.*, p. 104.
9. *Ibid.*, p. 102.
10. *Ibid.*, p. 108.
11. Carter G. Woodson, *The History of the Negro Church* (Washington, D.C.: Associated Publishers, Inc., 1921), p. 15.
12. W. D. Weatherford, *American Churches and the Negro: An Historical Study from Early Slave Days to the Present* (Boston: Christopher Publishing House, 1957), pp. 53-57.
13. *Ibid.*, p. 57.
14. Quoted by Weatherford, *op. cit.*, pp. 54-55.
15. Franklin, *From Slavery to Freedom*, p. 95.
16. Woodson, *History of the Negro Church*, p. 10.
17. Quoted in Woodson, *History of the Negro Church*, p. 13.
18. H. Richard Niebuhr, *The Social Sources of Denominationalism* (New York: Holt, Rinehart and Winston, Inc., 1929; reprinted by The World Publishing Company, 1957), p. 248.
19. Quoted in Woodson, *History of the Negro Church*, p. 10.
20. *Ibid.*, p. 24.
21. *Ibid.*
22. Franklin, *From Slavery to Freedom*, p. 80.
23. Quoted in Weatherford, *American Churches and the Negro*, pp. 31-32.

24. Winthrop S. Hudson, *American Protestantism* (Chicago: University of Chicago Press, 1961), p. 22.
25. *Ibid.*, p. 60.
26. Niebuhr, *Social Sources of Denominationalism*, p. 237.
27. Woodson, *History of the Negro Church*, pp. 72-73.
28. *Ibid.*, p. 73.
29. Franklin, *From Slavery to Freedom*, p. 247.
30. *Ibid.*, p. 162.
31. Frazier, *Negro in the United States*, p. 346.
32. Woodson, *History of the Negro Church*, p. 94.
33. *Ibid.*, pp. 95-96.
34. Weatherford, *American Churches and the Negro*, pp. 176-179.
35. Woodson, *History of the Negro Church*, p. 149.
36. Niebuhr, *Social Sources of Denominationalism*, p. 154.
37. Hudson, *American Protestantism*, p. 73.
38. S. Paul Schilling, *Methodism and Society in Theological Perspective*, Vol. 3 of *Methodism and Society* (New York: Abingdon Press, 1960), p. 59.
39. Richard M. Cameron, *Methodism and Society in Historical Perspective*, Vol. 1 of *Methodism and Society* (New York: Abingdon Press, 1961), p. 53.
40. Weatherford, *American Churches and the Negro*, p. 91.
41. Woodson, *History of the Negro Church*, pp. 142-143.
42. Quoted in Weatherford, *American Churches and the Negro*, pp. 114-115.
43. Woodson, *History of the Negro Church*, p. 41
44. *Ibid.*, pp. 120-121.
45. *Ibid.*, pp. 260-261.
46. *Ibid.*, pp. 259-260.
47. Franklin, *From Slavery to Freedom*, p. 199.
48. *Proceedings of the Meeting in Charleston, South Carolina, May 13-15, 1945 on the Religious Implication of the Negroes* (Charleston, S.C.: 1945), pp. 20-21.
49. *Ibid.*, p. 59.
50. James Weldon Johnson and J. Rosamond Johnson, *Books of American Negro Spirituals* (New York: The Viking Press, 1940), Vol. 1, pp. 25-26.
51. Miles Mark Fisher, *Negro Slave Songs in the United States* (Ithaca, N.Y.: Cornell University Press, 1953), pp. 25-26.
52. For a list of spirituals, *see* John W. Work, *American Songs: A Comprehensive Collection of 230 Folk Songs, Religious and Secular* (New York: Theodore Presser Company, 1940).
53. Fisher, *Negro Slave Songs, passim.*
54. *Ibid.*
55. *Ibid.*, p. 176.
56. See the definition of Christianity in Charles S. Johnson, *Shadow of the Plantation* (Chicago: University of Chicago Press, 1934), p. 20.
57. *Ibid.*, p. 179.
58. *Ibid.*
59. *Ibid.*, p. 183.

60. *Ibid.*, p. 70.
61. *Ibid.*, p. 145.
62. Myrdal, *American Dilemma*, pp. 860-861.
63. Frazier, *Black Bourgeoisie*, p. 78.
64. *Ibid.*, pp. 89-114.
65. Cameron, *Methodism and Society in Historical Perspective*, p. 152.
66. Frazier, *Black Bourgeoisie*, p. 78.
67. *See* Myrdal, *American Dilemma*, pp. 861 *ff*.
68. *See* John T. Gillard, *The Catholic Church and the American Negro* (Baltimore: St. Joseph's Society Press, 1929), pp. 35 *ff*.
69. *Ibid.*, p. 9.
70. John T. Gillard, *Colored Catholics in the United States* (Baltimore: The Josephite Press, 1941), pp. 112 *ff*.
71. Albert S. Foley, *Bishop Healy: Beloved Outcaste* (New York: Farrar, Straus & Co., Inc., 1954).
72. Albert S. Foley, *God's Man of Color* (New York: Farrar, Straus & Co., Inc., 1955).
73. For a helpful understanding of denominational activities, *see* Robert Moats Miller, *American Protestantism and Social Issues 1919-1939* (Chapel Hill: University of North Carolina Press, 1958).
74. Bureau of the Census, *Religious Bodies: 1936*, Vol. I. *Summary and Detailed Tables* (Washington, D.C., 1941), pp. 850-863, 900-903.
75. W. E. B. DuBois, *The Souls of Black Folk* (Chicago: A. C. McChurg and Co., 1903), pp. 190-191.
76. Mays and Nicholson, *Negro's Church*, pp. 266 *ff*.
77. Frazier, *Black Bourgeoisie*, p. 43.
78. Based upon Bureau of the Census, *Religious Bodies: 1936*, Vol. II, Parts 1 and 2 (Washington, D.C., 1941).
79. Based upon *Yearbook of American Churches*, ed. Benson Y. Landis (New York: National Council of Churches in the U.S.A., 1962).
80. Myrdal, *American Dilemma*, p. 873.

Chapter 4

1. Kyle Haselden, *The Racial Problem in Christian Perspective* (New York: Harper & Row, Publishers, 1959), pp. 67-69.
2. *Ibid.*, p. 31.
3. *Ibid.*, pp. 32-33.
4. Thomas J. Harte, *Catholic Organizations Promoting Negro-White Race Relations in the United States* (Washington, D.C.: The Catholic University Press, 1947), Vol. 24, p. 155.
5. Winter, *Suburban Captivity of the Churches*, p. 116.
6. *Ibid.*, p. 125.
7. Lenski, *Religious Factor*, p. 318.
8. Myrdal, *American Dilemma*, p. 866.
9. *Ibid.*, p. 941.
10. DuBois, *Souls of Black Folk*, p. 206.
11. James M. Gustafson, *Treasure in Earthen Vessels: The Church as a Human Community* (New York: Harper & Row, Publishers, 1961), *passim*.

12. Charles S. Johnson, *Into the Main Stream* (Chapel Hill: University of North Carolina Press, 1947), p. 313.
13. Ephesians 1:22-23, trans. J. B. Phillips (New York: The Macmillan Company).
14. Ephesians 4:18-19, trans. J. B. Phillips.
15. Ephesians 2:19, trans. J. B. Phillips.
16. Galatians 4:7, trans, J. B. Phillips.
17. Galatians 6:5-8, trans. J. B. Phillips.
18. The First Letter of John 4:18-21, trans. J. B. Phillips.
19. Ephesians 4:25, trans. J. B. Phillips.
20. Lenski, *Religious Factor*, p. 318.
21. Myrdal, *American Dilemma*, p. 803.
22. Lewis, *Blackways of Kent*, p. 133.

INDEX